BEYON

Stories of Collapse and Rebirth

Ted Bernard

Author of Late-K Lunacy

Illustrations by Alexa Miller

BEYOND LATE-K
Stories of Collapse and Rebirth
By Ted Bernard © 2023

Subjects: Fiction, science fiction, post-apocalyptic fiction, futurism,
North America, Ohio, 21st century

Cover art and illustrations: Alexa Miller, alexamillerdesign.com

Editing and design
Peter Geldart, Danielle Michaud Aubrey
Petra Books 2023
petrabooks.ca

Softcover 978-1-989048-87-0
Digital; 978-1-989048-86-3
5.5" x 8.5"
Times Roman 10/12
American Typewriter 10, 12, 14
ca. 75,000 words
illustrations
204 pages

"Dystopian stories are usually set in a bleak future marked by oppression and misery. I love how Ted Bernard's stories take us instead to a future that feels like the past. The world has indeed fallen apart, and the characters in Beyond Late-K must live, like our forebears, with no cars, electricity, telephones or internet. There are troubles galore, but it all feels like a possible, even likely future. Everyone we meet seems real, for the lives Bernard portrays are illuminations, not desecrations. From the perspective of a new and difficult world we gaze back at '*the pointless materialism, the folly of permanence*'. What a hard-biting and fascinating book."

—John Thorndike (author of *The World Against Her Skin* and *A Hundred Fires in Cuba*)

"Picking up where his Late-K Lunacy left off, Beyond Late-K is a candid exploration of how various characters in the future cope with the '*harsh simplicity*' of a world decimated by ecological disaster and climate change, global pandemics and societal collapse, nuclear destruction and even ubiquitous infertility as they try to maintain their humanity—a challenge we might all have to face in the all-too-near future. We need good-hearted visionaries like Ted Bernard—a passionate expert in sustainability—to show us the way and inspire hope that we, too, can not only survive but also create a better world respectful of all life."

—Kathleen Davies, author of *Sacred Groves: Or, How a Cemetery Saved My Soul.*

For Ariana, Celeste, Donna, and Olivia
Each a pearl of brilliance, tenacity, and affection.

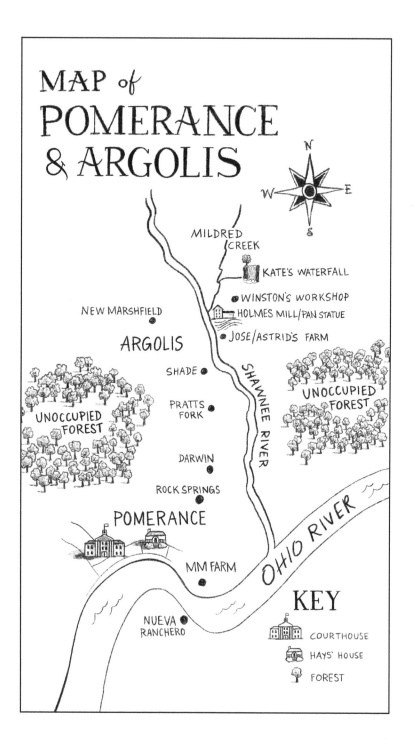

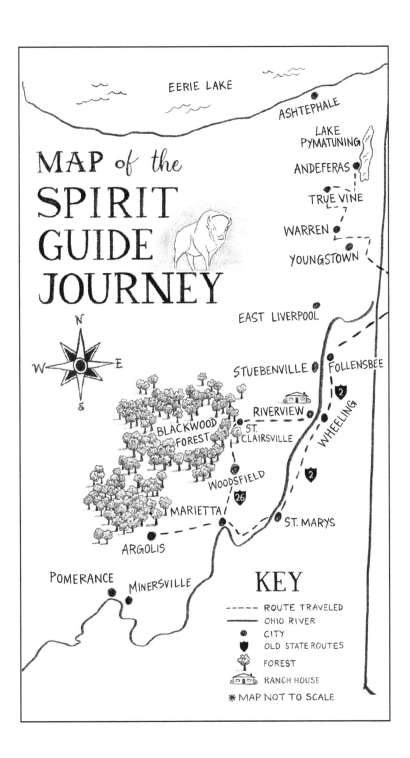

Table of Contents

ONE

Points of No Return

Safiya, 2012-2021

From a certain point onward there is no longer any turning back. That is the point that must be reached.[1]

1

SAFIYA KAMAL WASN'T KNOWN TO BE CAUTIOUS. She rarely second guessed herself. "Go for it, Safiya," her Egyptian mother would tell her. "In our new country, there are no limits. Take risks. If you happen to go down a wrong path, make the best of it." That advice came back to her years later in a world vastly diminished, her new country a barely functioning remnant. As was her history and

---

[1] Franz Kafka, *The Trial*. Knopf, New York, 1937

inclination, she wasted little time on the world she left behind; there was no turning back. The world ahead was not without promise.

One spring evening when her mother was still alive, Safiya and her younger cousin Nur hovered at the edge of a cocktail party in Ottawa's outer suburbs. They whispered softly as they studied the aliens across the room — rich white people in vacuous conversation. Safiya was nominally here to protect Nur who'd been invited by Drew somebody. The trouble was, Drew was nowhere to be found. Safiya and Nur were ready to slip out when Marcel, a muscular French-Canadian, sidled up.

"Hello girls," he said. "Are you thinking what I'm thinking?"

"And what would that be?" Safiya flinched at his pick-up line.

"Well, that this is one of the most uninspiring parties you've ever attended. And you'd commit to handing over your first born to anybody who could help you escape."

"As a matter of fact, we were just planning to leave. But making light of childbirth is cruel."

"I was kidding about that but not the escape."

"What did you have in mind?" asked Nur.

"Let's go across the river to a night spot I know in Gatineau. We can have drinks, nibbles, listen to a good band. Then I can take you guys home."

"That sounds like fun," Nur said. Safiya threw up unspoken cautions. "Come on Saf, we just agreed it was time to leave."

"Okay. But we don't even know this guy's name."

"I'm Marcel Bourque." He offered his hand. "And you?"

"Safiya and Nur," volunteered Nur, her finger pointing.

Marcel proved to be the perfect gentleman. Their conversation was lively. After predictable small talk, they landed on common ground. They'd attended the University of Ottawa; they discovered mutual friends and acquaintances; and though they bantered about politics, all three preferred the left-leaning NDP/NPD. They exchanged phone numbers and before midnight, he paid the check as they parted ways with friendly handshakes. Neither woman heard from him in the ensuing weeks.

Three months later, he called Nur, asking her out for dinner. She demurred, explaining that she'd drifted into a relationship with an Egyptian-Canadian, a member of their orthodox community. He had impressed her parents.

She told Marcel she was tempted, "But right now I think I'd better say no. Call my cousin. She'd be delighted to hear from you."

Marcel made the call before Nur had a chance to talk to Safiya. He took her to the Caffé Mio in Wellington Village, an Ottawa neighborhood. A Wednesday, the small restaurant was half empty.

"What would you recommend?" she asked.

"If you like poultry, the duck confit; red meat, you cannot top their *tartare de boeuf*."

"Fish?"

"Trout, maybe. I've not tried it." Marcel had a relaxed manner, a velvety tone to his voice, a smile that consumed his whole face, hazel eyes with crinkles at the edges. Six feet tall, he seemed super fit, a body builder maybe, pushing thirty, she figured.

They ordered a bottle of wine. The bartender delivered their choice, flashing a friendly smile at Safiya. He was middle-aged and also of Middle Eastern descent.

"Hello, my dear! Safiya, right? I don't think I've ever seen you here."

"Oh, hello, Mikael!" A warm smile spread across her face. "Yeah, I'm Safiya. Great to be here and yes, it *is* my first time. Meet my friend, Marcel."

The two gentlemen shook hands. Marcel said he was a regular. While serving the wine, Mikael responded with typical guy talk, as though they were long-standing mates. Jovial blather about politics, the Ottawa Senators, the restaurant business, the sinking value of the dollar. Talk empty of meaning for her.

When Mikael retreated to the bar, Marcel said, "Nice guy. Does he own the place?"

"Well, his family does."

"Uh huh. How did you come to know him?"

"He and his family are members of our church. You know the Coptic Church over on Strandherd?"

"Ah, no. I live in Gatineau where we had drinks last time. I'm a Catholic but a lapsed one. I haven't been to mass in a decade." He changed the subject. "Speaking of that night, my friend Bob Leyton, the host of that boring party, later told me that he noticed my departure 'with two beautiful women'."

"That's a stretch."

"No stretch, Safiya. You two *are* spectacular. You especially."

She tilted her head, called up her dubious face, and gently placed her hand on his. "Thanks, Marcel. But didn't you call Nur first?"

"A case of bad judgment."

Dinners arrived — the duck for him and a pasta dish for her. Crème brûlée with espresso and brandies afterwards. They talked softly. Refilling their brandies, Mikael assured them that there was no pressure to turn over the table. The ambiance — low lights, discrete waiters, seductive jazz in the background — put a soft sheen on the evening and made Marcel, who was not classically handsome, look alluring. Having consumed more alcohol than was her norm, Safiya's perception blurred. The evening seemed unreal, as if they were reflecting on a distant past they'd shared in some exotic place. A Greek island perhaps.

The brandy was to blame. Safiya found herself falling into an all too familiar gauzy trap, drifting toward a point of no return she'd promised to avoid. On the boozy walk to the car, she coaxed him into a doorway, loosely wrapping her leg around his. They groped and kissed, and though there was a clear path to his bedroom, he reined himself in and dropped her off with a quick hug at the door of her parents' home.

In the weeks that followed, Marcel Bourque wanted to be with Safiya Kamal constantly. She was compliant, enjoying his company despite more than occasionally longing for something, someone new. This had been her history. Glom onto a steady; live with him maybe; talk of a future; get bored. Restlessly seek and lure another while deceiving the previous. Lust, lies, secrets, exhilaration. There was something about the pattern she could not resist: the drama, the risk, the uncertainty, the temptation, landing a catch to freak-out her parents. Getting to the brink. Abruptly retreating.

While continuing her hunt, she'd had little opportunity to escape possessive Marcel who offered her thrice weekly sex in his elegant flat high above the Ottawa River. Not surprisingly, all was beginning to lose its luster. Just as she contrived to meet a handsome and recently-divorced member of parliament, Marcel made mention of marriage. The icon on her dashboard flashed red: *Shut down your engine immediately.*

The MP, introduced by friends at a downtown pub, took her aside and bought drinks. They laughed and flirted. He was obviously enamored, hitting on her with a confident, relaxed charm. She responded with a transparent, though subtle brush of her hand along his jaw. He suggested dinner. For nightcaps, they retreated to his place just down Clarence Street. She woke the next morning in his bed, more fulfilled than she'd been in weeks, her heart pounding joyfully, her mind a swirl, her situation a pickle.

This time she could not wiggle away from the amiable, controlling Bourque and the weight of two sets of parents prepared to sanction their marriage. Bridging the cultural and faith traditions of their families — his father a French Canadian married to a devout Catholic from Dublin; her mother and dad both Egyptian Christians — the wedding was co-officiated by a Roman Catholic priest from Montreal, where Marcel had grown up, and the local Coptic Bapa. More than two hundred attended the ceremony at St. Mark & St. Mary of Egypt Coptic Orthodox Church in Ottawa. She was twenty-two; he, twenty-seven. Unbeknownst even to their friends, on the day of the wedding Safiya was in her first trimester of pregnancy. They had but seven months to adjust as a couple before Claire was born. Safiya quit her job to raise the child. Not long after, Marcel was transferred by his investment firm from Ottawa to Oshawa, four hours away. They decided he should rent an apartment and commute on weekends. Each Friday night he arrived exhausted and detached, not the Marcel Safiya remembered, the Marcel who once thrived on her every need. Fourteen months later, she was pregnant again. Having probably wandered down a wrong path marrying Marcel, she realized now that she could not abandon the marriage, the child. She felt trapped.

Though Marcel detested the idea of another child, Safiya would not even briefly consider aborting the pregnancy. The most intense fight of their marriage sent Marcel packing early one weekend. Pushing for an abortion had turned Safiya into a livid and aggressive "psycho bitch — What's with you, Safiya?" he asked. *Christ, has he forgotten he'd almost dragged me to the abortion clinic?*

The baby, Salma, arrived just as the North American economy was suffering a deep recession following the H7N9 pandemic of 2013. It had been months since the virus found its way to Canada and it was still spreading rapidly. No vaccine had been successful. Hospitals were brimming with dying patients, their maternity wards repurposed. Salma was delivered in an outlying manger — a private birthing circle. Marcel, present at the birth, seemed uncharacteristically giddy at the arrival of their second daughter.

A month later his company was bought out by an American firm. He was transferred to their head office in Columbia, South Carolina. With a toddler and a baby to look after, Safiya informed Marcel that until he became settled in his new job, she would stay in Ottawa where her family could help raise the girls. She never intended to move to South Carolina, a dead end in her mind. All she ever wanted was in Canada.

One weekend in mid-winter Marcel was back in Ottawa. Safiya noticed that when he'd run off to the gym, he'd left his laptop open and on. Though their marriage had been on thin ice, she would normally not have pried into his virtual life. But on a previous weekend, after he'd read the girls to sleep, he'd taken a call. Without grabbing his coat, he stepped outside. Despite the bitter cold, he was out for half an hour. Afterwards, frost bitten, he went immediately to the shower. When he returned, she asked about the call. He said that his boss in the States wanted him to check into something. "Nothing major," he assured her and retreated to the study with his computer. When he emerged two hours later, he came to her and apologized profusely. She did not believe him.

Now, she went straight to his email account. The inbox was open. She found dozens of messages from realzoe@gamecock.com: love blurbs, plans to meet 'my sweet Canuk', excursions to Hilton Head, disgusting sexual details, realzoe egging him to "Ditch the bitch." "What of my girls?" he wrote. "They'll survive," she replied.

Safiya hated being deceived. Yes, there was ambiguity. Hadn't she cheated on him back before the wedding? Shouldn't she be cutting him some slack? On the other hand, hadn't she been faithful throughout their marriage? It was a fact. For her little family, she had pledged no longer to be a huntress. Now realzoe, a real estate broker with deep southern roots, had fucked up everything. Realzoe was in love with my husband. Where has monogamy gotten me?

When Marcel returned from the gym, she confronted him with full bore fury. It frightened them both. She screamed, "Get the fuck out of my house and don't come back." Claire, now five, with Salma, three, stood in the hallway in their footie pajamas. They'd never witnessed a fight like this. They began to cry. In less than an hour, he was gone. They could not understand why Papa was leaving on a Saturday morning.

Although a portion of Marcel's pay arrived at her bank account each month, they'd arrived at a point of no return. Divorce papers arrived by courier. Attorneys wrangled, contested technical matters, battled over custody, extended the case to their benefit. Cross-border complications delayed things further. Meanwhile, beyond their small lives, the global order was set to teeter for the second time in a decade as another pandemic began to immobilize North America.

In April 2020, Marcel called Safiya from a hospital in South Carolina. His voice was raspy and thin.

"I hope I'm not interrupting something. I thought I should call to say I'm seriously ill."

"How seriously?"

"Doctors are concerned. I'm short of breath, running high fevers and may have had a mild stroke. My heart is not beating normally. I'm on oxygen. This is not to say I'll be dead in a week but could you please think about bringing the girls to me? I am alone. Seeing them might help me fight this."

"What about Zoe?"

"She's gone. Abandoned ship last year. Moved to Florida." His speech was slurred. There was a pause. "Safiya? You still on?"

"Yes, I'm here. Alright," she sighed. "Let me try to make arrangements. The world is a mess. Some airports are shutting down, many flights have been cancelled. I cannot promise I'll be able to pull this off."

"Please try. Soon."

She did. She wished her ex-husband no harm. As she prayed for his recovery, she prepared herself to face critical moments, feeling apprehensive of an uncertain future.

2

At Ottawa International Airport, the tension was thick enough to wear. Emerging from a taxi, the two girls in tow, Safiya found hundreds of edgy travelers in lines that snaked around and out of the terminal. Had it not been for Canadian civility, things might have spiraled out of control. She hated to think what it would be like south of the border, navigating two U.S. airports before landing in South Carolina.

Her father, a well-regarded Ottawa surgeon and medical director, found them outside the airport. He hugged Safiya and squatted to kiss his granddaughters. "Ah, my sweet girls, you're looking so beautiful and ready to help your mum."

To Safiya he said, "Alright, hold your place. Let me try to find my airport operations friend. She's in there somewhere."

Twenty minutes later, Dr. Kamal returned with two uniformed officers.

"Okay, girls, follow us," he said. That's when Canadian hospitality devolved into hostility. A mother in line just behind Safiya shouted, "What gives these people the right to jump ahead? We've been waiting just as long as they have." Before the echoes of her complaint faded, Safiya's family was inside the terminal.

At the Air Canada ticket counter, Dr. Kamal paid for three first class seats to Columbia, South Carolina as he slipped a $50 note to the agent. Safiya and the girls were then escorted by the uniforms straight to the security checkpoint. Safiya hugged and thanked her father. She, Claire and Salma said their good-byes with blown kisses, unaware that this would be their last time in Canada, their last hugs from their beloved patriarch.

Fifteen hours later, after tumultuous passages through O'Hare International Airport and Charlotte Douglas International Airport, they boarded a commuter flight from Charlotte to Columbia. As a Sunbelt city, Columbia had dodged the worst of the Great Recession and Bird Flu pandemic. Although the national and global economies had wobbled in those crises, Columbia thrived. This time, the concurrence of a global pandemic and a botched government response was leading toward social and economic disruption at an unprecedented scale: surging cases of the virus overwhelming hospitals, care homes, and workplaces; unemployment, evictions, foreclosures, school closures, and the shutdown of businesses large and small.

At 3:30 AM, finally in a hotel room across from the hospital, all three collapsed onto the king-sized bed.

It was mid-morning, the sun streaming through the third-story window when Salma awoke hungry. "Wake up you two!"

Quickly dressing, they descended to the hotel restaurant. After breakfast, they walked to a nearby intersection to cross to the hospital. Life in South Carolina seemed normal with light but fast-moving traffic, many pedestrians at the crosswalk, and a crush of people at the main entrance of the Providence Health Hospital. In Safiya's mind, this was a terrifying milieu for their first family trip to the States. Maybe she should have been more cautious.

Inside the hospital on the ground floor, she was discouraged by reception staff from seeing her ex-husband. "He is in a critical care wing on sixth where visitors are prohibited. No, you cannot see him. Please go home Madame."

She thanked the receptionist and, with the girls scurrying behind, she headed straight to the sixth floor. At the nurses' station, she made her case.

"I've come all the way from Ottawa in Canada. My ex-husband, Marcel Bourque, begged to see his daughters. They know he's gravely ill. They want to be with him, to help him heal."

"I regret to tell you, Madame, Mr. Bourque is in intensive care and is quarantined. He cannot have visitors. I don't know how you got up here. You don't belong. Mr. Bourque is battling a novel coronavirus; it has attacked his lungs. He is gasping for breath. He is contagious. Anybody going to his bedside must wear personal protective equipment. We do not have extra sets for visitors. Besides, we do not want his room to be contaminated by people from outside."

"Is he conscious?"

"He is."

"Would you then tell him that we are here?"

"Let me repeat, Madame. You cannot see him. What possible good could come of this?"

"I cannot answer that; it depends on his immune response. I assume it would help him. You are preventing us from achieving a greater good by refusing his request to see us at this terrifying moment in his life."

The masked nurse studied Safiya's weary eyes and the plum-colored sacks beneath them. Her eyes moved to the two girls, dressed elegantly. Neither had uttered a sound.

Breaking the silence, Salma blurted, "Ma'am, do you not have a heart?"

The nurse pondered the five-year old's audacity. She touched her mask, gently pressing the nose piece. She dropped her hand. "Let me check with my supervisor."

Five minutes later, she returned. "We cannot take the risk of exposing you and your daughters. I want you to understand that this is a lethal virus we don't fully understand. Mr. Bourque seems to have a severe case of the disease."

"I do understand," Safiya said.

"But Mom!" Salma protested.

The nurse continued. "What we can do, Ms. Kamal, is to let you and your daughters speak with him and see him remotely."

"Oh please, yes."

Safiya was given a number to call. She gathered Claire and Salma to her phone. The first image they saw was the attending ICU nurse in a protective gown and cap, a mask and face shield. The nurse turned the phone toward Marcel. He was attached to two intravenous feeds. Supplemental oxygen fed through his nose. A tube hung from his mouth. His skin was milky gray. He stared at them with watery blankness. The nurse prompted him.

Marcel cleared his throat. "Hello my dearest Salma and Claire. Hi Safiya."

"Hello Papa," the girls responded. "We are glad we can see you," Salma said.

There was a long pause. The nurse held the phone. Marcel spoke hesitantly, as if each word was a load he could barely lift. "Me too. I'm glad to see you too. Thank you for coming. It must have been a hard trip. In a few days when I am better, we'll be able to be together, hug each other."

"That's great, Papa," Claire said.

"Mind the doctors and nurses," commanded Salma.

"Okay, I promise. Let me speak to your mother."

Safiya took the phone. "Hello Marcel. Are you still feeling rough?" "Yeah, sort of. Maybe a bit better. I just want to thank you for making the trip. I hope I can make it up to you once I'm back on my feet. But first, please check in with my friend, Larry Bentsen. He's also my lawyer......nurse will give you contacts."

"Okay. Don't worry about anything now, Marcel. Just rest."

The ICU nurse spoke. "Alright Ms. Kamel," he said. "We'd better let Marcel go back to sleep. Why don't you three say goodbye?"

They thanked the nurse manager and left her with contact information. On their way out, code blue calls rang throughout the hospital. In a corridor on the ground floor, they wove around a queue of laden gurneys. The first in line were two and three deep outside the ER — a grotesque traffic jam: desperately sick patients coughing and wheezing, some wailing for oxygen — their plight in an overloaded hospital frightful. As the pandemic claimed thousands in the following weeks, that hideous scene infused Safiya's nightmares. Much later, she thanked God that she and the girls had not become infected that day.

Safiya read the girls a bedtime story about how a group of forest animals rallied to save their friend, Mortimer, a baby pig, who'd become stuck in mud at the edge of the river. After the girls had fallen asleep, a call lit up Safiya's muted phone. It was the ICU nurse. Marcel had lost his battle. At 34, he had become another Covid-19 statistic: one of more than 30,000 US fatalities to that date.

Breaking the news to the girls would be difficult. Safiya tossed and turned, wondering how to do it. When sunrays edged around the curtains, she'd been up for two hours. She called Marcel's lawyer and began to search for a way to return to Ottawa. It would not be easy. All flights from Columbia had been cancelled. Car rental agencies had few choices at exorbitant prices and crossing the border in a rental car was no longer permitted. Among other obstacles, one seemed insurmountable. Supplies of gasoline had been disrupted by infections raging through the petroleum and logistics workforces. The car rental agency predicted she would find few or no stations selling gasoline. Safiya decided she could not take a chance and turned to public transportation.

When the girls awoke, she sat between them on the bed, her arms around each. "I have some very sad news. Your papa died last night. The nurse called me after you fell asleep." Snuggling more closely, the girls wept softly.

"I am so glad we saw him yesterday," Claire blubbered.

"Now what, Mom?" Salma asked.

"Now we are going to find our way home," Safiya said.

In mid-afternoon, they walked out of the hotel lobby with their luggage. There were no taxis but the hotel van took them to the bus terminal. "Y'all are pretty lucky," the driver said. "After this, there ain't no gas 'til next week."

The trip took ten minutes in light traffic. Few cars traveled the freeways that surrounded Columbia and, eerily, there were no long-distance rigs. The bus terminal was rundown and dated. There were bays on either side, arrivals on the left; departures on the right. A bus parked in the departure bay had no logo or familiar identification. It did not look roadworthy. Safiya had no other options.

She settled the girls in the waiting area while she found the ticket agent. She reserved three seats on a bus leaving in six hours for Charleston and Wheeling, West Virginia and on to Pittsburgh and Buffalo. She paid in cash. Once they got to Buffalo, a fourteen-hour trip, she would find a way to cross into Canada at Niagara Falls. After that, it would be seven more hours to Ottawa, assuming there was gasoline.

She shared snacks with the girls from a supply she'd snitched from the hotel restaurant. Having been born into privilege, Safiya had never traveled this way and it frightened her. She and her parents had always flown in first or business classes with access to airline member lounges in airports. She looked around at the other people. They were poor, working class, mostly African-American, except for one elegantly dressed hulk of a black man who spoke a strange English and paced, like a panther, back and forth across the lounge. Almost everyone carried pillows. Their clothes were threadbare; their shoes worn. They could ill-afford travel. Now in the midst of a pandemic they needed to be someplace else. She heard a cough wracking a frail grandmother slumped against one of her grandchildren. She hadn't covered her mouth. No one was wearing face covering. Safiya vowed to sit as far away as possible from that poor woman. But who knew how many others were infected, some without fever or cough but heading toward a serious illness that was highly contagious?

Their bus, arriving from Savannah, was two hours late. It chugged into the arrivals bay, its brakes squealing. A dozen passengers disembarked and scattered into the darkness. After refueling, the bus shifted to the departure bay. Seeing that, people lined up at the door. Safiya counted twenty-four including themselves. They were near the front of the line. They inched forward as the driver checked boarding passes and loaded luggage. On board, Safiya passed through a handful of sleeping Savannah passengers and led the girls to the back.

After settling in and helping the girls get comfortable, Safiya cast her eyes down the aisle. The bus was less than half-full. Out the window she noticed a middle-aged white man who'd not been in the waiting room running toward the bus. He and the driver climbed aboard. Like Safiya and her girls, neither that man's manner nor his dress suggested he would be on a dilapidated bus heading toward Buffalo in the middle of the night. On the other hand, a terrifying disease was spreading and disrupting everything. Maybe his plight was similar to hers. He showed the driver his ticket and passed by some empty places to sit two rows in front of Safiya. He turned round ostensibly to check the whereabouts of the bathroom. Safiya's radar flipped to high alert. His move was clearly a quick survey of people in the rows behind him.

3

Like an aged tortoise, the bus pulled away from the terminal, turning right onto Buckner Road which led to the interstate highway that would take them north. Had there been traffic, the creeping bus would have caused a backup. But there were no cars or trucks at this hour. Safiya put aside the troubling thought that even this bus might run out of fuel. She needed to be positive; she needed the girls to believe they'd be back with their granddad soon. The bus chugged up the ramp to the interstate haltingly gaining speed. Safiya had yet another worry. The bus seemed to be on the brink of breakdown. Yet it somehow kept on rolling, the drone of its diesel lulling almost everyone to sleep. Not Safiya.

The well-dressed man seemed equally alert. He leaned back in his seat and feigned dozing but every few minutes she noticed him leaning into the aisle to look toward the driver. She watched and fidgeted. Her intuition told her it wouldn't be long before he made some sort of move. She feared he would target them. Nobody else seemed worthy of a burglary or hostage taking.

The well-dressed man rose and worked his way forward. His right hand went to the inside of his suit jacket. As he walked down the aisle, nobody stirred. In Safiya's mind, time stood still. The man approached the driver, bent over him, whispered something, shoved a handgun in his ear. He audibly ordered him to pull off the road. The driver applied the brakes. The bus screeched to a stop. Pulling up the hand brake, the driver flipped on the interior lights. Passengers awoke. The man yanked the driver into the aisle, the gun still pressed to his head. He announced in clear, accented English that he was hijacking the bus.

Passengers screamed in protest. Kids, rudely awakened, wailed.

"Shut up," the man said. "Everybody! No one's going to get hurt if you just shut up and stay exactly where you are."

"Where are you taking us?" a passenger shouted.

"We're going to Washington, DC," the man replied.

Someone else screamed, "You'll not get away with this, you bastard."

The man moved his gun away from the driver's head and pointed it at the ceiling above that person. He pulled the trigger. The bullet crashed through the roof.

"Next time, sir, it'll be your brains splattered all over this bus."

Passengers sat stunned in the silence.

The man shoved the driver back into his seat and instructed him to turn the bus around. As he was doing so, the man moved up the aisle, passenger by passenger, stashing in his pockets the few dollars people were forced to cough up. One elderly Latin fellow, spread his hands, palms up, and said, "*No tengo dinero, señor.*" With the butt of his pistol, the man clobbered the Latin man's head. Bleeding, he collapsed into the arms of his daughter.

"You brute!" she screamed. "My dad had nothing. He is a defenseless good man."

The bus went dark. The hijacker fired a shot forward shattering a window in the entry door. "Turn on the lights," he commanded.

The driver hesitated. "TURN-ON-THE-FUCK-ING-LIGHTS!"

In the darkened bus, the next few seconds were all the panther needed. He leapt out of his seat and lunged at the well-dressed man. With arms like tree limbs, he immobilized his prey. They toppled to the floor. The man lost his grip on the gun. Without hesitation, the panther took hold of the man's head and neck. His immense hands pulled his head right, while twisting his neck left. On the second pull, something snapped. Safiya muffled a squeal. The hijacker twitched, gurgled softly, slumped toward oblivion. The panther released his grip and crouched over his prey. He emptied the man's pockets. The lights came on as he stood up. A boy who had scuttled under the seat, handed over the gun. To cheers and applause, the panther waved bunches of dollar bills in each hand and began retracing the man's steps, returning the money. The driver reversed the bus and headed back north as the panther pulled the body out of sight.

Over the next five hours, the bus labored through the mountains of Virginia and West Virginia. Before dawn, the driver weaved his way through the empty streets of downtown Wheeling and pulled into a dimly-lit terminal. Unfortunately, the nationwide rationing of gasoline and diesel had not stretched fuel supplies sufficiently to reach this outpost. Explaining the situation, the driver advised passengers to disembark and wait inside the terminal.

"Please be patient," he said. "A shipment is due, maybe even later today. As soon as it's here we will proceed to Buffalo."

People wrapped themselves in coats and blankets and filed into the poorly heated bus station. A cloudy, raw mid-winter morning dawned on the huddled travelers. Their shared experience on the bus, the terrifying hijacker and his sudden demise, drew them together. They shared their meagre stocks of food and struck up conversations about their plight, their families, their sense of the future in the early days of a global pandemic.

The driver and ticket seller never returned. As food and patience ran short, the community that had formed so naturally began to dissipate. Passengers said their farewells and dispersed into an almost empty city. The tall hero named Moises was the first to depart.

"Come on girls," Safiya said as they gathered their few belongings, "we're going to find a way to get through this."

"*Maman*," cried Claire. "I'm scared."

"Don't worry," her younger sister advised. "It's going to be fun."

All around them, a dangerous virus lurked. Safiya was petrified. Were she to become infected, she could die. On that very day, thousands were succumbing. She couldn't imagine her daughters wandering alone in a devastated city with no way home. She had but one goal: to flee this wretched place as quickly as possible. Hungry, unwashed and ruffled, they strenuously avoided others; scrounged food and blankets; found a map and some winter coats. The first night they slept on pews in the cavernous sanctuary of the Cathedral of St. Joseph. In the morning, they filched silver from the collection box and matches and candles from the alter. The second night they found themselves on the floor of a shuttered mall, earlier scarfing up dimes and quarters, a half dollar or two from broken dispensers and shattered ATMs, and harvesting a few cans of beans from the shelves of a mostly plundered Wal-Mart.

As they slept, just before dawn, a vast shadow loomed over them. Startled to wakefulness, Safiya, cried, "Please do not hurt us; we're just trying to survive."

"Do not be frightened," the panther said in a gentle cadence. "I bin followin' you. I will help you and protect dees preshus wee girls." Safiya's instinct to trust his words proved to be one of the wisest moves of her life. It yielded a lifelong guardian, hard worker, and comedian with bizarre takes on life. What had promised to be a fraught day now was less precarious. After a breakfast of stale crackers and leftover baked beans, they followed Moises out into the steely morning. Cautiously weaving their way around obstacles and people, they arrived at the wide river. They needed to cross it. Two hours later, the four vagabonds made their way over a crumbling four-lane bridge into Ohio. The next day, after sleeping in the Mt. Zion Baptist Church in Bridgeport, they wandered southward, the river at their left, to a place on the map called Riverview. At the top of the bluff, they followed a once-tarred road. At its end, on the bluff's edge, was a substantial ranch house. They broke into its kitchen and dropped their belongings. From the deck was a stunning view of the mighty Ohio, once one of North America's most prominent rivers. This abandoned house soon become their home.

Moises said, "We bi at de end o' de road, Madame."

"This is the point we were meant to discover," she replied. "From here, there's no turning back. There's just one thing for us to do."

"And dat be what?"

"Forge ahead."

"Forge ahead?"

"Yes, we must put our minds and hands to something useful. We've got to make something, do something that people desperately need. Something they'll pay for."

"All will bi well," Moises said.

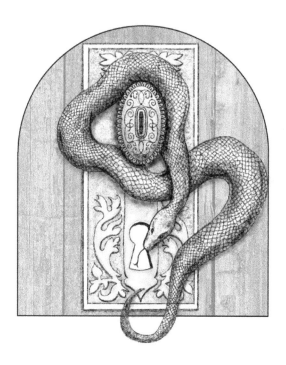

TWO

Hestia and the Witch of Andeferas

Andeferas, Mid-2030s

The lifting of a single thread unhems the world.[2]

1

THE EVENING AT THE EDGE of the shimmering lake is deathly quiet. As the man stares at the water, he sees deer bending to drink, as if nothing had happened. Maybe there are no deer. Maybe merely willows at water's edge. A tiny dwelling huddles nearby. Partly an underground burrow, like that of a groundhog, at the far edge of the village, the hut is lost to the eye against the autumn hues. The footpath to the village curves away toward the east, away from the fiery sunset. The silence is deep and relentless. Had he not lost faith, it may have

---

[2] William Kloefkorn, *Swallowing the Soap*. University of Nebraska Press, 2010, p. 49.

granted solace across the vast lake, a hint of destiny beyond his shrunken self. But his convictions had long ago been annihilated. The sun, a scorching blister, seems motionless just before it dives into the lake. He rises, stretching painfully to summon the hideous toll. His anxious mind tries to unravel what he once thought certain.

He calls to his wife, Freya, who has also survived. She emerges from the darkness of the hogan, a tall woman, wild steely hair pointing every which-way, her ruby cloak stretched across broad shoulders, a leather belt drawn tight to her waist. She moves toward him, moccasins soundless in the sand.

"Where are the others, Ethelred?"

This is how things were at Ashtephale (once called Ashtabula) in the wake of the attack, the bloodshed and looting, the torching of our village, the abductions, the retreat of the Nanticokes in their giant-oared warships across Eerie Lake. Ethelred, in a fugue state, gazed at the remains of our village, naught but smoldering ashes in the distance beyond Freya. He was speechless, his hands shuddering as he backed away from her.

My older brother, Silas, and I descended upon the scene from the artesian spring at the rocky copse that saved our lives. Later we collected what remained of our belongings and marched south to higher ground. This was before the arrival of the Argolians, but after babies died of poisons and pregnant women bore the agony of many miscarriages. And after the days and nights when the western horizon glowed, and thunderous blasts resounded from the Perry Megalith. And after a handful of children, who had huddled with me and Silas in that rocky shelter, became our most compelling purpose for building some kind of future.

2

On bright October days like this, it is my habit to stroll the potholed streets of Andeferas (once called Andover) nestled on the shores of Pymatuning, a long lake at the edge of this abandoned place, our reason for landing here: the abundant drinkable water, the fishing, the security of vistas to the horizon. On Wednesdays and Fridays, with the key from my pocket, I open the little brick library just west of the weedy public square. Despite its decrepit condition, the library shelves a trove of books people once cherished and an archive of times long gone. Others of our clan browse the open shelves, the books sometimes falling unbound with pages that crumble in your fingers. My duty is to handwrite copies of the most treasured volumes, page by page, to prevent further wear and tear on the originals. Me, a young woman with a steady hand, what my elders describe as lovely penmanship for a left-handed person.

Silas insists I'm wasting my time hunched over crumbling books like a medieval nun. He thinks I should be with the children all day long, happy as I am being childlike, though I've just passed my nineteenth birthday. All well and good, "But shouldn't somebody here be trying to preserve our heritage?"

"Probably, but not you, Hestia. It should be an older person with less imagination and sparkle."

Our mother and father are dead. We grew up in Ashtephale on the shores of Eerie Lake before the fatal raid. Our mother burned to death when the village was sacked. Our father, taken prisoner, was last seen in shackles on warships heading north toward what used to be Canada. Our world had unraveled in a heartbeat. As if some malevolent deity had pulled a loose thread and the whole garment had come undone.

Silas thinks more time with the children would comfort my troubled soul — the grief of our losses. I don't tell him that I had already thought that. Nor that Mirabel and Rosalie scolded me. They said I was trying to elbow them away from the schoolroom, and they spread rumors that I was stepping out of line and putting down Freya. Nothing could be farther from the truth. But truth is not necessarily of value these days. People make up stories.

Silas understands me; wants what's best for me. Except for matters of his own sexuality, he is more forceful than I. Some weeks ago, we sat together on a bench on the shores of Pymatuning, speaking from our hearts. "I so miss mother and father," I blubbered. While Silas was stoic, I cried my eyes red. It was a hazy autumn morning; the sun had risen above the distant forest. He wrapped his arm around me, his hand cupping my shoulder, comforting my spasms as gently as the breeze off the lake. We stayed there a long time, until I had no more tears to shed. And then he said, "Maybe it's time to move on, Hestia."

"Here we go again."

"No, I mean literally move on. Like, go south or west and get far away from this wretched place. Grab a couple of motherless kids someplace and start a new life. I am sick of being judged, of being the boy people say is more like a girl."

I'd heard that opinion before but his idea of migrating was novel and it shocked me. I never imagined leaving Andeferas, let alone kidnapping children.

3

In the library basement are the archives — stacks and stacks of papers and documents gathered from neighborhoods in this bedraggled town, abandoned farmhouses, single-wides and double-wides with their caved roofs and busted windows, and from former businesses downtown and in decrepit so-called malls.

To my knowledge, Kirke, the village clairvoyant and mystic, for years has not allowed anyone to descend the stairs at the back of the library. Why, no one can say. It is rumored that she replenishes her ritual powers there. A few years ago, people petitioned for access to the archives but the movement was silenced for no apparent reason. In the months following, we had little time to think about the banned catacombs. We were too concerned with feeding ourselves, staving off death and trying to bear children. Plus, we were determined to sustain the upstairs part of the library so as to raise literate children who could think for themselves and make arguments based on evidence rather than gossip and hearsay. Reading, we reasoned, fends off superstition and educates discerning children — despite the daily toils of living, despite Kirke's unsettling spells and her otherwise bizarre behavior, despite the pitiful number of kids.

Freya appears at the doorway. But for the daily harvest platoons that include every abled body, for weeks she and I have merely exchanged obligatory farewells as the sun set on exhausting days. And though she is my most cherished elder, we seem to have drifted apart, like fishing skiffs on windy days on Pymatuning. Freya is our nominal leader, mediator, and grandmother. She is also Village Council clerk. With kindness and humility, she manages to guide our fragile clan. Even in times of hunger and sickness she implores us to work toward better days. With the exception of Ethelred, Freya's husband, most of us behave as though Freya's guidance is a merciful combination of grace and wisdom.

Ethelred is cut from different cloth. His skin is thick as a wild boar and he's sour as wild grape mash. He verbally abuses Freya. And with everybody else he is harsh with his words and seems to abhor anyone who disagrees with him. He suffers no fools, accepts no criticism. Poor Freya.

I sit at the long cherry table, the opaque brightness of sun streaming through the surviving window, all others having been replaced with plywood. I study the cubed rectangular shadows of the window panes splayed across the table, a pleasing geometry. Freya is restless. She paces from one end of the room to the other. Stopping about four spans from me and squinting into the light, she asks, "Has Kirke gone down to the catacombs recently?"

I stand up and look into her eyes, searching for something behind the question. "Not since mid-summer. Unless, of course, she possesses power to pass through walls."

"You do understand why I'm asking?" Freya's tone is impartial but the look on her brow is not. It worries me.

"I have lived only one-third of your life, Grandmother. But yes, I believe I know your motive."

"You are wise beyond your years, Hestia. That is one of the many reasons I love you more than all the waters of Pymatuning, and why I must entrust you with knowledge you may one day wish I had not spoken."

Freya takes hold of my shoulders and guides me back into the chair. She sits across the table from me. "Kirke is the eldest among us. She has survived through all our deprivations. Her skills as a soothsayer have helped us, year after year. But since the death of Gideon, I have felt forebodings."

"Forebodings, Grandmother?"

"Yes, something nameless. And the feeling has been gnawing at me like an appetite that cannot be fulfilled. Something I cannot explain further. Ethelred will not even consider my misgivings."

"Perhaps Kirke is dwelling in darker realms. Her totem is the serpent."

"Yes, I have wondered about her recent hallucinations. She can be frightful. Her darkness is disquieting and lately, just as her witchery seems more and more bizarre, her temperament has become restless and a touch mean-spirited."

"Does she intend to take us to the underworld? Has she given herself to Shaitan?"

"Change is difficult for all of us, Hestia, but more so for Kirke. She has cause to be weary of life. Yes, there's the devil but let's not overreact. Let's not give Shaitan more credit than he's due."

With that, Freya leaves the library without further word, which strikes me as lacking her usual grace. Our small community seems to have devolved into a place of superstition and occult fantasies.

4

Things have taken a gloomy turn. The harvest has been pathetic, the lake is more choked with algae than ever, and it's unbearably hot and muggy for late October. The heat and humidity are making everybody a little crazy.

"Seems like we have no choice but to sweat and bitch." Rudi, overseer of community food stocks and keeper-of-the-peace, is venting his opinions on Silas. They're passing back and forth the last of a joint on a Sunday afternoon in the shade of a half-dead willow. At least the marijuana is thriving. The algae on the lake emit the stench of rotten eggs. A hazy sun descends through a thick deck of clouds. There's nary a breeze. As though it were mid-July, insects swarm and dive-bomb their heads.

"I give us four, maybe five more seasons before things get really bad," Rudi says. "Grain crops failing what with flooded fields in spring, mid-summer droughts, and rust and scale. Fish in Pymatuning are getting snuffed out; goats wander away and never return; our generation can't seem to get anybody pregnant. Kirke casting useless spells in the middle of the night."

"Maybe the kids will fare better'n us," Silas replies. "We've got what? Nine kids. They're happy enough and in a few years, they could pair up and make babies."

He takes the last puff, scratches his neck, swats a mosquito.

"Fuckin' mozzies," says Rudi, wafting the air with his vest, which is filthy and rank. A bit stoned, he's sprawled across a rough-hewn bench put there back when the willow was whole. "Ninesh not an even number, Shilas. Besides, there are six boyz and only three gaols."

Rudi wandered into our village five years ago. After his parents and most of his friends and relatives perished, he ran away from Meadville. He was seventeen. He's a friendly, open-faced guy with patience to go along with extraordinary strength. Unlike Silas and me, he can hardly read, though he's clever enough with numbers to keep track of corn husks in the barrels, shocks of wheat and rye, bags of beans and potatoes, and how far everything will stretch through tricky winters. He can trap rats and weasels, and is a deadly accurate bowman. Recently, the whole community feasted on his first wild boar of the season.

Silas wants to ask Rudi about Kirke, more curious about than fearful of her spells. Rudi struggles into an upright mess. He's speaking slowly, slurring his words. He cannot coordinate his eyes and reveals that, like a shooting star, he's hurtling through space, finally rolling off the bench onto dusty ground. "Damn hard landing," he roars. "But Kirke, she's just a blithering old hag; ain't got no more juice, can't heal a sick dog. She's bent so low her jugs are draggin'."

Bernard

"You better be careful, man. You may be risking bad fortune on all of us."

Rudi cannot contain his stoner brain. "May Kirke's spells be forever cursed!"

5

A year ago, Kirke, more than seven decades into life, came home to find Gideon on the floor and gasping for breath. Gideon, a burly gray-bearded, harmless beast of a man, had long ago seduced Kirke. Gideon was a herdsman; Kirke a witch. Their barren partnership persisted despite decades of quarrelling and tribulation.

When Kirke found Gideon, she ran to him in panic. Though she struggled to heft him upright, she failed. His slumped torso was too heavy.

"Bloody hell," she screamed and ran toward the library.

It was Friday. Dutifully copying Robert Herrick's poems from my favorite book, an anthology of English poetry, I was lost in his 17th Century rhymes and musings about a place called Devon. Kirke burst through the door and grabbed me by the shoulders. She looked bereft and muttered nonsense. I had no idea what to do. Before I said a word, she turned and raced to the back of the building and down to the catacombs. I followed her. Realizing this was borderline madness, I halted halfway down the stairs.

I'm not here to tell you what happens when you encounter a witch in action. I cannot recount witchcraft details, or patterns of cosmic wisdom, or arrays of spells and omens, or Kirke dancing between planes of existence, or any of the various realms of magic and premonitions, of talismans, divining rods, wands, caldrons, cats, toads or owls. Looking down at Kirke, mostly obliterated by swirling ribbons of some kind, I hear her voice — a raspy cackle — speaking a tongue I'd never heard. Using a stockman's pocket knife with a bone handle belonging to poor Gideon, she cuts red fabric into more long streamers. In retrospect, the scene is the most detestable of witchy tropes I've ever conjured.

Terrified, I retreated upwards, butt-step by butt-step while trying to put what I'd just witnessed out of mind. The best, or was it the worst, was yet to come. As I stood on the top step and backed across the threshold into the library, the witch wafted past me, her face winched tight with terror, her body naught but a wisp of gossamer, the red streamers rippling behind her like a wake. She floated toward the closed front door and then shrank to a scaly viper no bigger than a medium-length copperhead that, with lightning speed, slithered through the keyhole. I raced to the door, ripped it open. Kirke was gone. Gideon died. So reported Freya the next day. She told me his body was never seen nor will he ever be celebrated in any sort of burial or memorial. These were Kirke's wishes. Friends of Gideon protested. Kirke would not yield. She was gone for days, apparently seeking respite in the surrounding woods and caves with occasional visits to the catacombs.

Nobody but Freya and I know the details of Kirke's flight the day of Gideon's death nor what could possibly explain them. Kirke retains her spell-casting role in our superstitious lot: a person with psychic capabilities that in the past have helped heal and perhaps improve our community. But now I know that her powers have ended up in realms none of us can wrap our minds around or pretend to be normal or good for us.

In the next few months, joining Gideon in the afterworld were three other senior villagers none of whom had histories of illness or disability. All had been elders on our council and all had at one time or another run aground with others on council. Their deaths stunned us and set off wild conspiracy thinking: Kirke and Shaitan were in cahoots; Kirke had not finished her mission to cleanse certain elements from our village; Kirke had cursed the Village Council. All I can remember about those weeks is that, beyond anxiety over who might be next, our community fell into bleakness that discolored everything from birthday celebrations to the basic tasks of survival — work in the fields, tending our herds and horses, caring for our children. Even song circles. Kirke was hardly ever seen but her dusky aura seemed to hover over every kitchen table.

6

As a strong-willed, studious and somewhat indecisive good person with no history of ill deeds, I will admit to an almost pathological curiosity. But where's the harm in that? I'd already watched a witch wriggle through a keyhole. That's hard to forget. Maybe you don't want to know what an impetuous writer might conjure up when she suspects a witch has taken down people she loves and what she might not merely imagine but what she might actually do. On the other hand, maybe you do.

I really did want to bury those weeks of my life and move on. It wasn't that I had no urge to share what I saw and what I did. I do understand that suppressing things can lead to more anxiety. But writing about a witch and her potentially malevolent intent, no matter how I might frame it, could overwhelm me. The disappearance of Gideon. The deaths of three elders. The creeping venom in our clan. The simple prospect of a witch gone bad. A witch we don't need.

The writer wonders how to do this. She'll be characteristically hesitant while avoiding Silas and Freya, figuring they would think her mad, though in fact they love her and likely would have understood. After dithering, she'll stitch together a plan. Soon she'll be moving about in the dark, staking out the witch's haunts: her house, the locust grove, Stillwater Caverns. There will be no sightings. Soon she will boldly follow her lantern into the catacombs. This will grant her an ironic quiver of pleasure, the very act of transgression. By the third week, she will have assembled a box of potions and powders, pages of scribbled incantations, and three tattered, much-perused volumes — *A Handbook of Witchcraft, The Complete Manual of Spells and Potions,* and *The A to Z of Successful Witchery* — replete with underlines and marginalia. By the fourth week, she will have absorbed enough of this trove that terrifying dreams descend upon her by night. Sleep deprived by day, she will obsessively fixate on her goal. Days will slip by with no progress.

In the course of her nightly rounds, at last she will catch a glimpse of something scampering out of the locust grove. Diffuse light from a rising gibbous moon will leave room for doubt: Could it have been a wild dog? A bobcat? She will follow at a distance. The canopy will open to illuminate a nebulous crooked figure scrambling through the brush like an ape. Though a face will not be visible, she will jump to a preordained conclusion.

In minutes, the suspect will vanish into the blackness of the cavern. Behind a towering boulder, our pursuer will stay put through the night. To no avail. As dawn lightens the eastern sky, she will assume her prey has escaped. She will return to the village to sleep the day away. In mid-afternoon, she is awakened by loud knocking.

"Hestia, are you alright?"

"Oh Silas. Yes, of course, I'm fine. I was just napping."

"When I didn't find you at the library this morning, I began to worry."

"Drat. I forgot today is library day. I guess I'm a bit off."

"Yeah, seems like everyone's in shock."

"In shock?"

"Haven't you heard? Seamus McAnneny was found dead this morning at his kitchen table."

"Dead? Oh heavens. I just saw Seamus at the library two days ago. He was his usual bubbly self, sharing gossip as he always does. Gosh, he is — er, was — only what? Fifty-something?"

"Fifty-eight."

"He has no partner. Who's looking after the body?"

"I've not heard. When Agnes discovered Seamus, she got in touch with Rudi."

Though she'd been awake in recent days for far too many hours, her exhaustion metamorphosed into manic energy. Shooing her brother away, she will power-walk to the other side of town. She will watch Seamus' house from a stand of oaks. A half-hour later, she will decide the place is empty. She will race to the back door and, as expected, will be able to simply walk through. People in Andeferas have few possessions worth stealing and everyone draws from the same food stock.

She will spook around the rooms looking for clues. No signs of a struggle, no blood or body fluids, no foot prints across the porch or on the linoleum, nothing disrupted. Convinced that spending more time here would be useless, she will reluctantly head toward the door. As she opens it, her eye will catch sight of a dark strand under the door. She will stoop to pluck a half-cubit long braid of what appears to be human hair. Her mind will flash to the witch's manuals. Human hair, cut during the full moon, has ritual significance. It is a spell-casting contrivance, adding potency and permanency. Once employed, it must immediately be buried.

She will tuck the braid into a small cloth bag and return home. Silas has an update. Rudi found no outward signs of trauma on Seamus' body. That's it. Seamus was taken down by an evil spell. Shaitan at work through Kirke. *"Not so fast,"* she will scold herself, then discard the thought. She is still manic and captive of an idea.

At dusk, dressed in a black top with hood and tights, she will return to Stillwater Caverns, this time boldly setting up at the narrow entrance. There's nothing on the walls of this cold and dark place. No pictographs or petroglyphs. Nothing here but silence; not the sluggish kind, but a silence that comes from deep in its cavy throat.[3] In her bag are Seamus' braided locks, a wand, a small jar of sparkly powder, and a handwritten incantation from the A to Z manual. The night is chilly.

---

[3] The writer — Hestia — acknowledges, without shame, images inspired by Wislawa Szymborska's mystical poem, "The Cave." In *Miracle Fair: Selected Poems.* Translated by Joanna Trzeciak. W.W. Norton, 2001, 84-85.

Whinnies of screech owls will rattle her. She will wait through the night. Kirke is a no-show. Homeward at dawn, she will wonder whether her upside-down routine is a wise choice, no matter her obsession. Sooner or later, lack of sleep will cloud her judgment and mess up her plan. Moreover, people will wonder why she's not showing up at the library. Silas especially. She will conceive a new strategy.

Day forty-five of her quest will look like this: at dawn she will sprint to Kirke's house to re-dust the doorways with fine talc she liberated from the catacombs. Yesterday's dusting reveals nothing. Later in the day, she will spend hours perched on a branch of a maple at the edge of the locust grove. Nothing is happening. After climbing down, she will check the ankle-height threads strung across the cavern entrance. They are intact. She will return home to sleep.

The next day at the cavern she will discover severed threads. Dashing home, she will prepare a satchel with food and water and a blanket for her night watch. At midnight, footfalls on the trail: two shadowy figures climbing the rocky path toward the cavern. In the darkness she cannot identify them. She will have prepared for this. She returns to her hideout behind the boulder. As expected, muffled sounds waft through the chill darkness. A thump. She bides her time.

As dawn splashes puddles of sunlight along the path, she proceeds cautiously. Inside the smokey cave, a fire, recently extinguished. From the craggy ceiling, bats hang by the dozens. A wave of nausea washes over her. Alongside the smoldering ashes, her lantern reveals a nebulous heap beneath her blanketed trap. Perfectly still, the heap nonetheless induces dread. *Am I about to eavesdrop on my own death?* With renewed gumption, she tears away the blanket.

Deader than a block of granite, Kirke lies face up beneath Shaitan, also motionless, his ass upward, his head buried in her cape. The writer conjures a grim scenario.

With both hands, she tugs at Shaitan's rumpled coat. She rolls him over. Consumed by the terror of an encounter with a devil, she gasps: Shaitan is not Shaitan. A bone-handled knife rises from his sternum. She trembles more, the lantern in her hand, as she stoops to confirm his death, a pool of blood accumulates across his belly. With his hulk now on the cavern floor, the witch, perhaps flashing a wistful smile, levitates — merely a moment — before deflating like a punctured lung into the firepit's embers. Flames engulf her.

The writer will long be haunted by these hideous memories — as if that morning had been an alter realm in which she breathed and moved — a realm parallel to the murky cave. An underworld of death and cremation. In time she will take pride, despite persistent aftershocks of guilt, in a riddle resolved. Stories of evil spells by an unhinged witch could now be put to rest. Not one of the deaths was the work of a witch with malicious intent. The collective failure of our clan to think clearly, to naively believe conspiracies and lies, and our senseless unbridled fear condemn us to bear the burdens of culpability and shame.

The man with the knife in his chest, a malevolent human if ever there was one, was Ethelred. Ethelred, the erstwhile partner of Freya, our cherished leader and beloved grandmother, herself a victim of decades of abuse and denial who now must wander our village tormented by regret and loneliness.

The writer will never know whether Kirke's spells tapped into a dark reservoir of occult power or whether they were simply figments of our hyperactive imaginations. On the other hand, she had witnessed the witch's transformation into a serpent and had seen with her own eyes her final act of levitation. Or had she?

THREE

Survivors: Kate and Macy

Argolis, Late-2030s

To survive is sometimes a leap into madness.[4]

1

KATE WALKED HOME along one of the neighborhood lanes in what used to be the town of Argolis. At the mill sorting documents her father had found in a dark corner, she had only been gone a couple of hours. She entered the house and discovered her aunt's body — lying with her head in the oven.

She knelt beside the still woman, found no signs of life. Wracked in disbelief, she tugged the body across the kitchen onto a woven rug in the dining area. Cradling her aunt, she lowered her head onto a pillow.

---

[4] Joy Harjo. *How We Became Human*. New York: Norton, 2002, p. 78.

And then she crumpled to the floor alongside her. Hours later, awakened by footsteps, she sat up abruptly, rubbing her temples, aghast at the corpse at her side. Her lips began to quiver.

Her father looked down on her. "Oh, sweetheart, poor Auntie Lara gone way too soon. We'll need to plan a memorial."

"Dad," she blubbered. "Auntie's head was in the oven."

They buried her in the place where her partners also lay, one the victim of gunfire thirty years earlier, the other, a few years later, of a fall from the mill roof. At the ceremony, people spoke of Lara's grit, the tragedies of her life, her deep knowledge of the forest and its birds, her never completed PhD. When the mourners had parted, Kate and Macy tossed stories back and forth — Lara's midlife slump and resurgence, her randy son David, the night she showed up to sleep with Kate's father, her illness and death at fifty-five.

"She was old and sick," Macy said. "Ready to die."

"What an awful way to go. Sure, her life was hard — so is everybody else's — but checking out this way? Would you have expected it?"

"Never. I mean, when we were kids, we heard about people who were starving doing themselves in. But nobody I've ever known has died by suicide."

Macy cast her glance at Kate and saw in her face a clouded solemnity. Macy knew that look, the bleakness lurking beneath Kate's cheerful guise. After all, Kate had been raised by a professor who taught about a desperate end-stage for the world, a stage called 'Late-K'. No wonder she felt hopeless sometimes. Kate turned away to watch the river in the blood orange twilight. An evening breeze flowed across their blanket and swooshed the maple. Mourning doves began their evening coos. Macy reached over to her friend. She spoke her name. They embraced, their hips responding with a longing neither chose to acknowledge, at best, an awkward hug.

Though their community sought to be resilient in forbidding times and seemed friendly enough day-to-day, when it got down to personal histories and sensibilities, as with any sample of humans in good times or bad, relationships were fraught with heartache and pain.

Years ago Macy, a scraggly waif, showed up one night in Blackwood Forest, miles from here. She was barely two, her mother dead of an overdose, her father never known. A couple took Macy into their home, raised her until they no longer could. They believed her to be cursed. Latent heroin in her blood. In her early teens they sent her over the hills to live with the widow Lara and her son. "I've got this stigma," she claimed.

Kate pulled away. They got up off the ground, dusted off. "You're not the only one," Kate said. "My story's as fucked-up as yours."

"I seriously doubt it."

"Can you say you never met your mum? Have you been raised, quote unquote, by a bloke too distracted to be a proper dad, a man swallowed up with guilt and constantly hounded by disgusting women who might have become dastardly stepmothers? It's no wonder we feel pathetic. Here we are fully adult, sexually unrequited, trying to make a future in a place with virtually no opportunities."

"Pathetic is right," Macy agreed. "But sexually unrequited? What are you saying? Should we revisit that story? Or should we forget it and begin a new one, basking as we are in cuddly dampness?" Kate bit her tongue. Trash-talking a hot phase of their lives was not a great idea. But let's not get ahead of ourselves.

Kate still lived with her dad, Stefan, the village's most respected elder. After Kate's mother bled-out at childbirth, he bumbled through single parenthood in the hardest of times. His daughter grew up independent, callous at times, and self-aware, thanks to a couple of aunties — as her dad liked to think of them — rushing in and out with garden produce, soup and baked goods, home stitched garments, and more than occasional bouts of intercourse remorse. Lara was the latest and best. As she became more and more ill, she retreated to a separate bedroom. Stefan hardly looked in on her, leaving Kate to her care. Her death may have restored a bit of tranquility and it did resolve two problems; Kate could get back to work, and Stefan could try to shed more guilt. But Kate could hardly bear the loss.

Homebase was a tiny isolated village in what once was southeastern Ohio. As survivors of Late-K and collapse, the few dozen residents lived crudely in abandoned houses and buildings along a river at the outskirts of the once thriving university town of Argolis. Neither woman could recall anything about the world at their birth, a world that elders grimly remembered but were reluctant to talk about. There was so much the girls did not know, no matter how many times they pleaded for details. All they were able to discern was that it was a time when connectivity meant something other than the engagement of people in each other's lives, and that something called social media induced waves of hatred and separation so extreme that the country ripped apart. Why humans and governments were unable to rise above this non-human thing had never been explained.

2

Within hours of Macy's relocation to Argolis, she was assigned the job of caretaking two strangers — the recently-widowed Lara and her son David. They lived in a leaky-roofed bungalow on the way to the mill. On her first day, Macy, then fourteen, wanted to bolt. But she had nowhere to run.

The bungalow hadn't been cleaned in months. Bedding, the few pieces of stuffed furniture, carpets and curtains were flea infested. The skinny kid huddled in a corner of the back bedroom had to be David. He looked vacantly at Macy and despite her friendly gestures, spoke not a word. His kinky dark hair was a greasy tangle hanging to his shoulders. On his filthy t-shirt were the letters *GEESE* in faded orange caps, a reference to the mascot of the defunct university just downriver. The boy's hands and feet were caked with grime. Hard to say if he was a brownish kid, like her.

The boy's mother, Lara, looked too old to have a toddler. Hands clasped behind her back, she paced the house like a fisher cat, murmuring a mournful language Macy couldn't pick up. Nearly everyone who checked in that first day gave Macy less than a week in the forsaken household they themselves had been unable to rescue; mother disturbed, father recently dead of a bloody accident, kid a malnourished ragamuffin, and the house decrepit and conceivably unsafe. People coming and going in desperate attempts to stave off a death of even one more villager. That Macy was capable of accomplishing what they'd failed to do seemed impossible.

But they underestimated Macy. The scope of her organizational zeal, the capacity of her heart, and her knack for scrounging everything from socks to cabbages astounded them. Although housecleaning would be a long-term project, within hours she managed to draw David out of his stupor, strip away his rotten clothes, shave his head and bathe him with lye soap in full view of the neighbors. From a nearby line, she filched underwear, shorts, and a top for him. What she unearthed was a curious, sensitive cinnamon-shaded boy.

Still, she was jungles deep in the weeds. She scrubbed the linens, beat the mattresses and blankets, established her beachhead in the pantry, slaughtered a stray chicken and boiled it for supper with sprouting potatoes she found in the pantry. She forced the distressed mother to settle down at the plate she'd set out. Lara refused to eat and out of nowhere reared up full fire, shoving Macy to the floor.

"Whoa! Easy does it, ma'am. I'll not be hurting you. This is your home and you're going to love what I can make of it."

Lara resumed her pacing but something awakened in her eyes.

At sundown, Macy read the boy to sleep and slumped onto her mat exhausted. She felt like a battered person.

After that, people stopped-by less and less frequently. When they did, they asked, "How are *you* doing?"

"I'm a survivor," Macy replied.

"Great!" they responded, relieved, as if they expected something far more dreadful. The word *survivor* was all they wanted to hear.

***

As David's childhood passed, Macy poured her love into him and learned to tolerate his annoying male habits — the pissing contests, the strutting — as a sister might of her little brother. Month after month, she was his sole caregiver, playmate, meal planner and homeschooler. This was the easy part. Lara and her late partner had laid a firm foundation. Macy had come to believe she was born to childcare. Even as Lara recovered her senses, Macy continued to be the crucial cog of the household.

Things went haywire when David reached puberty. In her bed, in the darkness, Macy parsed each day and wondered how to cope with the new testosterone-crazed David. She tried to draw lessons from her own adolescence when she drove her own adoptive parents bonkers. But it was useless. Boys just seemed so blatantly incorrigible, wanking every time you turned around, subservient to their persistent pricks. *Stupid. Stupid.*

One afternoon, after Macy and David had finished the day's lessons, a pillow fight devolved into a wrestling match, lapsed into awkward body contact, spun toward breast groping and comically blown open-mouthed kisses. Macy was anything but amused. She did her best to shrink and squirm away. "NO DAVID, NO! GET OFF ME!" But her five-three frame was no match for the ungainly boy who overnight had become huge, his feet elevens, his height heading upwards toward six, arms flailing like willow branches in spring. David's upper half was boy; the lower half, bumbled toward man.

Macy was sure that David would not intentionally abuse her. But in the present scuffle the playing field wasn't level. She was in a pickle. As luck would have it, Lara wandered into the room and everything skidded to a halt. The scene seemed to crack open Lara's worst fears. She screamed, "What the fuck you doin', son?"

David rolled off. They both scrambled up. He was cowering, shedding tears. The bulge in his shorts vanished but not the stain. Macy ran out of the house. She never heard the scold. Nor would David speak of it. Her childcare world had toppled.

3

A few weeks after that skirmish, Kate, wearing a straw hat, walked along a riverside path heading north. It was summer; long days stretched toward ten o'clock. The river meandered peaceably. The rocky path was bordered by thick undergrowth, brambles snagging her legs. Midges danced in coordinated swarms. Late in the day, the sun's long rays spiked between the trees. *Hey, coyote pups yapping!* She imagined the pups roughhousing, wild as can be, careening madly through the woods like they'd never done in their short coyote lives. Sounds of the wild were so common those days they might be disregarded. Not by Kate. Thanks to Aunt Lara, her senses were finely attuned. She heard the coyotes but not the snap of a branch behind her.

Ahead she saw the tributary rippling forth to join the river. She turned upstream. *Did this charming little brook ever have a name?* Kate had discovered it five summers ago. When she traced the course upward for the first time, she could still remember the cool waters on her feet and legs. Tall oaks and maples and poplars formed a canopy. Her first kingfisher sighting; ovenbirds singing "teacher, teacher"; a vireo in the undergrowth. The best was yet to come: a sixty-meter cliff at the valley head, a grand waterfall cascading over it and into the deep plunge pool where she stood at its sandy edge. With no thought of risk, she climbed out of her clothes, dove into the chill, came up to break the surface, and swam sturdily back and forth, her body tingling and awakened in the clear water. From then on, this moist verdant valley with its towering precipice and hanging greenery became her place of solace and sensuality. A place to power through the muggy summers, where the cool days of autumn could be imagined.

After a few more minutes of climbing Kate could hear the waterfall. On the sandy beach, she removed her sweaty clothes, set aside her bag and notebook, tied her flaxen hair into a ponytail, and waded into the water quivering pleasurably. When it was breast deep, she kicked off and swam a lazy crawl toward the falls. On the other bank, she paused beneath and became one with the cascading waters, which in turn flowed down through the valley of the brook, into the Shawnee River running through the village, and far away to the ocean. Soon, she lay down under the roof of the vast sandstone cavern behind the falls. As the light softened, she sank into dreams that transported her away from her weary, menial life — a life that rendered her oblivious to lots of things, including comings and goings in the village. Her dad nagged her to be present. *As if he should talk.*

At that moment, she had no clue that a brown boy — adolescent and horny — had been stalking her. In a small notebook, he monitored her pathways through and around the village, her hours at work, her time with friends and at home, even her dad's daily movements. At night, as though writing fiction, he added fanciful details: she's a shape shifter, she wears a silk negligée and no underpants, her breasts are like puffy pears, her siren songs lethal as she longs for a young prince.

By the second and third week of his surveillance, he noted that every few days she departed the village before sunset and returned at nightfall whistling softly. Where she had been, he cannot say. It kept him awake, obsessed as he was. The whole scene was sick, he knew well. But what's a boy to do in a small village with few girls? So far, he dared not follow her. Until this evening. And though he had almost no experience in the forest and was fearful of its creepiness and of catamounts in the night, he reckoned that if he were to chicken-out or if she'd wandered too far, he could always turn back.

The boy knew that his fantasy girl and his tiresome nanny were age-mates. The village has so few young people that it would be ridiculous if they weren't friends. But they seemed not to be together much these days. After the fracas that angered his mother, there was no way he was going to share this project with Macy, heretofore his closest friend.

"Macy does her best to avoid me," he told his little friend, Danh, age eleven. "I guess she thought I was getting too frisky. She's just mad at me. She'll get over it."

"I don't understand," said Danh. "What's frisky mean?"

"Never mind," David said. He realized that the pillow fight was never going anywhere. He just got carried away. Macy might as well be his sister. Brothers do sometimes spy on their older sisters to learn the ways of girls and what they look like without clothes. He had read this in a book. Instead of spooking Macy again, he would learn these things from a different girl.

He hung back on the tributary bank, allowing his prey to get beyond earshot. Moving cautiously forward, it wasn't long before he began to hear a rumble — deafening almost, like a mob of gnarling black bears. He slowed to reconsider. His mind had been twisted by evil things in fairy tale forests. The boy in him advocated turning back. The man-boy, though, reasoned that the girl must know what she's doing. He insisted they push onward. Man-boy prevailed. He tiptoed carefully toward the roar. In the dusky light, he veered slightly away from the bank, unsteady now on sloping ground, nearly tipping into the rushing water. Something sharp broke his momentum, dug into his leg, pulled him up the bank, and would not let go. He slumped to the ground with a yelp. The throbbing pain was like nothing he'd ever known. He thought he might die. "Help!" he blubbered.

Kate awoke. *Was that cry a part of a dream?* Squatting to pee, she heard it again. She ran to the pool, swam hard to the opposite bank, toweled off, dressed quickly, and stuffed away her sweaty things. Not quite dark, she hurdled down the path.

"Help, help, please!" the call again from below her somewhere.

She plunged off trail into the thicket. The going was rough and the tangle only got worse. She tied her knitted bag to her waist. At every turn, she was spiked and whipped by berry canes, spice bushes, locust saplings. Tripping, she scuffed her knee and squatted to duck walk, the better to worm her way downward beneath the tangle. She called out, waited. No response. She feared it was too late. Picking up a sound, was it the last fluted notes of a wood thrush? She stopped to listen. Not a bird, a whimpering downhill and to her left. On all fours over stony ground, she scrambled further downslope, pausing at the bottom to listen again. Her legs and hands were scuffed, her smock torn, her mind grappling with the likelihood of a dying person when she came upon the boy, sprawled upslope, his head gashed by a mossy rock the size of a pumpkin. He seemed unconscious.

"I'm right here," she said softly, kneeling and laying her fingers on his neck. It was throbbing and hot. His hair soaking with sweat as saliva oozed across his cheek, puke on his shirt. He'd peed his pants. She recognized him as Lara's boy, Macy's foster child. What on earth was he doing here?

From her bag, she removed a flask and poured water over his forehead and lips. He opened his eyes, lifted his head. "I hate zha forst!" His face and lips swollen, he searched Kate's face wildly as he tried to sit up inducing a fountain of bile down the front of him. Kate instinctively recoiled, noticed his leg. Radiating outward from two red punctures was a patch the size of a catalpa leaf, blackened purple and yellow at the edges. It encompassed most of his calf which had become the circumference of a maple sapling.

"Snake bite."

He sputtered, "Yeah, zha buggah."

"Was it brownish-orange with darker bars and a rust-colored head?"

"Maybe." He drifted off again.

"Copperhead," she said. "Lots of pain in the leg? Numbness?"

No answer. She grabbed him by the armpits, dragged him to flatter ground. She splashed more water over his head. Dashed to the stream to refill. He rolled over, propped himself on his elbow, his eyes glassy, hands jittery. She was sucking on the two punctures in his calf, spitting out blood, serum, possibly venom.

"Come on, David, we've got to get you home, then find Dr. Todd." Dark now, the trip took three hours, hobbled and disoriented as he was, a lump of excruciating pain. At David's height, Kate was stronger than any girl in the village, but her willowy frame was no match for the boy's ungainly stagger, and she was perpetually thwarted by his rounds of collapse.

Almost midnight, they reached Macy's. There was light in the kitchen window.

"Macy, come quickly!"

Macy found Kate slumped on the doorstep, David whimpering in fetal position on the grass. Though the girls met rarely these days, Kate had never been happier to see Macy. She wanted to heap praise but had no words.

4

Five years ago, things were better. One bright spring afternoon that year, Kate showed up on Macy's doorstep. A Saturday, Macy had finished her chores. Their friendship, at times tumultuous, was good that spring, good enough to enable their repressed adolescent imprudence to well-up, right on the doorstep. Imprudence nowadays in no way compares to what was possible and common in the old days. After all, neither girl needed a driver's license — no vehicles, no petroleum; they had little opportunity for wild sex — few eligible boys or girls; and they had not dallied on porn sites, not suffered through bullying or sexting — not experienced poor connectivity on the internet, not complained about mobile service, and never had been shamed on social media. Yet with raging hormones and the right setting, inevitably, what may be called imprudence could turn to a local form of recklessness in a heartbeat.

Macy, the older and more venturesome, said, "Hey! Great timing. David's napping. Let's run away."

Kate was reticent. "Oh, I couldn't leave dad alone. He'd never survive."

"Not literally."

With no more talk, they scampered out of the neighborhood like children, skirted around fenced vegetable gardens and ran across goat and sheep pastures kicking aside turds. They jumped a fence, plunged into an abandoned lane overtaken by Japanese honeysuckle, grape vines, and clumps of sumac. Macy stopped to check out mushrooms growing on a rotting log at the shady edge. "I know this one," she said, "Folks down in Greig County call them shrooms. They're magic."

At the end of the lane was their hideaway — a mostly intact, single-wide immobile home. In the past, it might have been spiffy, not repulsive like now. Vines and undergrowth virtually camouflaged the place. Its vinyl siding was encrusted with mildew. Windows broken, the roof slumped on one side. Macy stopped short of climbing the steps to the door with the cracked window and rusted lock.

"Come on, let's gather a bunch of dry sticks. I want to build a fire," she said.

In an old pot, they boiled water. From her pocket, Macy threw in a handful of mint leaves. After chopping the shrooms into small pieces, she added them to the brew. The pot simmered, yielding a musky smell. She stirred the brew.

"Smells like a heap of dead moths," offered Kate.

"It's not the odor we're concerned about, my dear. When it cools, we'll sip. But first we must wait."

"What are we waiting for?" Kate asked, though she intuited what may be coming. They climbed the steps. Inside they encountered the decaying remnants of an unknown family's home two generations ago, including all manner of contraptions the girls could not name. On the hanging door of the refrigerator Kate fingered faded kids' art and a 2019 calendar.

Pointing at the fridge, she asked, "This closet thing was a cooler of some sort?"

"Yeah. You would stick that wire into the wall over there. And somehow it would make cold air but only when the door was closed."

"Hmm," said Kate. The notion of a cold closet in a kitchen was bizarre.

They headed down the hall to a cubical where there was a big mattress, once rodent-infested, but no longer. Macy spread a freshly laundered sheet. They had been here before, playing cards, blabbing incessantly, idly fantasizing about places far away. Neither had travelled more than a few miles from the village.

A warm breeze threaded through broken windows. The girls began to sip the acrid brew and splayed out on their backs.

Macy rolled onto her side, scrutinizing her friend, whose shape seemed to be rhythmically pulsing, like a frog gullet. "Have you ever thought about us making out?" she asked.

"With each other?"

"Yeah, I mean, you're one beautiful long-legged white girl with lovely small breasts and I'm one short-legged brownish gal with much bigger breasts. And I'd guess that we both have horny yearnings. It might be fun to, you know, explore our differences."

"Fun? It wouldn't be much fun if we got to be known as lesbians."

"In this village, are you kidding? There are hardly any quote-unquote normal couples here. Nobody would bat an eyelash."

"What if I want to have babies? What if I've already done it with a boy?"

***

Kate's swirling mind leaped to a brilliant autumn day when she and Lara strolled together along the river to the confluence, where the Shawnee River flowing through the village met what folks once called the Ohio. It had been a dry fall. Neither river had much water to work with. The breeze was subtropical. No birds sang. But the air sparkled with such clarity you could imagine sailing right up to the crescent moon high above them. They sat on the river bank.

Lara spoke of her first partner.

"Adrienne. A woman, right?"

"Yes, a woman. It's possible, my dear."

Kate said, "Wow, I need to think more about this. And you, you then fell in love with a guy?"

"That's right; two, in fact. Life offers opportunities and, you know, women's and men's tastes do change and evolve through life. And now I'm with your father. He's kind to me. We have many things in common, you especially. He loves you very much, you know."

"I do know that about my absent-minded father, who never speaks of love," Kate said.

"Now what about that boy you had a crush on?"

"Yeah, Jason. You know his parents, Em and Nick. Jason and I are the same age."

"Uh huh," Lara said. Like everybody else, she was reluctant to speak about Jason.

"Well, Jason and I found our way into a dark corner one night in the Argolis ruins. We ripped off our clothes, kissed and, you know, with our hands and fingers, reached our peaks. We were too chicken to do more. But we might someday."

"When that time comes, let me know, okay?"

"Sure, I promise."

Kate knew Lara had her best interests in mind. As things played out, though, it would have been impossible to have that conversation.

Kate and Jason had marched toward critical thresholds rather faster than expected, back in the ruins, miles from the village. Neither thought it was a good idea to trust an adult with intimate details of their first real sex. In retrospect, it was neither romantic nor satisfying. They were frightened. He pulled out just in time. Or did he? She was seriously hurting and wanted nothing to do with rehashing painful moments that should have been beautiful.

Over the next three weeks, they worried. They were edgy and they managed to hurt each another. They both wished it had never happened.

"If you hadn't put that hairy beast in me, we'd be much better off," Kate told him.

"Hairy beast? That's not what you called it that night."

Right on schedule her period arrived, within two days of which Jason joined an excursion on wagons heading north. Now, almost a year later, Kate had no idea what had happened to him and the others. And there was some reason why asking about the expedition was forbidden. The memory of Jason and her sexual fantasies faded in equal proportion to her fear that the expedition would never return.

***

On the bed in the hideaway, Macy told Kate she doesn't really care if she's had sex with a boy. "So have I, when I was thirteen. He wasn't exactly a boy and I wasn't exactly keen."

"Were you raped?"

"I wouldn't have called it that at the time. Let's say I was curious enough not to resist at first."

Kate had no response. Her world had begun to shimmer as spectacular iridescent geometric shapes encircled the bed, like flights of butterflies, leaving sparkling tracers in their wake. The windows were golden auras. Nauseous, she barfed over the side of the bed. Better. As though time had stopped, she felt herself melting into her surroundings. She was the hawk. The oak. She was Mother Earth herself. She soared toward the goddess.

Macy studied her glassy-eyed bedmate. When the time was ripe, she proceeded to undress, folding her clothing and placing it neatly on the floor. Naked, she climbed on top of euphoric, semi-aware Kate. While removing Kate's garments, Macy gently caressed her neck and arms, her face and nipples. She kissed her lips firmly enough for Kate to respond with urgent open-mouthed kisses. Though Kate's breath was sour, it was hotly propelled by fervent exhales and childlike cries. Macy moved her tongue around Kate's mouth as if calling her in for more. Kate's hands greedily guided Macy's tiny hips, round and round, her head cocked back, her throat emitting gasps. There followed a timeless succession of events that soared — orgasm to orgasm. In each other's arms, they fell into blissful slumber. At sunset, they rose unsteadily and aimed toward the village.

In Kate's mind, the blur of that afternoon yielded few specifics and recurring tremors of guilt, not to mention a daunting headlong plunge into the unvarnished quandary of these times. *Is survival even worthwhile?* We cannot replace ourselves, especially with sex between likes. This in the midst of such gut-wrenching convulsions and pounding headaches that, much to her dad's dismay, forced her to retreat to the darkest room — Lara's room — for almost a week. And her thoughts, when she had any, never strayed far from the brew Macy administered to her but barely drank herself.

On the seventh day of her agony, from the porch, Macy knocked and called through the screen door. Squinting and pressing palms to her forehead, Kate shuffled across the kitchen.

"Sister," Macy said, "that afternoon last week was fucking awesome."

Kate mustered a tentative smile but her sallow face could not hold it. The moment of brightness vanished. Kate wondered. Macy's my friend, my sister, right?

"Come on, let's go find some more shrooms."

"Not if I have anything to do with it."

Macy reached across the doorway to place her hand on Kate's cheek.

"No!" Kate grabbed Macy's wrist, tossing it aside.

"Hey, hey, calm down."

"No calming down. You took me for a fool. You. Me. We need to forget about it." She turned her back and slammed the door. On her way to her dark chamber, she soberly realized their sisterhood, such as it was, was seriously tarnished. She began to feel angst about many things, especially those that had nothing to do with her. Her dad's inevitable ageing and decline, the wagons that went north, wounds and diseases the village doctors could not cure, the corn blight, a legion of others.

5

David's libido roared back, finding himself erect more often than not. Macy tolerated his distracted behavior as long as he completed his assignments and accomplished his chores. His mum, Lara, wasn't home much and seemed unaware of where her son was on the maturation curve. As for David, he was sure of one thing: he could not talk about sex with either of them.

After his swollen leg returned to normal and the bite wounds healed, Dr. Todd told him he no longer needed treatment. It had taken weeks. Lacking antivenom, the doctor had monitored David's vitals, applied poultices to prevent infection, and checked for signs of clotting. David would experience lifelong muscle pain and some weakness in his calf. Otherwise he was healed.

"You're a lucky boy," the doctor said. "Years ago, I treated Professor Zielinski for a snake bite. His copperhead must have been more virulent or maybe it was a cottonmouth. The wound was nasty. Prof Z. limped the rest of his life. Ah, but that was before you were born, son. Main thing is to keep away from places copperheads like to nest."

David has not forgotten his quest. But the warm weather was long gone. Now in mid-winter, people huddled round their wood burning stoves and fireplaces. When they ventured out, they rushed from errand to errand, bundled up from head to toe. You couldn't see a fucking bit of skin. Updating his notebook was challenging, though his imagination continued to churn out cheese — *She goes forth through the woods and fields at midnight on Garthmore, her trusty steed.*

David no longer worried about stepping on a snake. It was his own snake that obsessed and unnerved him. On a midweek day in February, Kate ran into him at the weekly staples distribution at the mill. She'd frequently checked on David's condition after the event, but once his future was no longer in doubt, she forgot that she'd never discovered why he was in the woods that night.

"Hello David. Long time no see. How's the leg going?"

"Oh, hi." David resisted calling her by name. Holding a five-pound bag of potatoes, he began to march in place. "My leg's, um, fine. I'm not even limping. I won a race against Danh who used to be faster than me."

Kate noted David's face reddening. "That's great," she said. "Say, now that your snake bite is history, can I ask you a question?"

"Um, sure."

"What exactly were you doing in those woods that night?"

"Well, I can explain about that, but I don't want to do it here. Could we talk somewhere, like, you know, more private?"

"Okay." Kate raised her eyebrows but, after all, this kid was only fourteen or fifteen.

They descended two stairways to Kate's office — the office of the village archivist, a cheerfully decorated corner room with west-facing windows with a river view. In an adjacent room, bins on shelves contained carefully labeled documents and folders. A library room with aisles of shelving and books was off to the left. Kate's small oak desk in the middle of the room separated her from David. Sitting in a straight-backed chair, he twiddled his fingers erratically.

Kate felt relaxed, not a stern bone in her body. She speculated that David's need for privacy might have something to do with her erstwhile bosom buddy. David's candid account of his teen angst, of his perpetual horniness tweaked empathy in her. When David got up to leave, she ordered him to cease his prowling. Then, she softly suggested, "Maybe we can talk more about this another time." That night, after dinner with her dad, she pondered how best to respond to David's confessions. She was significantly his senior and ought to have sent him packing. Having no inclination to be his counsellor, she realized that she could not just dismiss him, kindly or not. For one thing, there was something erotic going on. The poor kid, like any kid his age, was trying to navigate puberty in these hapless times when we're so thin on the ground. As for what to do next, she could not think clearly.

A week later, on her way home, David transfigured out of the darkness. Matching her strides, he said, "Maybe this would be a good time for that talk you mentioned. I noticed your dad and Mr. Hays leaving the village."

"I thought I told you to stop stalking."

"I wasn't stalking *you*. I just saw them earlier today taking off with packs and heading south."

"Uh huh. They're scoping out the idea of repopulating Pomerance, the old Ohio River town."

"So, want to have the conversation at your house now?"

"Ah, David, I'm a little anxious about you. Things could get out of hand, like they did with Macy."

"It's okay. I don't want to do anything like that. I just need to talk with someone who's not Mum or Macy."

"Alright, as long as you promise to be a gentleman, help me stoke the fire and feed the animals. I'll warm up some soup."

Over the next several months, two lonely humans, in the most troubling of times, satiated themselves in all the ways one could imagine — the older and more experienced mentoring the younger, a tender soul, who learned how to hold back and blow past thresholds of pleasure Kate could never have imagined. It was not the summer of 1942. It was the winter of 2037. What was left of the world now was far more ravaged and needful. And, as in 1942, these young bodies became a haven to escape the trauma of a world that no longer made sense.

Would they evolve as potentially reproductive citizens and parents for this beleaguered village? That's not how things worked in the past, and not how they worked now.

David graduated from Macy's tutelage to that of Kate's father. Practically and ethically, it became impossible for David to lie perpetually about sleeping with his teacher's daughter. By the same token, Kate knew full well she could not sustain the affair. Meanwhile, Macy, no longer having a young man to mentor, left the village.

Emotionally hollowed out, Kate plunged forward stolidly, a twenty-something grieving her gone aunt, her testy sisterhood with Macy, and yearning for Jason's return, a prospect as murky and troubled as the summer day she buried her aunt. She knew she should take comfort in her walks and swims at the falls, barred owls calling in the night, her smallness in the scheme of things. But she could not shake off her apprehension. *If our meager generation is destined to fail, why endure this madness? What's the point?*

FOUR

The True Vine Sanctuary:
Hestia and Salma

Andeferas, 2030s

1

SEVEN YEARS AGO the Brothers of the True Vine took possession of Saint Theobald, a defunct Benedictine priory and retreat center. Surrounded by forests and meadows, the priory had been abandoned after the last priest died. Reputedly, this band of mostly young brothers, a monastic order of unknown origin, had been driven from their previous locale by a handful of incensed villagers.

The Brothers of the True Vine would have been of no interest had their origins and practices not been steeped in mystery and had they not been so close geographically. For years, as far as people in Andeferas had known, there had been no occupied settlements nearby. Given their history, that's the way they liked it. But the former priory, less than a half-day's ride by horseback, was beginning to unnerve them.

"The Brothers, what's their religion?" Silas asked his sister Hestia as she was ladling venison stew to accompany the freshly baked corn bread that infused her small kitchen with delightful aromas. She was adept enough cooking on a woodstove to be praised by the older women as an accomplished homemaker. At twenty-three, Silas was four years Hestia's senior and her only surviving relative. Silas admitted to incompetency in the kitchen and was prone to show up at dinner time.

"Darned if I know what religion," Hestia replied. "Their sanctuary was once some kind of Catholic place and the brothers all dress like medieval monks. But they say no prayers before eating and we saw no statues of Jesus or Mary or anybody. Is that their names?"

"I've heard of them, I think."

"No crosses either. All the old churches have crosses."

"Strange. Did you see anybody besides the brothers there?"

"Yes, it appears that when they migrated, the brothers were not alone. There were other adults and possibly some children there, as well as herds of farm animals. I'll tell you more later. Let's just eat and not think about those monks for now."

2

Villagers in Andeferas had no awareness of the monks until a party of them pulled into their village square. It was a bright spring day, the air thick with lilacs and honeysuckle, the soil singing of rebirth. In their one-horse cariole, the party consisted of three bearded monks and one girl with beaded cornrows, stunning in a kitenge shirt-dress and tight brown pants. As the villagers had almost never seen visitors, the sight of strangers set off alarms. People around the square instinctively retreated, locked their doors, and hovered in upstairs windows.

From the library, Hestia boldly marched out to the square. Out of the corner of her eye, she saw Victor Graber charging toward the carriage brandishing his Winchester 94, though neither he nor anybody else in the village possessed ammunition. Dozens of antique weapons were reputedly locked up in the basement of the former Methodist Church. In the early days, weapons had turned up everywhere but live ammunition was rarely unearthed. The village wanted nothing to do with guns.

Hestia shushed Victor away and turned to the carriage.

"Hello! And welcome to Andeferas." She bowed into an open-armed courtesy.

"Je suis, me, myself, *je m'apelle Mahakash Yapa.* Bon goo'day Madame," the elderly monk said, his eyes twinkly. The other two, much younger, brown-bearded and cow-eyed, looked on silently. The girl, with skin the shade of desert sand, smiled demurely, her hands at rest in her lap.

Though the Monk's language sounded like French, Hestia wasn't sure. She called across the street to Silas who, with Rudi, was repairing the cupola atop Agnes Spornsmith's cottage. There was an old grandmother back in Ashtephale who spoke the language and Silas, who had befriended her grandson, was always at her house. Maybe he could help.

He and Rudy climbed down and came across to offer handshakes to each of the monks and were particularly solicitous to the girl whose flapping eyelashes might have triggered typhoons in a young man's loins, if that was her intent.. She looked to be about the same age as Hestia. So far, she hadn't uttered a word.

Using hand signs and ludicrous broken French, Silas led them back across the street to Agnes' house. After introductions, the main monk and his two brothers, the girl, Rudi, and Silas gathered at the dining room table. Hestia helped Agnes quickly warm up and serve bean soup, beet greens, and crusty oatmeal bread.

"Welcome," said Agnes. She apologized for the simplicity of the meal.

"Thank you Madame. No apologies needed. We are honored to be here at your table," the girl said in clipped English. "I am Salma." Sweeping her hand toward the brothers, she continued, "As you've heard, our Abbot here is Mahakash. His companions are Brothers Forthwind and Tybalt. We come from a place once called St. Theobald Priory. The brothers have renamed it The True Vine Sanctuary."

There was something discomforting about Salma's deliberate English, as though she were reading from a book. In a life with little drama and much tedium, Hestia began to imagine a mythical tale spooling out Salma's rebirth from the hardscrabble lot of peasant waif to the exalted role of Abbess of the True Vine. How absurd! Her dress was anything but a nun's habit, and the sensuality of her every gesture said nothing of obedience and cloistered contemplation, let alone chastity. The three monks nodded vacantly, as though the conversation was in a foreign language, which it apparently was.

Hestia spoke up, "Salma, if you don't mind me asking, how did you become interpreter for the monks? And where did you learn English?"

Salma's eyes threw up a barrier. "Oh no, that's certainly not my role at True Vine. But for this excursion, the Abbot believed he would need an English speaker. I was selected. As for English, I was born speaking it." Silas and Rudi seemed to have been stricken dumb, as though lost in a fog of infatuation.

Agnes' eyes shifted back and forth between Hestia and Salma. The silence in the room made her nervous. Allowing Salma to translate, Agnes spoke slowly of her girlhood aside Eerie Lake, their former village of Ashtephale: its grand fishing, orchards and gardens, the tranquility of the place, the day that she and her late husband, Duvall, met; their family that included Maria, their only child, and Great Aunt Bertha; the explosions at the Perry Megalith; the tragic poisoning of their twin grandchildren — babies at the time; the blood-soaked day that turned Ashtephale survivors into refugees a decade ago; their arrival here at Andeferas, an abandoned village miles and miles south of the lake. She said she was happy to learn of nearby neighbors and told Salma and the monks that she feared that without more children our community would wither.

The Abbot's eyes widened. He and Salma exchanged glances. "We also are grateful to learn we are not alone in this empty country." Salma interpreted the Abbot's words. As the brothers rose from the table, Salma said "The Brothers of the True Vine are looking forward to showing you their sanctuary soon."

3

It took three months before the people finally organized an excursion. Those who'd had lunch with the Brothers told their story at the Village Council which met in the sanctuary of the former First United Methodist Church. Like all the other churches in this village, it possessed neither clergy nor congregation. Nowadays nobody had time nor interest in the archaic faiths that drew ordinary people to these pews. They apparently had fallen into step with the increasing secularization in the prior world. From church records, it was clear that there were just a handful of Methodists when the world came unhinged.

The church, despite its resident bat and rodent populations and moldy hymnals, provided a central place and people met there frequently. After several hours of wrangling and wasteful tangents, the Council came to consensus that a single short foray to the Brothers of the True Vine would do no harm, especially if our delegation offered no commitments. The Argolians, three men and two women from a region far to the south, agreed to harness up one of their Percherons for the trip. As to who would travel, the decision was made by drawing straws.

"What are you wearing on the journey?" Hannah asked Hestia. The two were lounging on a steamy late September afternoon in the shade of two Norway maples outside the library. Days this hot tediously strung on and on into what used to be autumn.

"Well, I have few choices, Hannah. We weren't as fortunate as you. Our community lost everything when our village was ransacked. And before we arrived here, someone had stripped this town of almost all garments and fabrics. What I wear has been handed down from older women. But to answer your question, it will be a denim smock that will reveal nothing of my body nor show the dust."

"Are you ashamed of your body, Hestia?"

"Oh no. When I see my reflection on the Pymatuning waters, I'm accustomed to my twiggy image. It is what fate has granted me. I'll probably fatten up once I bear some children. That is, if I can find a mate, with, you know, proper manhood. Here in Andeferas that seems more and more unlikely. Maybe my fertility, assuming I have some, will go to waste."

"Don't give up, Hestia. You're a fine-looking young woman. You must be grateful for what you've been given — a healthy, lithe and strong body, beautiful hands, a sparkling smile and abiding wisdom. As for landing somebody with manhood, we must leave that to Pan."

"Pan?"

"I'll tell you about Pan another time."

Hannah was in her forties and rather lean herself. She had alluring almond-shaped eyes that often masked her pranks. Her humor bordered on slapstick and she loved to mimic people around her, even the men. She could also solemnly tell of her own experience as a reticent girl with little hope of becoming a mother. Then a bit later in life, she met Manuel, a handsome Mexican, fell in love and gave birth to a beautiful brown-skinned child, Samantha, now seven. Hannah spoke too of life's hardships — the collapse that squelched her education, the pandemics, how much she missed Manuel and Samantha. For her part, Hestia imparted stories of her dear parents and how broken and lonely she felt without them. In such moments, she and Hannah formed a friendship, and for the first time in her life, Hestia felt completely in accord with another adult.

Hannah and four other Argolians had travelled many weeks northward from a place near the Ohio River to recruit people to join their community, which, like Andeferas, was at risk of failing. After their long journey, it took just a few days for them to comprehend the predicament here, ironically similar to their own — the jealousies and superstitions, the apparent barrenness of many young adults, the virtual depopulation of this country — its wild emptiness, and the low probability that a sanctuary of monastics could help resolve anything.

"After we visit the Brothers of the True Vine, I think it will be time for us to head home," Hannah said wistfully.

"Oh Hannah, I shall really miss you."

"Maybe we're not meant to be separated. Would you ever consider going south with us?"

"Good grief, what a thought! My heart tells me that it is both enticing and frightening. Could Silas go too?"

"Yes, of course."

That night, after dream beings alternatively aroused and threatened her, Hestia lay awake, her mind swirling with questions and fears. *Could Silas and I really break away? How could I leave my dear grandmother Freya and the other women who've made me who I am? Would I survive a long trip? Would I be accepted in a foreign place? Could I bear children? Will my breasts make milk? What sort of man might suit me? Who is this Pan?*

4

As the party set off, the day was already sultry. The rising sun cast shadows across patchy forests and grasslands that surrounded the village. Nick and Jason, his son, piloted the Conestoga wagon. Jason, a strapping boy about the same age as Hestia, had occasionally hung out with her at the library. She wondered whether he was flirting but she couldn't tell because much of what he said was nonsense. And she'd never been wooed by a young man.

Like a ship at sea, the wagon roiled down the once-paved southbound road — a faded Route 6 on a rusty sign, now a morass of potholes, cracks, gullies, collapsed bridges, and brush encroachment. It's no wonder the wagons in Andeferas had long been sidelined by broken axles and wheels with severed rims and spokes. Nobody in the village had the skill to repair them. Along with other junk, they slowly rotted in a thorny patch referred to as 'the heap'.

In addition to Hannah, Hestia, Nick and Jason, Agnes and Rudi rounded out the expedition. After travelling all morning, Nick turned on a narrow dirt road going west and then onto an almost hidden lane on the right marked by a sign which read, 'Brothers of the True Vine Sanctuary'. The lane passed through a cool patch of mature oak and maple. Further, on both sides, were carefully-tended orchards with ripening peaches, plums, apples, and nuts. A dozen or more workers labored in a distant part of the orchard, their heads covered by scarfs topped by wide-brimmed straw hats. They were picking fruits and nuts, and dropping them in bags slung round their necks. They moved through the trees in formation, apparently supervised by one elfin monk. As if visitors travelled this lane daily, the pickers never took their eyes off their work. In the opposite direction were vast vineyards, the ripening grapes in fulsome clusters tended by yet another group of field hands.

At lane's end, Agnes disembarked onto a brick-paved courtyard surrounded by freshly-painted buildings interconnected by pathways with grass verges and gardens of flowers and shrubs in glorious bloom beneath the shade of tall longleaf pines. "How splendid this courtyard! Compared to our village square with its burned-out buildings, rubble-strewn lots, and weeds and thorns," Hestia said.

"True, my dear," Hannah replied. "But one cannot judge a book by its cover."

A sprightly elder monk popped out of one of the buildings, his tunic and rope sash swishing back and forth, his sandals clip-clopping across the bricks. His broad smile revealed missing teeth.

"*Bonjour. Comment allez-vous?*"

Agnes called forth her rusty grade school French. "*Bonjour Monsieur! Bien merci.*" From there she was forced to revert to English. "We have travelled from Andeferas; we are returning Abbot Mahakash's invitation to visit your sanctuary."

"*Oh, mon dieu. Oui, oui! An-de-feras.* Why you not phone ahead on *le téléphone mobile?*" He chuckled at his own little joke. Hestia wondered. From personal experience, she knew that dozens of mobile phones had been extracted from abandoned buildings and pockets of bleached skeletons in Andeferas. They'd been thrown into a box at the back of the library.

The monk continued, "*Pardon, Madame, mais vous voyez... L'abbot... Il est impossible. L'abbot est mort.*"

"Oh, how very sorry we are to hear that."

"*Merci. Maintenant,* zere is non abbot. *Moi? Je m'appelle Valmore.*"

Agnes was tongue-tied and Bother Valmore had exhausted his English. He nodded and peered into the wagon, saying *bonjour* to each of us. He was intrigued by Henrique, our massive Percheron. He stepped toward him, flashed a bashful smile up to Nick and Jason, and gently tickled Henrique's withers. Henrique whinnied with pleasure, nodded his tawny head, and deposited a mound of poop on the monastery bricks.

Out of nowhere the African princess Salma appeared, dressed in tight-fitting denim pants and a braided top with a V-shaped neckline. From her dainty ears dangled hoops with crystals that sent forth tiny rainbows as they wafted back and forth across her long neck. She smelled sweet, the fragrance of heliotrope. Rudi's eyes grew big. A more perfect woman he could not imagine.

"So, you've finally come," she said, aiming a tight smile at the distant horizon. "Since Brother Valmore's English is limited, I will be your guide." She instructed the party to follow her.

Hestia whispered to Hannah, "She never said welcome."

"Strange."

Nick, who missed little, heard Hannah's assessment and softly murmured, "Do you trust this person?"

"There's something worrisome about her," Hestia replied.

"Do you know that I am fluent in French?"

Hestia searched Nick's deep brown eyes and though he was a brawny, charismatic, handsome man who often joked, today she saw not a hint of braggadocio. "Let's keep that a secret for the moment," she told him.

Hannah nodded in agreement.

The visitors followed Salma into the building from which Valmore had emerged. He turned left; Salma, right. Following her, they weaved through several parts of the former garth and chapter house, stopping for explanations about the meeting and meditation spaces, the chapels, the library, and other unnamed spaces — all unblemished as a cloudless day in spring. Hestia ached to browse the shelves of the library. When she asked Salma for permission, Salma replied, "No, it is closed. We must move on."

"So much for that," whispered Hannah.

In an adjacent building — the kitchen and refectory — they descended a stairway into the basement. Salma explained that they were about see how the brothers had converted the Our Lady of Lourdes Grotto into a wine cellar. Barrels and casks lined every bit of the grotto walls. Hestia could not imagine how many tuns of wine or mead could be drawn from each barrel. The one barrel of almost undrinkable dandelion wine distilled in Andeferas was no match, and they had never harvested enough honey to make mead. Even more astonishing was the overhead lighting. A string of lights flooded the vault more brightly than most of the visitors had ever seen. Some had seen the meager lights in Holms Mill but not such eye-squinting orbits casting searing shadows with astonishing intensity across a room.

Rudi gasped, "Holy shit! Pardon my language."

Nick said, "Yeah, these people have somehow harnessed electricity. It's a lifetime since I've seen such brightness indoors."

"Incredible," said Agnes. "Electric lights. But how?"

"The lighting throughout the priory comes from solar panels that Brother Kornhower revived in our first few months here," Salma explained. "I will show you the panels later."

Changing the subject, pointing to her left, Hestia asked, "What is in that other room?"

"You need not be concerned about that," Salma replied.

She continued the tour outside along a serpentine circuit that was once a 'Stations-of-the-Cross' path. What exactly that meant was never explained. The brothers had repurposed it as 'a challenge course' meant to enhance their fitness. For the visitors, it was a lovely stroll along a manicured pathway through shady woods with raised beds of low-growing foliage plants. When Hannah asked where the brothers found such beautiful plants, Salma claimed she had no idea.

Circling back toward the priory buildings, they passed an array of glass boxes attached to steel frames anchored in the ground. Incredibly, these boxes generated energy from the sun to make light in the grotto. Hestia could not fathom how this worked, and despite questions, Salma was unable or unwilling to answer.

Off in the distance, cattle and sheep and horses grazed in fenced green pastures. Behind hedges, just to the east of the priory, they saw four two-story buildings apparently enclosing a central plaza. "Are those living quarters?" Hestia asked, pointing toward the hedges.

Salma pretended not to hear the question, instead announcing, "Now, citizens of Andeferas, we shall dine together."

In the light-filled refectory, a long table had been prepared with platters mounded with meats, fruits, vegetables, breads, and cheeses — a feast such as few Andeferians had seen, certainly not in recent years. The monks filled steins with intensely sweet and strong mead. After a few sips, Hestia told Hannah that her brain was beginning to feel tangled.

"Intentional dulling of your curiosity," Hannah suggested.

A number of new monks joined the luncheon. Nick sat strategically between Salma and these monks, all of whom were cut from the same cloth: youthful and fully-bearded, in brown-hooded tunics with a cowl and scapular, leather sandals with treaded soles, no socks. Rudi looked them over and asked if their robes were required. They did not or could not respond.

Brothers Valmore, Forthwind, and Tybalt joined Jason, Agnes, Hannah and Hestia at the other end of the table. The conversation never strayed from basics: How sweet these grapes! Is this whole wheat bread? Do you eat like this every day? Where do you find the honey? When these pleasantries no longer sufficed, the monks seemed comfortable with silence.

In hushed tones, Hannah and Hestia tried to make sense of the day. "Have you any notion of how Salma fits into this picture?" Hannah asked.

"None whatsoever. She's strung tight as a length of wet rawhide."

"Yes, she makes me anxious with her mix of curtness and sensuality." Hanna said.

"Rudi has certainly paid special attention to her."

"Poor boy; she's not his type. Maybe we could invite him to go with us. There are marriageable girls in our village."

"He'd jump at the chance" Hestia said. "I have a raft of other questions."

"Like what?"

"Where do these people come from, and why? Who were all those field workers we saw? Why so much wine and mead? What was in that other room in the grotto? What religion do they practice? What's under the monks' robes?"

"I may have insights to share later, except not about what may be under a brother's robe."

Hestia wondered: *How did I manage to think up such a lewd question?*

The three monks aimed curious, friendly gazes at the women — a tilt of their heads, raised eyebrows, crinkled eyes, Cheshire-cat grins. "*Il est temps de faire la sieste,*" announced Brother Valmore. "*Hmm, um, Siesta... er* nap *en Anglais.*"

Hestia said, "*Oui!*" and smiled back. She waggled her fingers toward him in a capricious, innocent way, that of the little girl who dwelled inside her.

It was time to board the wagon. With Salma translating, Agnes offered formal thanks and promised to tell the people of Andeferas all about this visit. Salma responded that the next time we meet a new abbot will have been appointed, and that she hoped there would be a next time.

After an exhausting afternoon with one stretch and pee break, the wagon pulled into Andeferas just as the full moon rose above the oaks and cast long shadows across the square. The weary travelers disembarked and wordlessly headed toward their darkened homes.

On her way to the library the next morning, Hestia waved at Hannah.

"Hestia, hi! Have you recovered from our long day in the wagon?"

"Well, yes. I guess I have. I'm not too exhausted but my emotions and thoughts are all over the place. What about you?"

"Same here," Hannah admitted.

Nick, tagging along, claimed to be fine, then asked, "Look, can we have a quiet conversation in the library?"

They gathered at Hestia's work table. Sunlight licked at cobwebs hanging above the table. The room was stuffy. Hestia opened the window and door to fresh air and the fluty trills of an eastern meadowlark.

"I've got some new information and speculations about the True Vine," Nick said.

"New information?" Hestia asked.

"Behind-the-mask details. Things Salma didn't want us to see."

"Was I missing something?"

"Yes, lots," Hannah said.

Nick continued, "You remember that at lunch I sat myself in the midst of Salma and two monks called Baltad and Humfroy."

"Did those monks speak or understand English?"

"No, apparently not. Salma spoke softly with them in a dialect familiar to my ear — Québécois. I pretended not to understand and spoke entirely in English."

"Did she suspect anything?"

"I don't think so. She spoke freely. I doubt she would have wanted me to home-in on their conversations."

"Why not?"

"Okay Hestia, this is partly reading between the lines, but it's clear to me that the monasticism of the brothers is something else entirely. In response to Salma, who asked how it felt to be returning to the refectory, Brother Baltad said that his two-week withdrawal from the material world for contemplation and meditation had aroused his appetites. 'Appetites, Brother?' she asked. 'Yes,' he replied and seemed to aim a crooked smile at Humfroy. 'I look forward to some lusty days,' he said."

"Do you get this, Hestia?" Hannah asked.

"Maybe. He's been fasting and he's hungry and thirsty?"

"Partly so," said Nick. "When Salma extolled this summer's excellent pinot noir and their crop of weed, his eyes lit up. Then, she asked whether, you know, his 'quéquette' was up for action."

"His what?"

"*Quéquette*. It's a colloquialism for penis — small penis actually. Like wee-wee in English."

Hestia blushed, "So, was his *quay-kit* up for action?"

"Aye, it was. Very up."

"What did Salma say to that?"

"Well, when she pointed at his bulge — *renflement fait par l'érection* — Baltad's bearded face turned red. "We'll have to attend to that," she said. Then Humfroy raised his eyebrows and asked, '*Et moi, Salma?*' Without cracking a smile, she said, 'Be patient, dear Brother. Gwendolyn is not quite ready.'"

"So, is Salma some sort of go-between?"

"Yes, I believe so. And I do wonder what other roles she has. Her churlishness and secrecy reek of authority and power."

"A weird combination in a monastery, wouldn't you say, Nick?"

"I would."

Hannah nodded in agreement. "Now, Hestia, all this is just between us right now, okay?"

"Yes."

"There's a bit more. Nick and I managed to sneak away from the group on the path back to the refectory. We wanted to see what was behind the hedges and temporarily borrow a couple of things."

"Borrow things?"

"I'll explain in a minute. We climbed over the gate, which was locked, and found ourselves in a courtyard surrounded on all four sides by what clearly was the cloister of the former priory. We entered through an unlocked door. Nick searched for the monks' quarters; I knocked on a few locked doors of what were obviously women's rooms. Then I found one open. From a small chest, I borrowed what I was looking for and returned to the gate. Nick was waiting for me there. We scrambled over the gate, ran across the lawn and into the woods just as the workers were returning for lunch. We saw something troubling about them."

"Troubling?"

"Well, the workers were all women, dressed alike in olive green coveralls, just like those we saw in the orchards and vineyards. From what we could tell they seemed to be less than thirty years old; maybe some as young as twelve or thirteen. They were quick stepping in columns, herded by monks with rods and staffs. They marched in silence."

"How many?"

"Thirty probably. They entered one of the buildings we didn't go into. We could hear children's voices and smell food cooking. We retreated quickly to join you before you entered the refectory."

"Good grief."

"Right," Nick replied. "Hannah and I met this morning with the other Argolians to tell them what we saw and heard. We asked if we could postpone our departure a couple of weeks."

"Why?"

"Well, we think the women marching across that courtyard may be held against their will. If that's true, we may be able to liberate some who choose to leave. Perhaps go south with us."

"What about the children?"

"Yeah, what about them, Nick?" Hannah said.

"I've no idea. We need more information, which is why we're prepared to stay longer. Whose kids are these? Are they offspring of these women? If so, the brothers may also be fathers."

"How do you propose to get the information? I mean, you can't just waltz in and ask Brother Valmore or Salma?"

"Reconnaissance," was all Nick would say.

5

A week later, as four riders departed Andeferas, thunderheads gathered in the southwest. Nick led the expedition on the broad back of Henrique. Hannah followed on her sorrel Morgan, Ulysses, a gelding she had ridden all the way from Argolis. Hestia was next on a gentle chestnut mare named Farleigh. And Jason brought up the rear on the Argolians' other Percheron, Benoît. The riders heading south, all dressed in black, might have been mistaken for brigands.

They'd been making good time when yellow-tinged black clouds coalesced to blot out the sky. The wind picked up. Passing through Williamsfield they sought shelter. Once a crossroads village with a post office, a restaurant, convenience store and gasoline pumps, grain silos, and farm implement dealership, Williamsfield was now just another ghost town. The few standing homes were overgrown with box elders, crabapples, hawthorns, and tangles of wild grape, Japanese honeysuckle, and multiflora rose. The post office was shrouded by Kudzu and Virginia creeper. Through its collapsed roof, a tulip poplar reached to the sky. Across the road, the Old Coach Grill and Tavern stood in sorry decrepitude, its vinyl siding disintegrating, its large sign dangling at a precarious angle, windows shattered, interior stripped bare. Adjacent and mostly intact was a long, windowless block building, a former stable or workshop with a wide barn door on the gable end.

Nick reined in, dismounted, and shouted, "Over here!" With a buck knife he hacked away at poison ivy and honeysuckle to free the door. "We'll wait out the storm here."

The building reeked of hay, dust, and uncountable generations of rodents — the scent of social and economic collapse. Despite the stale air, the place had the feel of a safe haven. Hestia reached into her saddle bag and unraveled a towel wrapped round a loaf of honey buckwheat bread. She served it with wedges of sharp cheddar and the first apples of the season. They snacked as the storm ripped at the building with gale force winds, torrential rain and hail. The roof creaked but did not give; lightning crackled with thunder that spooked the horses. They could smell ozone and burning wood.

Jason paced back and forth, calming the horses. They nibbled oats from his open palm. Rubbing their necks, he cooed, "There, there, big fella; nothing to be afraid of."

"That one o'mine's a mare," Hestia corrected.

"There, there, young woman; nothing to be afraid of."

"Was that aimed at my mare or me?" Hestia asked.

"Both of yer," he said.

"Strikes are coming damned close," Nick said. "I smell smoke. Are we on fire by any chance?"

"Not that I call tell, Dad."

"Better say your prayers." Hannah flashed a smile at Nick.

"Prayers? If there's a god and she wills me gone, prayers ain't gonna help."

In thirty minutes, the storm tracked away to the northeast. They remounted. Just down the road they found the fire. A two-story home set back from the road, once referred to as a McMansion, spewed forth a mighty column of black smoke and acrid odors of sizzling carpets, plastics, roofing, who knew what. They dismounted and filed past the inferno, each taking stock of the pointless materialism, the folly of permanence, and why, after all these years, the fire happened today for them to witness. And of course, the obverse: If they had not been here, would there even have been a fire?

"Some farmer thought he'd really made it in life," Nick said. "He built this suburban replica of highly combustible materials and full of shit that had little to do with quality of life. He was proud of it. He thought it would be in the family for generations. He couldn't imagine that his generation would never be able to recover from the inevitability of Late-K or that a fire many years later would be the final word on his legacy. Now there's nobody but us to perform last rites and pronounce his dream officially dead."

"I want to cry," said Hestia.

"What's the use?" Jason asked. "We're suffering at least as much as he did."

"At least, we're alive," Hestia added.

From Williamsfield, they galloped through the cool, damp air into the lengthening shadows of late afternoon. Arriving at the Brothers of the True Vine Sanctuary, they cut right along a two-track wagon road skirting the orchards. By good fortune, there were no farmhands on this side. They circled around to the solar panels and downslope to a small stream under a grove of tall sycamores. Nick and Jason rigged a hitching line while the others led the horses to the stream. Once the horses had been watered, fed, and secured, the team squatted in the shade to review their plan and prepare for the unforeseen.

They split in two directions. Nick and Hannah headed to a hummock overlooking the rear entrance to the cloister. From her pack, Hannah retrieved items she'd borrowed at the priory the week before. In the shade, she donned the olive work coveralls, a head scarf, and a straw bonnet.

Hestia and Jason scurried past the vegetable gardens and beds alongside vast pastures stretching to the northwest. At the stable and tack barn, they took stock of the horses and mules and the wagons and carriages. From there they scrambled toward an ancient open oak, slid under a fence, and squatted behind the tree.

***

Nick and Hannah crouched below a stand of pin cherries at the top of the rise. With binoculars, Nick scanned the courtyard and lodgings.

"All clear," he whispered.

"Okay, here I go and may Pan guide and protect me." She ran to the unlocked gate and ghosted into the woman's cloister.

Nick stayed put. He heard whispers and giggling. He looked up to see two children, a boy and a girl, sitting on a branch above him.

He spoke softly, first in French, then English. "Hi kids, you having fun up there?"

The girl, perhaps five or six, replied in a mix of Québécois and English, *"Oui, c'est l' fun!* Want to come up?"

"Merci, but I think I'm too big for your tree. It would break. *Nous tomberions tous en bas."*

She laughed. *"C'est d'valeur!* I've never seen you before."

"Je suis un lutin.

"Franchement? You're not scary like *les lutins* in Giselle's stories."

"Oui. Je suis inoffensif. Tell me your names."

"Je m'appelle Marie. Mon frère s'appelle Jules."

"Bonjour Marie et Jules! When do the brothers and workers come back from the fields?"

"Maintenant! Je peux les entendre. Et toi?"

"Oui. S'il vous plait, do not tell them about me, okay. *Gardons notre secret."*

"D'accord, Monsieur Lutin."

***

Hestia and Jason sat silently under the oak. They watched workers carrying armloads of squashes to a box wagon driven by none other than Humfroy, the sex-deprived monk. Hestia wondered out loud whether Gwendolyn was now ready for Humfroy.

"Ready for what?" Jason asked.

"If we're not locked up and tortured, I'll explain later."

Soon the overloaded wagon, pulled by an impressive Canadian Warmblood, clinked and rattled past them. The troop of workers, flanked by three monks on each side, followed. Silently, patiently, Hestia and Jason scrutinized the monks as they passed. Then they slithered on their bellies closer to the path. As the last of the fieldworkers approached, they leapt forward, each clutching a worker, snuffing out their astonished cries. Despite determined resistance, they were able to haul their prey under the oak. Jason calmly explained to them that he and Hestia would not hurt them. They merely wanted to ask a few questions, after which, they would be released. The women quietly complied.

***

The two children shimmied down the cherry trunk. Giggling, they each tugged a moment on Nick's beard. *"Je te l'ai dit qu'il était vrai,"* Marie said as they skipped toward the cloister gate. Nick waved *au revoir* and watched the workers and monks filing past. Before the trailing monk, a novice, could lock the gate, Nick slinked up behind him. He swiftly covered the monk's mouth and nose with a cloth infused with the oil of cannabis. The monk crumpled as Nick muscled him onto his shoulder, dumping him in the copse of trees. He stripped the monk of his hooded tunic, providing an answer to the question of undergarments. Nothing but a bulbous gut overhanging spindly legs. He let out a soft chuckle at the sight of the bleach-white novice, now stoned. Donning the novice's robes, Nick rushed to the gate.

Dusk softened the late summer landscape, draining away its colors. A whippoorwill began its incessant calls as the four regrouped under the sycamores. Their spirits were high; their plan had succeeded. Though they were anxious to compare notes, they knew they must depart before Salma realized something was amiss. They mounted up silently, heading into the gathering darkness of the heavy summer night. Riding steadily, they pulled into Andeferas just past midnight.

6

Two days later, in response to frantic knocking, Hestia found Jason at her back door.

"Morning," he said. "I need to talk to you."

"Alright. Is it something urgent?" She opened the door and swept an inviting arm toward the kitchen table.

"You might say that."

"Have you had breakfast?"

"Actually, I haven't."

"Good, I've got some apples and hot oatmeal along with mint tea and cream."

They faced one another in Hestia's tiny kitchen. With a man not her brother, Hestia realized she'd never been in such intimate space. As he gobbled the food in his bowl, expressing appreciation with each bite, Jason seemed unaware that his presence was accelerating the beat in Hestia's throbbing chest. Finished, he pushed his chair away, stretched his long legs toward the wall, and flashed a smile that crinkled his eyes at the corners. The smile, the broadest and least guarded she'd seen from him, opened a portal to Jason's heart and maybe even his childhood as the son of two spectacular parents, Em and Nick.

"Hestia, here we are — now many hours beyond our mission to the True Vine." He dropped his head, drew in a deep breath, and ran a gigantic hand through his kinky mop. From there, nothing. The lengthy silence prompted Hestia to blot out all thought, promising or bleak.

"Sorry," he apologized. "I'm having a problem with, like, um, like speaking what's on my mind."

"It's okay. The True Vine mission, and what it may mean for our future, is not to be taken lightly. If that's what this is about."

"Well, it is. Yeah," he said quietly and lifted his moistening eyes to Hestia, astonishing himself and sending chills down Hestia's spine. He brushed away a tear. The longer they held the stare, the more charged the air in the room became.

"From the first time I looked into your eyes, weeks ago, I've been telling myself to ignore the urge to kiss those eyelids, those lips. I kept talking myself out of it, especially after a couple of stupid ploys at the library. There's also, I admit, somebody who might be waiting for me in Argolis."

"I've wondered."

"Hmm, you could tell?"

"Well, I've never been courted, if that's the right word. So, I wasn't sure what kind of signals were coming at me."

"Now you know."

"I do. I'm flattered."

"You, just being you, kind of takes my breath away, Hestia. You have such a solid, cheery sense of yourself, of what to do, what to say, who you are. After our time together on the expedition, I've tossed and turned, not slept well either night. I decided I had to come here this morning. Hestia, what I want to tell you is that I am highly attracted to you and I would like to deepen our...our friendship. Especially if you decide to head south with us."

"And what about that girl who's waiting for you?"

"I'm guessing she's moved on. I know I have. Things didn't go well for us just before I left. We had a sort of unpleasant parting."

"In that case..." Bounding through space, Hestia planted a hungry kiss on his lips.

Later that morning Hestia and Jason walked arm-in-arm to their meeting with Hannah and Nick. When they entered the room, Hannah winked at Hestia. "Ah Hestia! Pan seems to have visited you two."

Hestia blushed. Jason said, "Pan? We got a statue of Pan back home. That one?"

"Yes, that one," Hannah said.

Nick paid no attention. He opened the meeting, asking Hannah to take notes. After an hour, Nick asked Hannah to read back her notes. When she'd finished, she asked, "Is there anything we're forgetting or overlooking?"

"No," they agreed.

"Alright then, time to take this to Agnes and Freya."

They met the two elders around a picnic table at Pymatuning Beach. The breeze off the lake was northeasterly and fresh, rippling the lake into small waves. A chipping sparrow trilled softly along the lakeshore. Because the expedition three nights ago was primarily a venture of the Argolians, apart from Hestia, nobody else yet knew of it. Nick told them that this was a time not only for hearing about what the expedition discovered, but also for thinking about what it means for Andeferas and "those of us from the Ohio Valley."

Hannah presented a crisp summary. When she invited Freya and Agnes to speak, both appeared glassy-eyed. Hannah embraced their silence.

"As you know," Freya finally began, "I did not visit the sanctuary, so I don't have your points of reference. But I can hardly imagine such a religious order. If I did not know you, I might rebuke you for trying to make me believe some sort of fairy tale. In all, it seems not only morally and ethically distasteful but also rather threatening. Related to that, I wonder why the brothers came here in the first place. Do you know why they were driven from their former location and why they sought us out?"

Hannah responded. "I don't know. And I think I can speak for the others that those were not questions we asked. Am I right?" She glanced at Hestia, Jason, and Nick.

They nodded.

Freya asked, "Are you sure that these so-called monks are sowing their seeds in the wombs of captive women? What kind of religious brotherhood would do that and then take their children away from them? This is utter cruelty, a form of sex slavery, is it not?"

"Yes, it is. I have no reason to doubt what the two women revealed to Jason and me," Hestia replied. "They also admitted to being high when having sex with a brother. Their marijuana sounds more potent than ours."

"They wept when they told us of being separated from their children," Jason added.

"Who then raises these children? And how many kids are there? What will become of them?" Agnes asked.

"There's a nursery and kindergarten staffed by a separate group of older women who no longer work in the fields," Hestia explained. "Our informants weren't sure how many children there were; they guessed at least a dozen — all born since they arrived here. They feared that the children would be sold to people from across the lake or other traders who show up from someplace called Wheeling. So far, it hasn't happened."

"The two children I encountered seemed like normal happy kids to me. I did not ask them about their parents," Nick said.

"What of the field workers?" asked Freya.

"The agricultural workforce is totally young females," Jason said.

"Where does all that produce and wine and marijuana go?"

"They said traders from across Eerie Lake and from the big river travel here a few times per year."

"Where did those worker-women originally come from? Are they held against their will?"

Hannah replied. "We were told that most of them were rescued from towns and cities in their former homeland, a place they referred to as Pin's Silvainya, during the last pandemic. Only the comeliest girls were chosen. They're not exactly imprisoned but they have no vision of any other existence and therefore cannot imagine escaping. They did tell us that they're not abused, apart from having to be shagged by monks from time to time — sorry for being crude here. Apparently, they are well fed, sheltered, and clothed in return for their labor. The monks, they said, are not evil, just playing their roles in the community. They did sort of save them. Their alternative might well have been squalor and deprivation."

"Goodness," said Agnes, shaking her head. "And did you offer them a prospect of escape?"

"Yes, we did." Hestia said. "The two women Jason and I spoke to were highly receptive. My heart leapt when I heard that."

"They, in fact, *begged* us," said Jason. "And this is when they claimed that getting away from Salma would be their greatest relief. They reckoned that almost all their co-workers would want to do the same. They also said they would not leave if they weren't able to recover the children they'd given birth to."

"What about coming here to Andeferas?" Agnes asked.

"To put it bluntly," Hestia said, "they are fearful of moving here. They believe Salma and the Abbot would find them and drag them back."

"Who is the Abbot now?" Agnes wondered.

"Brother Valmore."

"That raises the question of Salma," said Agnes. "Did you find out why she seemed so unpleasant and cold? I was quite perplexed by her."

"Perhaps. Strange as the explanation may seem," said Nick. "I overheard a conversation about her in the monks' chambers. One monk explained to another that Zoroaster, who created all things on earth including humans, is not to blame. According to scripture, humans were initially insensate; then they gradually evolved into completeness, able to love and feel empathy, as we all are able. But not Salma. 'She comes from another place, a dark planet. She will never have feelings. It is a fact,'" he said.

"I hardly know what to say," murmured Freya. "Maybe Salma has Asperger's."

"Asperger's?"

"A kind of mental illness that may render people incapable of feeling and empathy. I remember people talking about it when I was a girl."

"Are those monks Zoroastrians?" Agnes asked.

"Beats me," Nick replied.

Then Freya said, "We may rue the day these brothers showed up in our square. The True Vine Sanctuary could be nothing but trouble for us. I'm so sorry, dear Hestia, that you have been caught in their ill-fated webs."

"Do not worry, Grandmother. I am strong in the face of the future."

"Indeed, you are," said Hannah. "Our challenge now will be to determine how this saga will inform our separate paths. It could certainly be seen as an opportunity for us. For you here in Anderferas, it may be a different story. And for that, my heart is heavy."

FIVE

The Ohio River: Hays and Avery

Pomerance, Late-2030s

1

AT DUSK, RUTHERFORD BOSWORTH HAYS rowed his aluminum fishing boat toward the skeleton of a former coal dock. Fifteen meters from shore, as was his habit, Oakley crawled over the side and dog-paddled into the weeds, his tail a flag aiming for the pathway home. He'd strayed into town a year earlier — a starving beast with a melancholy demeanor, mostly Basset, some spaniel Hays guessed, with his low-slung body, long ears, curved stubby legs, and wrinkled brow. Ornery at times, once regularly fed he became a good companion, a rare thing these days of roaming packs of wild dogs and coywolves. Hays lashed the boat, grabbed his tackle and catch, and followed the dog up the bank. It was an early autumn evening, the frogs and crickets amping up their serenades, sunset showering gold dust across the green ridges overlooking a river once known as the Ohio.

Hays limped up the weedy path keeping an eye on the clock tower of the bedraggled Greig County Court House that overlooked Main Street and the river. The clock read 7:45. Though it had not ticked for decades, it was correct twice a day and almost precisely so this evening. Not that it mattered. He chugged his way along weedy Main Street and up the hill to his house, a big Victorian just east of the Court House. Sturdily built by a coal baron in the 1920s, the house had been renovated by subsequent families through the years. But for reasons unknown to Hays, it was foreclosed and abandoned around 2005. Now it was a wreck. Its Sarasota Sand/Goddess Gold paint job had thoroughly peeled, the roof leaked, gutters hung at useless angles, few of the windows opened, and the front door was unlockable. Four years ago, Hays and Melissa threw their duffels on the porch and moved in.

"Home sweet home," he said and slapped his thigh. Oakley climbed a step or two, his bad hips and crooked legs tuckered by the long walk. "Shucks, dog." Hays bent over and with a groan lifted Oakley up onto the porch. His tail wagged him through the door and straight to his empty bowl. Hays dropped his fishing stuff, went to the kitchen with his catch. Oakley slurped some water, milled about underfoot, uttering guttural pleading barks. He was on the rowdy edge. "If you want yer supper, you best put that thought to rest," Hays advised. He set out a bowl of corn mush and bacon fat. In minutes the bowl had been licked clean. The dog ambled across the kitchen into the living room, heisted himself onto the moth-eaten plaid couch, rolled over on his back and drifted off to a land of watery dreams.

Hays lit two candles, peeled and boiled potatoes, fileted, battered and fried his fish. He poured himself a home brew from his root cellar and carried his meal to the porch, a habit he and Melissa had fallen into almost every night through the long dusks of summer and early autumn. After dinner, they'd refresh their drinks and listen to the frogs down at the river, hear the peents of nighthawks, watch bats and swifts swoop across the darkening horizon. Occasionally, another of the human residents of Pomerance would come by. But in these washed-out times, people mostly kept to themselves. It was alright.

Melissa grew up in this town when it still thrived thanks to abundant coal mining jobs, when classrooms and churches were alive with white Appalachian Ohioans, when Main Street provided all the goods and services one could want in small town America in the 1980s. She graduated from Greig High School, married a classmate. Together they restored a small house a few blocks from the Victorian. Melissa worked as a checker in the local grocery until she gave birth to twin girls. When the mine shut down in 1998, he lost his job and turned mean. He beat Melissa with his fists and one time with a baseball bat. She reckoned the girls were next. In the dead of night, they snuck out of town to a shelter. She enrolled in Gilligan University of Ohio, completing her bachelor's degree in her early forties. Her ex moved on to abuse someone else.

Melissa and Hays met at Jerry's Riverview Restaurant and Bar during the tumultuous years after Late-K and the collapse. He'd lost his wife, Jo, to the bird flu. Melissa's twin girls had finished their degrees and fled to the big city. Despite their age difference — Hays almost twenty years older — they fell in love. Melissa moved to his farm deep in the woods about 15 miles from Pomerance. When they could no longer sustain themselves there, they moved to Argolis, joining a community of survivors west of the shuttered university. In time, with a few others, they closed the circle to resettle Pomerance on the river. After a couple of years of a life as good as it could be during those times, Melissa died.

Off in the distance, across the river in what used to be West Virginia, Hays heard coyote families, miles apart, baying, their pups yapping and squealing. The night sounds — the cicadas, the heart-rending final flutes of the wood thrush, the wind through the sycamores — were all of a piece: the rhythms of an eighty-five-year-old who'd survived two wars, one in combat, two pandemics, and a planetary collapse. He was the oldest person anywhere, at least as far as he knew. Once a hearty beer drinker and pothead, as a courtesy to Melissa, he'd disciplined himself to one brew in the evening, an occasional shot of Ohio Mash corn whiskey, and the not so rare toke. When the moonshine and weed ran out, he'd hike a few miles to badger his supplier; a task that could always be postponed but was helpful in reassuring him that the world beyond Pomerance had not collapsed all over again.

The days, too, whether in mid-winter bleakness or the haze of oppressive summer humidity, rolled by somehow. His household routines marked the passing time, balancing his moods enough to have patience with the dog's bottomless appetite or unceasing pleas to play throw-the-stick. Rarely did he rebuke the animal and then only to hear himself on any given day: "Would you please get off my fuckin' case for a few minutes?" As if that thought had beamed into the house, Oakley jumped off the couch, clip-clopped across to the porch, slumped at his feet, and rolled over. Hays rubbed his soft belly. "You hear them doggies 'cross the river, Oak?"

***

Hays awoke as usual before sunrise in the lemony pre-dawn. From what used to be the master bedroom at the top of the stairs, he crossed to the bathroom and performed his ablutions with grateful thanks. "*Ngợi khen Thiên Chúa!*" He exclaimed loud enough to be heard at the courthouse, "for this awesome fuckin' water", which, after months and months, inexplicably began gushing from the tap and leaking from the toilet a few days ago, and "for the most aromatic dump this week, just flushed to who-knows-where." He'd uttered Vietnamese praise each morning of his life beginning one day in 1974 when he went down in the jungle with bullets in his leg. Delirious and dehydrated, he was cradled and transported to the thatched farmhouse of an ancient shamanic woman. Using medicinal plants and juju he could not remember, she healed the enemy soldier. She removed the slugs, drew out the sepsis, closed the wounds, and fed and cared for him as she would her own son. When he was well enough and walking without a cane, under the cover of darkness a village elder led Hays to an ARVN encampment.

That month of human grace and healing, Hays had thankfully, if often crudely, celebrated for more than sixty years. This morning a vague but weighty sense of consequence had awakened him as if the day beheld something different. He dressed and went down to the kitchen. Oakley, who'd once slept with Hays but could no longer climb the stairs, leapt off the couch with a morning woof.

"Time for breakfast, is it?" He filled the dog's bowl, made a mug of coffee from a full box of rusty tins of Nescafe he'd discovered in a shuttered grocery. A rare find, it was parceled out in a single spoonful, and only on days of consequence. He limped across to the porch to watch the sun rise above the hills upriver and to survey the riverscape. There was the Great Blue Heron, yep, nabbing her breakfast on the opposite bank. A Red Tail keening downriver. On this side, the ripples and sleek bodies of river otters he'd been watching all summer. Parallel to Main Street, Avery Caldwell out on her morning jog along the river. He waved and called, "Come on up when you're through. I'll fix some eggs."

Avery was a delightful twenty-something who'd migrated across the river with her dad last year. She then encouraged her brothers and their families to move as well, adding about twenty percent to the population of Pomerance. The Caldwells seemed committed to settle in and help sustain a modest recovery of the old river town. Hays busied himself clearing the sink of a week's dirty dishes, putting out a half-dozen eggs and other ingredients, setting the table, filling the dog's water dish, and reorganizing Melissa's knickknacks as if calibrating chess moves. The elf checkmates the bear while the porcelain China queen looks on. "Why the fuck do I continue to play with these dust collectors?" he mumbled out loud.

"What's that you're playing with, Boss?"

Avery crossed to the kitchen with a stop at the bottom of the stairs to scratch Oakley under the chin. "What a good boy," she crooned. "Warm and cuddly. Not like that master of yours." The dog thwapped his tail and yowled soft sounds. Avery was the only one who ribbed Hays mercilessly and got away with it. She was also the only one who called Hays 'Boss', short for Bosworth, the middle name he'd ditched a few years back. Most people couldn't manage Rutherford, his first name. Nor could he. Hays was what he went by these days. Except with Avery.

"Caught me. Just killing time here. I ought to clear out most of this shit."

She surveyed his kitchen, checking out the yellowed books and knickknacks, the cooking tools shoved into a beer mug, fishing gear, and a mess of papers, nails, screws, hinges, and other gizmos on the counter. She realized that given Hays' age, somebody, maybe her, someday, not soon she hoped, would have to do just that. It was a daunting thought.

Among the women Hays had hung out with in the latter decades of his life, Avery was unique. Despite the years that separated them, she treated him like a dude nowhere near as decrepit as he felt. And, as if he were her only confidant, she shared intimate stories about her emotional states, her menstrual cycle, her far-fetched longings, her sexual history. She relished his storehouse of memories about the way the world used to work, and the corrupt and dastardly politics of yore. She embraced and mimicked his crassness, contested but secretly admired his convoluted logic, and because Hays was a presumably safe target, flirted shamelessly. Hays loved the attention, loved the woman. Sure, he felt lust in her presence, low frequency lust at least. Just the other day as his eyes roved over her long neck, chiseled cheeks and full lips, he'd said, "I have to say this, my dear. Your slender body's nothin' but perfection and yer fetching face and fine ass are the most pulchritudinous features ever packed into one female."

Smiling, she reached across the space to wiggle his ear. Above his white beard, she saw rouge and she was happy. "Tha' tain't all," he continued. "Yer comical, rosy outlook elevates my spirits better'n booze or weed. It doesn't make much sense these days but don't you ever change."

"So, what's the news of the morning?" he asked.

"Not one helluva lot. Peed in the bushes on my way up here. How's that?"

"Headline news," he said.

"Yesterday, though, there was something."

Boss raised his eyebrows, cracked the eggs into a bowl, added goat's milk and a dash of hot sauce from home-grown jalapeños, some cilantro and collards from his kitchen garden, and beat everything a while. He dumped the mixture into a frying pan with a bit of ham from one of Macy's pigs, and scrambled with care. He dished out the eggs, doled out the last of his cornbread, and handed her a plate. "Hope this all goes down well."

"Looks delicious."

"Looks can be deceiving." He paused as the phrase brought back a troubling memory he couldn't pin down. Then he launched into his scrambled creation.

"Something? Something could mean almost anything, Avery. That you're opening with a vague word must mean you're about to divulge information that's astounding or ominous or merely noteworthy. Is it about your family?"

"No, we're all fine. We had everybody at our place last night. Grilled some pike dad caught with sweet potatoes we just dug. I made a cake with wheat flour Thad Symonds just got in."

"All good. 'Cept you didn't bring a piece of cake for me."

"Cake's all gone. What did you expect with three kids in the family?"

"Them rug rats. I guess they need cake more'n I do."

"Yeah. Well, back to the 'something'. It's a mix of noteworthy and ominous. Pay attention now."

"Yep."

"Yesterday, I rode over to Macy's to pick up a bag of tomatoes and some squashes. We sat on her veranda, drinking mint tea, just catching up. I hadn't seen her in a while. You know, since her place is right on the river, she pays close attention to any sort of human traffic."

"Uh huh. After them locks and dams blew out in the twenties, more folk do seem to be drifting past us. Humanity ain't totally hosed, I guess. People migrate. That's what people do; that's what you and your folks did. Jacob Yoder, the ex-Amish fella, told me some guy's rehabbed a sternwheeler up in Marietta. Gonna be powered with firewood. Plans to be a river trader. Then there are rumors about Macy's interactions with river drifters. A horn-toed lad from upriver spent a day or two with her recently, I heard."

"Bloody rumors. I don't want to get into that. She's a grown woman who occasionally feels lonesome."

"Who doesn't? I love that mutt there but he's a bit low on the enlightenment scale and his attempts at humor are getting stale."

"What about his virtue?"

"He's just a dawg, for Christ's sake."

"Shut up, Boss. This is serious. Last Thursday a strangely rigged keelboat with sails tied up at Macy's dock. Two shaggy bearded guys — one was huge — came onto her property. The tall one, old enough to have gray in his beard, the other, a good-looking spindly youth."

"Uh huh."

"The big guy spoke with a strange accent, she said. He asked questions. Creepy questions."

"Did they threaten her?"

"No, but they freaked her out."

"How?"

"Well, they left without a fuss but not before asking whether the village and people around here had kids — were there pregnancies? When she said no, it's a problem. They said, 'Maybe we can help.'"

"Where'd these guys come from?"

"Wheeling," she said.

"And what did Macy think they meant by that?"

"She assumed they'd be back to rape her."

"Holy crap. Ought to hang them fellers up by their testicles."

"Boss," she said staring him down across the table.

"Punishment's got to fit the crime. Hangin' by the balls might not be severe enough."

"Boss," she said again and paused. "If you think justice that crude should be the rule, you're more deluded than I'd realized. Do you really think it makes sense to talk about a lynching based on nothing more than innuendo? I mean, my dad would likely have your ass."

Boss pretended not to hear. "Shit. I had a feeling this morning that something heavy hung in the air. This must be it."

"What?"

He began maniacally stroking his beard, his head shuddering. "Oh, just a sixth sense I got. Rules, yeah, we need 'em, but we can barely feed ourselves. Sometimes, when it comes to justice, maybe we just gotta take things into our own hands."

"Well, count me out. It's true we've got almost no kids and none on the way. I've heard that adult survivors of the last pandemic from all over the place have been mostly unsuccessful conceiving and bearing children. That would include me, probably. Plus, my window's closing with no half-promising prospects."

"What about me?"

"Ha," she replied, a dismissal that had nothing to do with Hays' virility. "If my brothers and their partners had not conceived, we'd have *no* children in Pomerance instead of three. I believe Macy, and I understand her fear. I'm chicken. If I were her, I'd be getting out of town for a spell."

"Aw, I weren't suggesting you supply the rope or tie the knot. I realize this ain't your gig. Macy, though, I seriously doubt she'd run and hide. She might even string up those guys herself. What did she tell 'em anyway?"

"She said, 'Get outa here, you pathetic assholes.' Something like that."

"Ata go Macy! Anything more?"

"They said 'you'll change your mind' and that they'd be back."

2

As Hays and Avery got on with their day, far upriver a keelboat pilot skillfully rowed the craft northward. Safiya Kamal watched the boat approach from her perch above the river. As it got closer, she descended a long stairway. She wore a sleeveless, linen smock with a diving neckline over a pair of jeans. With her long legs, bare feet, and swift descent, she was a ballerina on her way to an encore, her movement liquid and graceful. For a woman her age with a daughter twenty-two, her apparent youth was unworldly, as though she'd dropped here fully and forever formed with skin the color of milky tea as smooth and unblemished as a newborn.

"Moises," she cried out. "Let me help you."

"Thanks, mum," he called back, though she was not his mother. Bucking the river current, he rowed the large craft toward shallow water. Then he stood. With the help of his pole and extraordinary upper body strength, he aligned the boat with the dock and threw her the lines. She lashed them fore and aft to cleats on the dock's edge and offered her hand to heist up the man.

"Dropped Aram down at Shadyside," he said. "Boy's got his eye on some pretty dunce down there. Big mistake. A nasty crowd. Rowdy, unpleasant drunkards. He'll row up here in the mornin', if he survives the night."

"Oh dear. I hope that last bit was in jest."

"Yeah, no worries, mum. He'll be fine."

"So, what did you find downriver?"

"I'd say there are more'n a dozen settlements from here to Pomerance where we turned back. We docked at as many as seemed safe. Talked to maybe twenty different folk. More'n half were open to our pitch, another few said nuthin'. One couple seemed too dim to respond. Another brown gal just upriver from Pomerance was a fair bit nasty. Cursed us in Canadian English."

"Apart from her, it sounds promising. *Des enfants?*"

"No, mum. At the waterfront anyway."

***

On the journey upriver, Moises and Aram had whiled away the hours of hard rowing and navigation with inane chatter, especially on days when the sail furled in brisk southwesterly winds. Moises was born on a farm near the city of May Pen. At the first signs of economic chaos in 2019 brought on by the titanic hurricane Natasha, he fled to the U.S. along with thousands of other Jamaicans, gradually making his way north, working first in Miami, then in Charleston, South Carolina. With enough cash in his pocket, he continued northward until a multitude of Late-K breakdowns stranded him in Wheeling. Now in his mid-forties, Moises had been toughened not only by a struggle to survive in harsh times but also by innumerable challenges to his manhood and race. A coal-black man — six-foot-six and more than 250 pounds — a titan with long arms roped by knotted muscles, he had often been singled out. He had stabbed or otherwise maimed more *losas* than he could count. Despite his hard shell and menacing capabilities, he was, at heart, a simple, convivial man with an outlandish sense of humor.

Aram was six when his parents were killed by bombs in the Syrian Civil War. With the help of a Canadian doctor working in Syria, he was granted amnesty and immigrated with the doctor to Canada. He turned out to be an elite student, graduating from high school second in his class and gaining admission to the University of Ottawa in medicine. During Aram's fourth year the deterioration of Canadian higher education led to closure of all universities. Unable to complete his degree, he found temporary work as a server in Caffé Mio, a popular

Ottawa café that had persisted despite the faltering economy and the looming pandemic. The business was managed by Mikael Mahakash, the youngest son of a prominent Egyptian-Canadian chef who owned restaurants on both sides of the Ottawa River. One evening Aram waited on Dr. Sadek Kamal who made him a proposition: "I will pay you to travel to Ohio to help my daughter." It was such a generous offer he could not refuse. Aram was now twenty-five. Unlike Moises, he was a quiet, introspective fellow, slightly built and almost a foot shorter. He had proved to be an amiable companion with intelligence and medical knowledge that added greatly to the pair's skills set.

"What'd you make of that short brown woman there on the north bank just after we turned back?" Aram asked.

"Attractive. Feisty thing. When I picture her in my sack, it set me juices flowing. Next time around I see if we be better friends. What'd you think?"

"More than meets the eye there but not my type. Her English was beautiful to my ears; it sounded Canadian. But it stung when she dismissed us as assholes." Aram, looking to fall in love, was pointedly not in favor of sleeping around. He did wonder idly what it would be like just to fuck for fuck's sake, how a guy like Moises could just sleep around.

"You never know," Moises said. "We surely go back dere."

Conversation lapsed. After a couple of hours, out of the blue, Aram struck up another topic. "Where's all this water coming from anyway? This big river just keeps flowing and flowing. It never dries up."

"Heard there was a gigantic, gushing, gold-plated fountain in Pitsbug. Big as de cornfield behind our cabin. The fountain water, dey say, it come directly from heaven."

"That's bullshit, Mois."

"You asked. Dere's also a twin river to the east dat flow the other way."

"What? You're crazy. That river would be flowing uphill. Who ever heard of that? Defies the Law of Gravity."

"Don't let gravity mess up good story."

"What about that couple down by Pomerance that wanted a kid?"

"What about 'em?"

"Very weird combination, didn't you think?"

"Yeah. Now dat I tink about it, dat filly was one tasty lil' bit. 'Member her short, spikey black hair, pretty face with dat pointed chin, raggedy shorts?"

"Not particularly. I'm thinking more about how lonesome she seemed and how desperate for a child. Plus, the old man — that sour-faced, sullen guy."

"Shit, Bro, yo' missed dat gal's fine assets. Yeah, her ol' mate was not exactly a stallion. Yo sure right dere. Slump over like limp dick. Maybe he be de last Amishman on earth. How did dey ever hook up?"

"Not like there are tons of choices for old guys, let alone for youngsters like me."

"Like you? You ain't no kid no more."

"More a kid than you, brother."

***

Moises and Aram appeared the next morning at Safiya's door as the rising sun began casting shadows across her porch. The start of a muggy summer day.

"Hello, you vagabonds. Come in. I've got wheat cakes, eggs, and sausages for you."

"Thanks, mum," they said in unison.

Safiya's house, a rambling wood-framed ranch built just before things came undone, was in remarkably good shape. She had decorated and furnished it with the best remnants she and Moises could squander from the abandoned towns of St. Clairsville, Bridgeport, and Martins Ferry. They sat on matching high stools around a kitchen island bar, popular when the house was built, around 2017.

Wolfing down their breakfasts, Moises filled the space with speculation about the people they had surveyed, observing that they all had some connection to the river for personal transportation, goods trading, lodging for travelers, and water to irrigate their crops. The big river — the Ohio River as it was beginning to be called again — had once more become a thoroughfare with traders, n'er-do-wells, and families heading south and west. Safiya agreed that the river would be the very heart of their venture.

After clearing the dishes, she got down to business. She paid their wages in silver, told them to take a few days off, and shared news of her daughter, Salma. Aram had never met the girl; had no picture of what she looked like. He was vaguely aware that the daughter was connected to their project. All Moises would say is "Dat girl be one hard-headed wench who don't exactly stir me passions, if you know what I mean."

Moises had also known Safiya's older daughter, Claire. "Now, Claire, she be one tender flower. Gone now," he once told Aram.

"Gone?"

"Yeah, man, almost soon's we got here, Claire got de sickness. No doctors nowhere. She done gasping fo' breath. She dead in couple weeks. Safiya be broken-hearted."

"Salma had some sad news" Safiya continued. "Mikael passed away. It was a few months back. He was seventy."

"Aw mum, sorry to hear dat," Moises said.

"Yeah, me too," said Aram. "If he hadn't taken me under his wing and sent me here, I may not have survived. When the university closed, I was a mess for a while. Imagine that. A Christian guy who didn't even know me, helping an ex-Syrian Muslim without a looney in his pocket!"

"I remember," Safiya said. "Well, those old religions don't amount to anything these days. I guess that's progress. As for Mikael, there is not much we can do but remember him well."

"I'll have no trouble doing that," said Aram.

"Yeah," Moises agreed.

Safiya changed the subject. "There's a new chap at the helm now. Salma's working with him. She thinks he'll be compliant. The first phase of our venture is therefore still on track. We'll have the horses and carriage ready for your departure the morning you get back."

"Ah, good," said Moises. "We be rested by den."

3

On that afternoon, Hays was tending to his chickens, collecting eggs, and pulling weeds from his vegetable beds out back when he heard a vaguely familiar voice.

"Rutherford B. Hays. You home, you bastard?"

"Yep," he called through to the front door. "Who zat?"

"It's Cameron. Can I come in?"

"Okay, bud. Meet you in the kitchen."

Cameron Caldwell, Avery's father, was a lawyer who once was an assistant district attorney in West Virginia. When Avery's mother was fighting the coronavirus, Cameron became fully dependent on his teenage daughter for caregiving. Unfortunately, her mom's pleurisy exacerbated by the virus proved fatal. Rachel Caldwell died in 2021. At sixteen, Avery became the surrogate woman of the house while finishing high school, attending and graduating from the College of Charleston (the final class at that college), and taking care of her two younger brothers. With the economy of West Virginia in ruins and survivors everywhere bailing for greener pastures, the Attorney

General's office closed and Cameron Caldwell was furloughed. He and Avery loaded up their belongings and fled the city. To this day, interdependence continued to define their lives.

Caldwell and Hays sat side-by-side on porch rockers drinking cool brews from Hays's root cellar.

After a spell, Caldwell asked, "How's things?"

"I'm breathing and taking nourishment. My shit still stinks."

"More good health to you," Caldwell said lifting his bottle in a toast.

"Here's to that, brother. Something else on your mind?"

"Of course. I never just drop by like that daughter of mine. Hope she's not a bother."

"Bother? Nah, not at all. She brightens each day she comes here. The dog would agree, if he could. One hun'red percent."

They both turned to look at Oakley, inert and stretched across the width of the porch.

"He's alive, right?" Caldwell asked.

"Yep, most of the time."

"Okay, I'm worried. Avery came home the other day talking about her friend, Macy. She told me about the riverboat guys from Wheeling and fretted about their intentions. This spurred me to pull out my notes, putting together codes and ordinances for our little community. You recall that I'd poked around the courthouse for clues about how Greig County used to work?"

"Yep. As I remember it, most of the shit from the Courthouse was obliterated by mold and all other manner of scum, not to mention consumption by Rodentia, right?"

"That's true and most of what I *could* read was irrelevant. We're not living in a complex society with sophisticated information and communication systems, and functioning state and federal governments. We'll have to pare things down. Start with a clean slate."

"Uh huh. I have a sense the other shoe's about to drop. Careful. Do not drop it on my dawg."

"Right. Well, today I've been hiking around town knocking on doors, asking peoples' opinions about setting up some legal codes and a skeletal local government. Everyone was either positive or neutral. Virtually nobody wanted to volunteer for anything. Small sample of about a dozen, but that's about a third of our adults."

"Ain't surprised you got zero volunteers. People are struggling."

"That's fixable. By the way, I did speak briefly with two other people who had encountered those men on the keelboat. Jacob, the Amish fellow, and his wife, Ella."

"Ella and Jacob. Yep. She's one bright little beauty who sure outshines Mr. Wither Dick. What'd they say?"

"Well, Jacob liked the idea of a local government and also seemed positive, not fearful of the boatmen. Those guys told Jacob and Ella that they might be able to help them attain their dream of having kids."

"Damn strange. What? Have they resurrected fertility treatments? Found a stash of Viagra?"

"I wouldn't want to speculate on that. But I would like to know what you think about some laws, a village council perhaps, a constable, a judge."

Silence descended over the steamy porch. Caldwell let it be.

Hays broke it. "Well, at the moment, with only a few dozen residents, we seem to get by without governance or law enforcement. It's more apathy than anarchy, I would say. But without some kind of structure — a council or something, we're probably missing opportunities to revive this place. And soon, what with the increasing river traffic, we might be wishing we could contain or stem situations that would be, let's say, unseemly."

"Are you saying you'd back me?"

"For all it's worth, yeah. But that's like asking a pit bull if he'd be interested in supporting the dog catcher. I sure as hell hope you ain't got plans to ban home brew, moonshine, and weed."

Caldwell drained his bottle and carefully placed it on a side table. "Highly unlikely. I'm glad we talked. Maybe you'd like to be our first mayor."

"Not in yer wildest dreams."

4

The overloaded carriage slowly retraced the route back to Riverview. One-hundred twenty miles, replete with obstacles, hazards, and detours, consumed two long days. Because of rumored gang warfare in Youngstown, they bypassed the city and pitched camp a few miles south. At sunset, behind a dilapidated farm house, Aram and Moises unhitched and tethered the horses, brushed, watered, and fed them. With help from Salma Kamal, they threw together a simple meal and laid out five bed rolls. Under a dazzling night sky, bone-tired, Moises and Aram joined the children in deep sleep.

Salma was restless. She paced in the moonless night. She bore responsibility for the mission but disliked her conspirators and was troubled about her inability to control a couple of wretched kids.

By morning, everything she spoke was laced with acid. Moises knew the tone and saw her puffy face and red eyes. "Beware the ogre," advised one of the Vine Brothers when they departed. Moises walked away from her. He and Aram and the kids retreated to open space along the road and kicked a ball and tumbled after it in the weeds.

Once on the road, the second day heaved forth, Salma sniping at the men at every opportunity. Which in turn made the children fussy. "Even worse than yesterday," she said out loud. "Despite their current value, these brats set new standards for the definition of misbehavior."

Marie scowled, "We are not brats. Are we Jules?"

"*Je ne sais pas,*" he peeped.

Moises tried his best to ignore Salma as he guided the coach straight south. At mid-day they reached the familiar big bend in the Ohio River at East Liverpool, yet another ghastly ex-town. After a brief break, they followed the river south along the legendary, though almost obliterated, Route 7 through more ramshackle and largely abandoned river settlements — Steubenville, Wellsburg, Yorktown, and finally, Bridgeport. It was dark when they drew up to the ranch house on the bluff.

5

Hays grabbed his walking stick and whistled Oakley to the door. It was the first of October, a crisp blue sky breaking through the lifting ribbon of fog in the valley.

"Hey boy. Wanna go for a W-A-L-K?"

The dog smiled and barked, bounding around and chortling with joy. The two headed southwards along the old river road. It would be an hour's walk each way on Hays' gimpy knees. Avery could run it in 15 minutes.

Oakley ran ahead like the pup he used to be, disappearing into the brush from time to time to follow clues he'd sniffed out. Just before Minersville, Hays took a left to climb the river bluff towards what was once known as Welshtown. Morton Abzug, supplier of Ohio Mash fine corn whiskey and acceptable but not too fine cannabis, lived just outside what once was a Welsh mining settlement. A few steps along the rutted road, Hays remembered his companion. *Where is that damnable critter?* He turned around and called, whistling, and clapping.

He waited and called again. "Consarned beast."

He retraced his steps back to the river road, scanning the way toward Minersville. A blurry shape appeared in the distance. "Oakley?"

He called again. The dog stayed put, sniffing at something just off the road. Hays closed in on the scene.

"What's up there, fella?" Oakley held his ground, nosing something in the bushes, puncturing the silence with sharp "come-have-a-look" woofs. It was the remains of something, the odor of decaying flesh prominent. *What?* He waded into the brush to see what kind of critter Oakley still nosed.

"Back off, Oak." Hays pushed him away. With his walking stick he poked at the form, rolled it over. "Oh goddamn," he managed to say. In the war he'd seen too many dead children — what the Army called 'collateral damage'. But here? He turned away to settle his stomach. After a moment, he turned back to the unsavory task. This had been a tiny human infant, or would one call it a fetus? Not more than three pounds and mangled almost beyond recognition. Its body was splotched in dried blood, scarred by multiple punctured wounds, armless on one side, dirty as hell.

"Where in God's name did this little thing come from?" he asked his dog. Oakley had a notion. He was already sniffing a path downslope through the thicket. Hays followed. He staggered through brambles that tugged at his coat and threatened to rip off an ear. After five minutes of agony, Oakley's trail broke into the open. The dog dashed across a pasture, his nose retrieving messages Hays couldn't decode.

When they were in sight of a familiar farmhouse overlooking the river, Oakley halted. He began circling round and round beneath a snarled apple tree. Hays ducked under the branches. At about nine o'clock in Oakley's circle, he stumbled across what appeared to be a groundhog tunnel. It wasn't. Hays inspected the shallow grave, marked only by a toppled cairn of local sandstone and extensive excavation. "A freakin' coyote."

Panting softly, Oakley rested in the cool grass, mission accomplished.

"Well, Oak, I ain't lookin' forward to what I have to do next. You stay here, boy."

Hays crawled out, took a few long moments to straighten up and collect his thoughts. Turning his back to the apple tree, he headed downslope.

He knocked on the weathered door of the farmhouse.

An attractive, black-haired young woman appeared. "Mr. Hays. What a nice surprise!"

"Hello, Ella. May I come in? I need to have a word."

She ushered him to a chair at the kitchen table and brought two glasses of cool mint tea. "Now, what can I do for you?"

"Well, Ella, I've had a really painful morning." He told her everything, finishing up with, "Look, I have no intent to say anything to anybody about this. Whatever may have happened, I have no judgment to proclaim. Only sadness." He sniffled and caught a tear on its way south. Took a sip of tea.

The woman's chiseled facial features melted like butter. She looked like she'd just returned from hell. Which she had. She held her composure a few more seconds, then broke into sobs that so wracked her upper body, Hays could hardly bear to watch. Finally, almost inaudibly, she said, "Oh God, please, please don't tell Jacob. Please. This would crush him. He does not know about the stillbirth in the barn. He wasn't even aware I was pregnant. We'd not been intimate in months." She took in a gasping breath and sobbed more on the outbreath.

Usually never at a loss for words, Hays sat there frozen. Finally, he said, "You have my word on that, Ella."

She wept softly now. "We've been trying for several years with no success. I've assumed it would not be our fate to have children. This time, though, seemed different. Miscarriages before never got this far, if you can call stillbirth a measure of improvement. I had to bury the little thing quickly. I guess I did a bad job of that too."

Again, Hays could not find words right away. "This is nothing but heartbreaking, dear. I don't know what to do exactly. I *am* sure that you do not want to see what my dog and I have just seen."

"No, I don't." She sniffled and wiped her eyes and nose, regained a bit of her gentle equanimity. "As much as I would have loved that child in life, at first, I did not want to even touch the lifeless thing that came out of me. It was just too awful for words. Then, I knew I had to commit it to the earth as soon as I could. Before Jacob got back from Pomerance."

"Well, Ella, correct me if I'm wrong. I think you would prefer me to re-bury the infant in a place Jacob and wild critters are not likely to find."

"That is so, Mr. Hays. Someday, a while from now, maybe you will take me to that place. Right now, I have all I can handle just getting from one day to the next."

"I understand. You can trust me, I promise."

Hays stood, grabbed his walking stick, and hugged the frail woman whose dreams of motherhood had been throttled once again. Saying nothing more, he and Oakley left her at the kitchen door and crossed the pasture up toward the road. *Life is fucking cruel and sodden.* But not in his eighty-five years had it been this cruel.

SIX

An Odd Couple: Kate and Aram

Argolis, 2040

1

ALL MY SUPPOSITIONS ABOUT LIFE in this godforsaken time went topsy when a handsome fellow politely took my hand in his and fixed his owlish eyes on mine. Wordlessly yet explicitly, he probed my spiritual well-being or my sexual preferences, or both and perhaps more. His name was Aram. He was of medium height and build, a tad shorter than I, his well-proportioned body wrapped in confidence with skin the shade of a camel. On that day my heart leapt, so long had it been that a man, apparently untethered, came into view. Now, the memory confuses me. The way I experienced his command of himself and his masculinity, the way my own femininity resurged in those intoxicating days. The way all this seemed to transcend the deprivations of our time as though it could elevate everyone around us. What astonishes me is who we were then. And who we are now.

***

Macy, my friend since childhood, is short and muscular. With the help of an ex-Amish neighbor and a bunch of Latin men and women who showed up from the south, she's spent the better part of a decade reviving a livestock, vineyard, and market gardening operation on the Ohio River. From clearing and burning brush, planting beds — grapes and pasture — to rehabbing pens, outbuildings and a farmhouse, her work has been legendary. Her farm now supplies vegetables, dairy, chickens, turkey, beef, pork, and fine wines to people along the river. Our friendship has certainly had its belligerent moments, but overall, we've more often found a workable balance between her feisty, social genes and my calmer, introverted ones. Macy needs company. I don't. She is bisexual. I'm not. Macy's hands-on. I'm more cerebral. Inexplicably, this oppositional cocktail has made for an enduring friendship.

I've been with a couple of rather unsatisfactory blokes, neither of whom were long term. I never wanted them permanently in my bed or even my life. That may have had something to do with the fact that back then I still lived with my dad. But even after I moved out, I continued to cherish my privacy. That and the pitiful dearth of more dashing partners have left me a circumstantially unattached woman on the downslope to thirty.

Macy, on the other hand, was swept a few years ago into the orbit of Mariah Gonzales, a bounteous, exuberant Mexican woman who expanded Macy's sense of the possible and helped scale up their farming enterprise. Now partners in all senses, Macy and Mariah have become a force to be reckoned with. Their farm, Mama Riah & Company, has not only thrived economically but also has provided employment for about fifty managers, field hands, vintners, poultry attendants, dairy workers, and livestock herders. To know of their success is to have hope in bright new beginnings in these otherwise drab days.

2

One resplendent spring day, on my chocolate mare, Karma, I rode down Old 33 with Stefan, my dad, on his russet Morgan, Colonel, passing through a string of abandoned places with names that reek of mold: Shade, Pratt's Fork, Burlingham, Darwin. We were on our way to visit our friends in Pomerance. Most of the people in Pomerance emigrated from our village of Argolis so every visit turned out to be a reunion. We planned a late afternoon picnic on the river followed by overnight at the home of one of dad's oldest friends. The sun beamed its warmth on our faces, long pallid from weeks of steel-gray skies. Star-studded dogwoods adorned the edges of the oak-maple forests on either side of the former freeway. Our horses' spirited gait told me they too felt the revival that always comes with spring.

"Rock Springs, coming up," shouted dad in the lead. He was smiling, boyishly happy, not his typical shielded self.

"Pomerance here we come."

We'd made this trip many times in the past several years as the fortunes of Argolis and Pomerance had become intertwined in what appeared to be a reawakening regional economy. New settlers in and around both villages brought new skills and energy, but unfortunately almost no children. Even the little Latin community across the river from the Mama Riah Farm had no children under twelve. It's stunning that nobody of reproductive age around here has borne a child for almost a decade. Despite all the speculation about how the last pandemic made male survivors sterile, nobody knows what's really true. Some young men allege it is the women who are barren. My experience is certainly not instructive. I desperately douched after sex every time. The last thing I needed was a kid. But without kids, all the promise of better times is nothing but delusion.

We trotted through the remnants of downtown Pomerance and up the rise past the shuttered courthouse to a stately, though crumbling, Victorian. Hitching our horses to a fencepost, we climbed a steep walk and steps to the porch. A dog woofed.

"Boss! You in there?" Dad called through the screen door.

A white-bearded man with a walking stick and a trailing low-slung dog came to the door. "Yep, I'm still kicking, Stefan. Goldamnit! You've got that luscious daughter along too. This calls for a celebration. What the fuck shall we celebrate?"

"How about my sixtieth birthday?"

"Sixty! Shit, Stefan, that must make me at least seventy."

"Hi Mr. Hays," I managed to squeak. He gave me an oh-too-long hug and bubbled with enthusiasm about the prospect of a party.

"Gotta get the word out on gossip-dot-net." The reference escaped me, but on the out breath, Dad shook his head.

Later that afternoon, we hauled our picnic baskets down to the Pomerance dock and amphitheater where a small crowd of a couple of dozen was gathering, each with their own food and drinks. Not surprisingly, almost everyone was an adult, though I did notice three kids, the youngest of whom looked nine or ten. Two men and two women from the Latin settlement, Nuevo Ranchero, had guitars and a couple of horns. They began to play mariachi and it tweaked something so beautiful and painfully absent in my life, that I could not restrain tears of remorse. Or was it joy?

Dad and I made the rounds with hugs from those who once were neighbors and more restrained greetings from people we'd never met. The Campbells, for example, whose three kids were part of their extended family. Macy and Mariah tied their flatboat at the dock and headed straight to us with hugs and friendly jabs. And, in the midst of everything, an odd two-mast craft came around the river bend, drifting downriver to the dock. One of those on board was Aram. It was the first time I'd laid eyes on that alluring Mediterranean man. He was last off, following a local couple I'd previously met and a muscular black fellow who was the tallest and sturdiest person I had ever seen or imagined. Even more memorable were the two white kids he hoisted affectionately on each of his massive arms. Those little cherubs seemed as though they'd been dropped directly from heaven. Heaven? Though it bore no religious significance to me, people once thought of it as a place in the clouds, which is ridiculous. Cherubs? I knew them to be celestial beings who graced the margins of a book of Christmas carols I perused cover to cover as a child.

Back at the Pomerance pier, the stunning crew that included Aram stepped off their throwback riverboat striking a pose to remember, right alongside the beautiful Ohio River. People just stared at them.

The young woman, Ella, stepped forward, beaming a smile outshining the sunrays bouncing along the swirling river behind her. She said, "I want first to thank Mr. Hays for inviting us to this party. It's delightful to be here. Next, Jacob and I wish Stefan the happiest of birthdays. We are glad you and Kate came down to Pomerance to celebrate. And now I have two guests I want to introduce. Please welcome Aram Masood and Moises Marley."

People clapped politely.

Someone, a middle-aged woman I did not know, shouted, "Welcome to the best little river town anywhere!"

Ella finished by saying, "And finally, may this beloved community be the first to meet Jacob's and my newly adopted children, Marie and Jules!"

Another tentative clap or two led immediately to hearty applause and whoops.

"Yay, more kids!" yelled one of the Campbell boys.

Jules and Marie couldn't manage to crack a smile.

Hays whispered something to my dad. Dad raised his eyebrows and shook his head.

***

A few days following the party, I found Aram on my doorstep. Unlike the warm day in Pomerance, it was wet and cool with bruised-bellied clouds yielding stormy rain bursts followed by quiet spells of fog and drizzle.

"Hello, Kate." He stared through the screen, his face a mashup of sopped puppy and boyish amusement. He hadn't shaved; I found his bright eyes and stubble sexy. And I wondered: *I hardly know this guy. How in hell did he find me all this way from the river? Why is he so nonchalant? Why is my heart leaping?*

"Come in out of the rain, you."

It was midday. We shared tea, sliced apples, and sandwiches. Afterwards we moved to my couch by the Jotul stove that I fed with crackling dry splits I'd hauled from the woodshed. There was great comfort and pride in the wood I cut and split almost a year ago. The room felt toasty and hospitable. Later we drank a couple of homebrews and smoked a joint while getting to know mostly superficial things about each other. I found the conversation easy. His face was often open and ready to break into a smile, as if he perpetually sought humor in things. Hardly a hint of sexual energy coursed between us the whole afternoon.

Discovering that Aram had been born overseas, I asked him where. He paused quite a while, disguising, I figured, something he'd rather not reveal. "A country no longer a country in what was once referred to as the Middle East."

"And your parents?"

He paused again, looking at the ceiling first, then at his shoes. During this pause, I considered him in detail and concluded he was quite a package. Finally, quietly, he said, "They were killed in a civil war when I was a kid."

He looked back into my moist eyes. "No need to grieve," he said. "With help from my adoptive family in what then was Canada, I dealt with it. For a while it busted my faith and confidence."

"And now?"

"I've recouped my self-esteem and learned to pray again."

I reached over and placed my hand on his. He recoiled ever so slightly. I realized he was a strange sort of man, an attractive sort with a bit of dark sensitivity.

As dusk approached, I asked him if he would be going upriver soon.

He said, "Kate, I don't know whether to continue my present work. I have doubts. And therefore, I don't know when or if I will head back to Wheeling. Moises has already set sail. When we met at the river, I was intrigued by you. But after your jarring musings about your motherless childhood and your absent-minded father, and how very lonely and unfulfilled you sometimes feel, I am beyond intrigued. The hardships here are great. Maybe I could stay. Maybe I could help." Looking back, I see that Aram, in just a few hours, had come to understand me at some middling level. I wish now that his native empathy and compassion had not diminished to a farthing.

He stayed the night, sleeping on the couch, while I trundled upstairs to my chilly bedroom. The buzz of the weed and our heartfelt conversation dissolved like fog after sunrise. Unfortunately, the fog in my brain did not readily dissipate. The man confused me.

The days of spring flew past. I travelled to the river to spend two weeks at Mama Riah's farm helping Macy transfer greenhouse starts to her beds and kicking back each night with her and Mariah and their friend Avery. We drank too much and smoked more than we should have. It was the best: warm sunny days and languid spring evenings in the Ohio Valley. It revived my zest for life. Or was it Aram? He, who had traveled the road to the river with me as far as Jacob and Ella's farm. With a resonant but basically passionless hug, we said goodbye there. He told me he felt honor-bound to fulfill a promise he'd made to help Jacob and Ella with chores and childcare. A man of his word.

* * *

In late June, he found his way back to Argolis. We decided he could move in with me. I told him to take the small room off the kitchen, once my study. He happily threw down his meager belongings. "A room of my own!" he said with no apparent derision. For the time being, he would sleep on a stack of quilts and blankets on the floor. He would have privacy, but the likelihood of finding a mattress in Argolis that wasn't disgustingly moldy, rodent damaged or bug-infested was dim.

Aram settled in and began to ask all kinds of questions about the books and objects he found on my bookshelf in his room. He seemed rapt in exploring and discussing books I'd read on a range of subjects he knew little about — Ohio history and nature, the Appalachian region, women's studies, the Millennial and Z generations. "What on earth are these?" he wondered. Some of the objects — tiny plastic animals, shiny agates, a jar of Legos, a doll, a couple of board games, some family photos — thrust him back to his own childhood and called up vague memories of better days in the country of his birth.

We were adjusting to living together, or should I say, sharing space under the same roof. Aram seemed to go from day to day cheerfully, though I suspected he had to work at it. Once, he confessed that he was somewhat of an introvert with a need to have time alone. By day, he spent most of his time at the village clinic with Dr. Todd. Putting aside his thwarted dream of finishing medical school, he soaked up everything Todd explained; he began a residency in family medicine in a clinic with no highfalutin drugs, no anesthesia, and very little medical equipment save the basics — stethoscopes, blood pressure cuffs, some surgical instruments, a couple of low power microscopes. On the other hand, the shelves of the clinic harbored a vast range of tinctures and plant-based salves and remedies Dr. Todd and his partner Sean concocted, including laudanum and marijuana for pain. For his part, Todd appreciated another medical brain in the village, gladly shared his library, and managed to pay Aram a few silvers a month.

In the evenings, when we put out food to share, conversation was always easy and often surprising. When he chooses, Aram possesses a bizarre and humorous sense of the troubled world, a sense that usually lightens my moody outlook. One evening, after a long day at the clinic, he waxed on about hair and nostral science; the need to honor your nose hairs. I felt an evolving fondness and always looked forward to dinner.

Aram wanted to talk about religion one night. I almost put a damper on the conversation by riffing off my dad's pronouncements on the subject. "You know, almost all religions humans ever devised had no way of testing and revising their core beliefs. So, each generation of believers was condemned to inherit the superstitions and ethnic hatreds of those who came before. Who in his right mind could support a faith in which ordinary people felt motivated to burn women at the stake for what their religion labeled blasphemy?"

"So, your dad raised you without faith?"

"Let's say he raised me with healthy skepticism and therefore a disregard for the religions that mostly imploded around the time I was born. Religious zealots of all kinds, according to Dad, have been nothing but divisive social forces because they could not get past superstitions and enmity that often led them to violence and genocide toward people not like them."

"I see that. My adoptive parents were Syrian Canadians. We attended mosque every Friday. I even went to a madrasa school a couple of years. In times of trouble, our mosque was looted. Shot up. Ten people killed. We were lucky. It was a Friday when our family was out of town. After that, young men from our community returned the violence trying to torch a cathedral. They got caught and were sent to prison."

"So, you understand how ancient religious hatred is carried forward?"

"Of course. At university, I walked away from my roots. Many of my Muslim friends did too."

"Why then do I see you prostrate on the floor of your room?"

"I'm praying, dummkopf." He smiled. "It helps me get nearer to God."

"The God who sanctioned violence of the kind you described?"

"I hope not."

"What comes back to you from God?"

"Honestly, not much. But some guidelines for life I learned at madrassa do bubble up to keep me from straying too far off the path."

***

By fall that year, Aram had become a familiar and respected figure in Argolis. He and my dad had become friends. Aram, jokingly at first, liked to refer to him as 'Dad', a practice, he explained, that was common between the young and elders back in the old country. He'd embraced Dad's weirdness and verbosity as quite wonderful. He said, "From your early description of him, I expected someone else. Absent-minded, yes. But also a gentle soul — an elder, who evokes in me an urge to look after and honor the man." For his part, Dad referred to Aram as the son he never had and heaped praise on his fervor for becoming the best physician's assistant in the Shawnee Valley. Of course, Dad assumed Aram and I were a couple. For obvious reasons, I did not disabuse him of that assumption.

One chilly evening in late October Aram and I sat together after dinner on the couch in flickering candlelight. It was too soon to fire up the wood burner so I draped a knitted shawl over us. Our bodies were pressed together side-by-side. Without thinking, I hunched closer to absorb more of his warmth. He took my hand. We sat in silence that way, then spoke softly about whatever came to mind — mundane things like rumors around the village, the vibrations of the house, where to get weed, whether each of us snored.

"This feels right, to have you here close to me," he said.

"Oh, is that so? Well, it feels pretty right to me too."

"Good," he said. "Despite the harsh simplicity of our lives, no television or computers or music or cars — things our parents took for granted at our age — and the fact that neither of us has had a bath in a few days."

"Let's not go there." I put my head on his shoulder. My breath shortened and I felt swirly below. His hand tightened on mine. Though I craved more and was tempted to keep things going by stroking his bristly jaw or nibbling his ear, I resisted. We dozed off, jerked awake after a few minutes, awkwardly said good night, and headed off to our separate beds.

For the better part of a month, Aram and I hardly saw one another and the tenderness of that snuggle on the couch seemed nothing but an aberration. On an especially blustery Friday, with a cold rain pounding the metal roof, I stoked both the kitchen and living room stoves, and baked corn pudding to go along with a pot of tomato vegetable soup and fall greens I'd harvested the day before. As the skies darkened toward evening, the aroma of the pudding and the crackle of the stoves lent a homey, drowsy aura. It made me happy.

After dinner and kitchen cleanup, I stretched out on the couch with a novel — *Mercy,* by Jodi Picoult, an engaging mystery about a family set in a quaint town fifty years ago in a place called Massachusetts. After being unearthed in a musty corner of an abandoned house at the edge of Argolis, the book had been devoured by several of my friends. Its faded hard cover was frayed at the edges, the binding was unraveling, and the pages were yellow. But it was legible. Even more intriguing, inside the cover, was an inscription — *For my Jennifer. Know that I love you, darling, and may you have a most wonderful 26th birthday. Yours ever, Norris. June 15, 1996.* Which led me to fabricate a tale about those Ohio lovers two generations ago. If she'd survived the two pandemics, the nuclear war, omega, and the floods and droughts and wildfires, Jennifer would be seventy now. That never happened. Jennifer's almost certainly dead. But when she was twenty-six, my age soon, how faithfully did she return poor Norris' love? Poor Norris? Yes, he was then known as a hopeless dweeb whose most common coping strategy was to ignore her. Men — arseholes then, arseholes now. But was Jennifer enamored at all at this point in her life with Norris? Or did she regularly sneak next door to get frisky with the more dashing Thaddeus?

Fresh on the heels of that thought, Aram slipped through the back door. He was thoroughly soaked. He stood at the threshold of the front room, a puddle collecting around his sopping feet. "Hi Kate. Mr. Clueless forgot his raincoat and boots. Got thoroughly drenched sloshing home from Sean and Todd's. Sorry about the mess."

"Hi. No worries. I've had the stoves going all afternoon so there will be plenty of hot water for a nice bath to take the chill out of your bones. After that, would you like something to eat?" As always, my maternal instincts kicked in.

"No. No thanks. Sean cooked dinner for us."

Aram came down the stairs wrapped in his bathrobe, a towel round his neck, wool socks on his feet. He padded over to the couch. I sat up and opened my hand to invite him to join me.

"Oh, thanks." He sat next to me as I wrapped my blanket over us both. He opened with banter about his day at the clinic making me laugh at the foibles of doctoring basically healthy patients with inscrutable symptoms and unrequited social needs. "I need to read more psychology," he said. With his relaxed closeness and the thought of his bathrobe as the only barrier between me and naked him, I felt my skin tightening with the beginnings, whoa, the middlings, of arousal. He sensed this and bent over to kiss me, a long series of full lips kissing in which he became a vibrant presence over me as, I presume, I did under him. We accomplished a succession of syncopated waves focusing on you can imagine where. I reached for the bulge and he gently sought out, through my sweatpants, my own throbbing parts. And that is how it climaxed, so to speak.

Giddy with pleasure, in my post-orgasmic dreamy voice, I asked, "Were you worried about entering me bareback?" I did wonder why he'd slammed on the brakes as we headed toward missionary one. "I know condoms are rare but I happen to have a small supply. I should have mentioned it." Just as I resorted to practicalities, which we were good at, my gaily decorated balloons painted with irrational fantasies drifted out of sight.

He propped himself up, a sober look in his eyes. "I don't want to have sex. I mean penetrating sex until I'm sure I'm joining myself with my life partner. These days the institution of marriage appears to be outmoded but I want something like that before I go all the way. It is how I will honor my parents. Both sets of them. And what little faith I still have."

Huh, I thought. *They're all dead.* I flipped him over, Amazonian style, and sat on his stomach, towering topless over him. "Would that be your first time, Aram?"

He nodded.

I laughed. "Are you shitting me?"

"I am not."

"There's a fine kettle of fish. The last virgin I encountered was fifteen. And you're how old?"

"Soon to be twenty-seven."

At that, I felt an unfamiliar mix of emotions assaulting both logic and reasonableness. Sure, I managed a measure of compassion, as a mother might have for her teenage daughter who'd just been rejected by her sixteen-year-old boyfriend. But I also felt anguish and, frankly, wrath. How could this interesting, yet weirdly pious, man be holding me ransom to a decision I thought I'd never face in the sensual wastelands of these days?

"What are your thoughts about this?" he asked.

"I've no fucking idea." I climbed off, pulled on my top, and bid him good night.

***

The days of fall inevitably bled into winter, though it bears little resemblance to the sub-freezing ice-bound seasons of yore. So I'm told. Aram was still my boarder. We managed to keep our interactions on friendly ground and focused on the practicalities of daily existence. There were occasions, especially on stormy nights, when we found ourselves back on the couch and once in my bed, driven by a mix of boredom and desire. Aram's four parents always hovered which meant we had to pleasure each other without crossing into the forbidden foothills of coitus. This was sufficient for Aram, the inscrutable, but offered only occasional ecstasy for me because it was emotionally more draining and exasperating than solo sex.

Beyond that, I came to recognize a darker side of the man who once seemed so light-filled and open-faced. One of those nights, when it appeared that he was keen to kiss and grope, I misread him. When I led with some nuzzling around his neck and ear, a bit of cheek-to-cheek, he jolted up off the couch. I was astonished. It was a level of acrimony that went beyond the chill of momentary rejection. He apologized, of course, but that dampened things for many weeks, even after a long conversation that more or less cleared the air.

One particularly cold night after I'd retreated to my bedroom and was on the furry edge of sleep, he tapped at my door. "Kate, could I just lie next to you for a few minutes of warmth?"

What could I say, 'no, go away?' I still did feel an almost maternal level of affection for him, trying as he was to navigate a path true to his upbringing and his understanding of the derelict religion he feigned to practice.

"Come here, yes, Aram. We can cuddle. Just cuddle."

We held onto each other front to front with no pretense of love making. Our bodies warmed and we relaxed into deep sleep. But not too deep, for two people to be fully comfortable in a small bed required adjustment and readjustment of front to back configurations until the first bit of dawn began to lighten the room. Aram slithered out of the covers and down the stairs to begin ritual prayers and preps for his day with Dr. Todd. I fell back into deep slumber. When I came downstairs more than an hour later, he was gone. He had thoughtfully stoked the stove and wood burner. The house was toasty, the tea kettle steamed, and mid-winter sunrays spiked through valley fog into the kitchen. It occurred to me that I ought to be feeling upbeat.

We'd slept together. Given that the phrase bore nothing resembling its normal significance and given that our relationship was ambiguous as ever, I couldn't decide whether we'd crossed a threshold or not. I tried not to think about it. As the days passed, Aram did not again tap on my bedroom door, retreating more and more inward. He didn't exactly avoid me but we hardly ever shared a meal. I could not fathom what of many possibilities would explain his detachment. So I let things ride. We shared the house and occasional polite conversations. Sure, he was a person with a good heart but there was almost no laughter. We acted like a disgruntled couple who had forgotten how to find joy together, and instead bitched and bickered.

As opportunities for communication and rekindling our friendship diminished, one morning I found myself speaking harshly when we were together in the kitchen. He was looking for a packet of dried apples he'd prepared and shared with me. I said something like, "Are you daft? Don't you remember that we ate those things weeks ago? Where's your friggin' head these days?"

"No need to speak that way to me, Kate."

"Well, it's the truth."

In the moments it took for us to spit out those few words, I realized we had fallen into repetitive bouts of prevarication, bouts that hurled us toward more and more hurt. It was a cycle neither of us wanted or relished. Yet we seemed unable to break it. I began to feel tense in my own house. It was a feeling I needed to address.

For many days after that, Aram and I continued to be dogged by the realities of life in the 2040s. For Aram, it was the tedium and fatigue of having to cover for an overworked doctor with scant advanced medical knowhow and too few tools. Winter made things worse. The flu was all about. Daylight was limited and it was almost impossible to perform any procedure in the poor light of lanterns. For me, Dad needed daily visits and care. Having slipped on his icy steps, he'd dislocated his hip, and broke an ankle. As his bones took longer than expected to heal, he became one cranky patient hopping around his cold house. He seemed to take for granted the meals I brought, and the firewood and ash I hauled. The point of this rant is to say that neither Aram nor I were on our best behavior when the day came to face our discontents.

Aram came home at eight o'clock after an almost twelve-hour day at the clinic. "We had to do an appendectomy under the electric lights at the mill; it did not go well. The patient bled out," he told me.

"Shit. Died?"

"Yes."

"Anybody I know?"

"Probably. It was Zach. Mikaela's partner."

"Double shit. That's awful. Esteban, such a sensitive and beautiful teen, is left without a dad. Just think what might have been, had this simple surgery taken place before Late-K led to Omega."

"Omega, Kate? That was thirty years ago. We weren't even alive then. It wasn't our fault. We did everything we could."

"Tell that to Esteban."

"We did. He and Mikaela were both there when Zach's heart stopped beating."

***

Up and down the Ohio Valley people were struggling with post-apocalyptic circumstances as they tried to survive and help their families and communities. Many of these people had fallen in love, and despite all the struggles, managed to stay in love or at least perpetuate their conjugal lives. Not us. I understood that fact even as Aram had distanced himself from me, and I from him. The challenge now was admitting the reality. It was going to be hard. Clear that our living situation was untenable, that our relationship was not about to catch fire again, I decided to ask Aram to find someplace else to live.

Aram cast me a stone-cold look, then turned away. Without another word, he walked across the kitchen and slammed the door to his room. In the morning, he apologized. He told me that he felt guilty for doing that, for having been so withdrawn, and for spoiling our friendship. He said that last night he was overcome with sadness and did not know whether it was real sadness or put-on sadness because he was so confused that he couldn't even comprehend his own feelings. After a long awkward pause, he said, "Yeah, I agree. It would be better to go our separate ways for now. I would not want things to get worse. In that case, there would be no hope for our future."

He had packed his belongings and stood at the kitchen door bundled for winter, his duffle slung over his shoulder and a small suitcase at his feet. He did not attempt an embrace or handshake. We seemed to be fixed to our spots on the faded tile a few feet apart, aware that neither had a playbook for this moment, memorable mainly for its stillness, which for me heightened the loss of something worthy, something insufficiently valued. Tears streaked across my cheeks. We were both to blame. He turned, opened the door, and made his way across my back yard, disappearing behind the fence into the dingy winter morning.

I walked over to dad's place. He was at his desk, his busted ankle propped up. I told him that Aram had moved out and that I'd asked Astrid to look in on him — Dad — for a few days.

"Oh, dear Kate. I am saddened by your news," he responded. "Gosh, I really do like and respect Aram. I had hoped you two would become partners, make me a grandpop."

This admission came as no surprise. But the way it poured out of him, so uncharacteristically tender, brought me to tears. All I could get out was, "Thanks." Wiping a few more sniffles with my sleeve, I admitted that I doubted we'd ever get back together.

He said, "You never know. For now, just be kind to yourself. Life does go on and I'll be fine."

3

In the last few shards of dusk, I knocked on the farmhouse door. The day had turned nasty with freezing rain turning to blowing snow that chilled to the bone.

"Oh my God! Look what the cat dragged in," Macy screamed.

"Hey girl, got a warm place for me and my nag? I'm desperately in need of a mid-winter respite."

"Absolutely!"

Mariah rushed to me with a fervent hug, her bounteous smile enveloping me with as warm a welcome as any blue girl could possibly want. It felt like a homecoming.

Later, after berthing Karma, soaking in a hot bath, and lifting a glass or three of Mama Riah's Rosé, we lingered long over dinner, catching up on months of Pomerance and Argolis gossip and news. Finally, I hesitantly spooled out the sorry tale of Kate and Aram, my voice slowing to tell of my sorrow.

I tried to put a wrap on the story by saying that, beyond Aram's commitment to a stale religion he really no longer believed in and dead parents, there was dark matter in other distant corners from which I was excluded. "Not that knowing about those places would necessarily have drawn us back together. But I do wonder whether it would have been possible to confront them and help him find redemption."

"Probably not," speculated Mariah who headed off to bed.

"I may be able to shed more light on that," Macy said. "But let's leave it to another day."

In the night I slipped in and out of dreams. Outside, snow was falling. I woke to a landscape softened and buried in pure white. In the pale morning light, as the sun rose, the snow sparkled like the Milky Way on a clear night. Along the river's edge, ice had formed. Icicles hung above my frosted window. It was perhaps our one day of real winter. As if the world had silently ceased its rotation, I felt I'd been offered a gift of some sort, a pathway for reconceiving life, grasping its wholeness, its consecrations, and knowledge of something for certain. I turned away from the window. The moment passed and I was back in the confounding place I'd just left.

At breakfast, talk turned to the day's chores. I was looking forward to putting my hands to something tangible. They deployed me to the horse barn. Of course, I went straight to Karma and she was pleased. She nuzzled my palm and nickered in anticipation of breakfast. I replenished her water and hay, gave her some oats, then repeated the routine for each of the farm's four Belgians, all whinnying their thanks. On a shelf, I found an array of grooming tools, some of which I'd read about but never seen. Apparently, Dad and other horse owners in Argolis had never been able to find these things in abandoned barns. For each horse, I started with their hooves, using a pick to clean away dirt and inspect their shoes. After that, I took a curry comb and with lots of elbow grease aimed at their hides, removed loose hair, dirt clods and dust. I finished with a soft body brush and a comb to untangle their manes and tails. As Macy's horses relaxed with a new human in their midst, the ambiance of a stable — soft whinnies and neighs, sighs of acceptance, friendly nickers, gas releases, undeniable horse odors of hay, sweat, poop and pee, transported me to a calming and familiar space. And I rejoiced that our little civilization had, with intention, reverted to real horsepower, the previous version having been crushed before my birth and present only in the unseemly rusted hulks all over the place.

After dinner, we sat in the living room warmed by a wood burner at full tilt, tipping more Mama Riah wine. Avery Campbell joined us. I was coming to enjoy Avery's whimsical takes on life. She seemed unflappable but also, like me, cynical, brutally honest and hardly optimistic about possible partners. "I'm deranged enough to think that maybe I ought to try seducing my best male friend," she said.

"And who would that be, Harvey Powell?" asked Macy.

"Harvey? Give me a break. Harvey can hardly spell his own name. Poor boy. And he can never remember mine."

"Then who?" I wondered.

She flushed. "Boss. Hays. I know he's over eighty but he's a character with plenty of zest. I love the guy. One day he told me my natural attributes were nothing but perfection. So there. I do admit to shamelessly coming on to him."

"Now there's an act of desperation," Macy said. "He may be all words, honey, much as I love the man. He did, after all, play a role in my upbringing. Now, I doubt he could, to put it bluntly, make a hard dick."

"Don't be so sure of that," replied Avery with a twinkle.

"You go ahead, girl. Conduct that experiment and let me know the results."

"I may just do that. But if I were you, I wouldn't hold my breath awaiting a report on outcomes."

I lowered my eyes. In no way was I of a mind to think about the sexual anatomy let alone the physiology of Hays, a dear friend of my dad, or of old men generally. I almost gagged. My mind then leapt to Aram's endowment and I had no trouble dreaming about that inside me. Even now.

As if she could read my mind, Macy said, "Speaking of outcomes, let's return to your ex-housemate."

"Okay. Aram," I said. "What is it that you know, Macy?"

"Well, I met Aram and his large colleague months before they recently floated back here. Going upstream, they stopped at our dock. From the vineyard, Mariah could see the boat's mast. She hailed me and I went to meet them."

"Why did they stop at your place?"

"At first, I feared pillage and rape. That proved to be wrong. In fact, they were surveying residents along the river about children."

"To what end?"

"I could not fully wrap my head around their motive at first, but their return clearly reveals what they're up to. Ella and Jacob, as you know, have two newly adopted kids, both of whom, according to Aram, were supplied by his former employer, a woman upriver near Wheeling. Back in October, when it came time to return, Aram decided to stay here."

"That's when he appeared at my door. He told me he was unsure whether he wanted to continue that work."

"I suspect he cannot live in a world of child trafficking."

"Is that what you call this?"

"That's how we're referring to it, yes. What else would it be?"

"Great Pan! Depending on how they source the kids and how the kids are treated, that surely would explain why Aram became more and more sullen, and less and less forthcoming. It may have little to do with being a lapsed Muslim."

"Right."

Assuming she had done her duty, Macy trundled off to join Mariah. Avery refreshed her glass and poured me another. The wine was doing its job.

"So, what are we meant to be doing?" I asked.

"I am probably the wrong person to answer that question." Avery went on to tell me about her dad's project. "Dad was once a lawyer and an assistant district attorney over in West Virginia. He and others in the village, including Hays, are working on forming a government. It would include a constable and a court for Pomerance and the adjacent shoreline along this side of the river. And they intend to find out about the upstream operation — the child-trafficking."

"Did Ella and Jacob pay for those children?"

"Probably but nobody knows for sure. And people are reluctant to ask, at least for now."

"Wouldn't it be tragic if they had to relinquish their kids at some point?"

"Absolutely. Which is why people seem willing to grant them a pass."

"What could one unofficial cop and judge in a small unincorporated place possibly do in these lawless days?"

"Nothing, as far as I can see," Avery replied. "And I've told Dad that. Still, I do want to know about their supply chain. I want to know whether mothers somewhere are grieving their snatched kids. If that's what Aram has on his conscience, it's no wonder he has hang ups."

I exhaled a long breath into the space between us. My conscience was telling me that knowing what I now know means life will never be the same. As if I needed to be told this. As if I didn't realize that along with the burst of traffic along the river there would be bad actors and illicit commerce. As if Aram could not really be one of those people. As if the Aram I loved, was not the real Aram.

SEVEN

Hestia and the Spirit Guide

Andeferas to Marietta, 2042

1

ONE MORNING WHILE PICKING the last of the huckleberries at the edge of an old field at the lakeshore, I saw a white bison lift his shaggy head above the shallow water and stomp his hoofs in the mud. I'd never seen a bison, let alone a pure white one. Startled by the sucking sound, I stood in awe at the size of him. I began to back away. He made a soft grunting sound and nodded his head as if to invite me to stay, his watery golden-brown eyes glowing with acceptance.

I wanted this beast to trust me, to send loving feelings across the species divide. I needed love that morning and maybe he did too. *Was I insane?* My emotional instability was all wrapped up in a decision about whether to leave the only people I'd ever really known. I took this ghostly creature to be a messenger.

Later that day in the library, I read that indigenous people believed that conversation with animals is a pathway to understanding and respecting the great circle, the ascendance of nature. The Koyukon of Alaska believed animas were humans in the distant past. They thus understand human speech and must be treated respectfully and ethically.[5] Native people also regarded rare white variants, like my bison, to be sacred and thus untouchable. They projected 'potent Medicine'. They were never hunted. Despite my innate pragmatism, I found this set of beliefs enhanced my sense of the possible. It stretched my world. On the other hand, was I so central in this bewildering world that a spiritually-potent animal would feel compelled to appear as an omen to me?

After work, in conversation with Freya, the grandmother I most respect, she assured me that her world would not collapse if I departed, even though she understood that it would probably be forever. I was confused. To be loved by this grandmother was bedrock for me. But her blithe dismissal of my possible departure? Without her encouragement, I may not have grown up so self-assured and comfortable in Andeferas, our small village. Known as a precocious independent woman, I was also village librarian. I had a reputation for loving kids, thinking for myself, and speaking my mind at Village Council meetings. Freya, more than any other person, had nurtured my growth and comfort in this world. If I emigrated, how would I fit into a new place with strangers? Was the white bison's Medicine drawing me toward unknown horizons or telling me to stay put?

The next day I found him farther from the lake in a vast meadow stretching to the western horizon. After bathing in the lake as the sun rose, I put on fresh clothing and strolled cautiously toward him. He paid me no attention until I got within twenty paces. Grazing in the tall grass, he looked up, his jaws rhythmically gnawing. From somewhere deep in his throat, he uttered rattling sounds. I moved within ten paces. He nodded and shook off insects buzzing his head. His tail whapped across his backside. I stepped closer, approaching him from the side as one would a horse. Though he outweighed me by many hundred stones, I felt no fear. I placed my hand on his head. He did not flinch. I reached up and gently scratched the forelock between his horns and cooed, "There, there. You are one very handsome spirit guide. I'll say that."

---

[5] Nelson, Richard K. *Make Prayers to the Raven: A Koyukon View of the Northern Forest.* p. 228. Chicago: University of Chicago Press, 1986.

He twitched an ear, shook his head slightly and moaned in appreciation. I backed slowly away, giving him space and the opportunity to graze again. He remained still, gazing at me as I turned and walked back toward the lake.

In the following days I sought further guidance. I found him each morning, always within sight of the lake. Always alone. Two days before my prospective departure, I sat on a small mound watching the morning sky brighten across the lake. To my left, the white bison, some twenty-five paces away, looked up at me. He bleated a greeting. I called out, "Oh, if I leave this place, how I shall miss you." Tears welled up. I buried my face in my palms, breathed deeply, wiped away the tears, and walked slowly to his side. I laid my palms on his shoulder. "Tell me, do I go or stay? Tell me."

As the sun's rays bled through the trees and lit up our patch of meadow, he responded with a monologue of grunts and moans. He went silent and looked into my eyes. I nodded my thanks. With nothing more to offer, he turned and trotted eastward, disappearing into the fog still clinging to the lakeshore.

***

Guided by the light of a waxing moon, Jason galloped into the village square just before midnight. The Argolians and I had been pacing aimlessly around the library. Jason dismounted, wobbly and exhausted. He did not acknowledge me or look my way. With his wide-brimmed hat, he batted away dust and sneezed. "Need somthin' to drink," he rasped. After chugging a stein of local brew, he reverted to his better manners and remained standing. "Thanks, I was really parched." The rest of us sat in a semi-circle to hear what he'd discovered. The situation at the Brothers of the True Vine Sanctuary had worsened, he said, and therefore we must prepare for up to twenty women along with one or more monks and hopefully some children. The children hinge upon the so-far unsuccessful collusion of nursery staff. The women would be devastated, he believed, if they had to flee without their birthright kids. But if it came to that, they said they would still choose to escape.

We agreed to gather in the square for departure by noon the next day. The Andeferas Village Council planned a going-off ceremony beginning with the pealing of the bells atop the former Methodist Church.

Early that morning I walked to the lakeshore. The white bison was nowhere to be seen. His absence marinated the silence. His disappearance into the fog yesterday was a moment I witnessed with certainty, a moment sodden with remorse. I felt strangely responsible. Thinking about it, I trembled at the portents that had begun to haunt me. From there, my mind went numb to the rising sun, the chorus of frogs and birdsong, the honeysuckle aroma of late summer. It was void of images, memories, names, truths. My guide was gone; my time here finished. Across the meadow, church bells rang. I rushed home to collect my belongings.

***

Our arrival in the mole gray of midnight set off dozens of hushed scrambles back and forth across the True Vine Sanctuary's residential plaza and through the gates where our people were posted. Women bearing backpacks and satchels, holding their squirming children rushed toward us, whispering, hovering, swarming — the ambience of dread sluicing the night air. I stepped down from the wagon to lend a hand, though it was not clear what to do. I had little idea of the plan. I walked away, leaden-legged and stiff. Bats swooped through night air which bore the faint scent of burning vegetation. A wildfire somewhere.

The erratic stirrings of anxious refugees mirrored the unruly chaos roiling my soul. Though only hours from Andeferas, I already grieved my decision. Jason, the man I presumed would become my life partner, had, as the day of departure loomed, become an unresponsive childish shell. He had not come to my bed for many days and barely spoke of our imagined future together. Was he preparing to reunite with his former love?

In less than an hour, the dozens of actors in this high-wire drama were either aboard one of the four wagons, two of which were being heisted from the Sanctuary, or ready to walk or ride alongside. I sat on a crowded bench in a wagon between Silas, my brother, and a childless True Vine woman named Giselle. None of us was in the mood for shallow talk or whispered speculation.

We rolled away from the Sanctuary as stealthily as possible, the creaking wagons and anxious whinnies and neighs of the horses and brays of other tethered animals notwithstanding. How long would it be before Salma and the monks were on our tail? Yet once we turned south on former Route 6, the adults began to chatter and whoop and the babies and children giggled and squealed in the dark. This joyful outburst of twenty-some refugees and a dozen kids gladdened my heavy heart as we headed toward our first stop at the outskirts of

Warren. Silas too felt the happy vibes. He wrapped his arm around me. "We're on our way to a new life, Hestia."

Arguably the worst night of my life, the second night of our journey, featured hungry infants and children screaming relentlessly, childless women in pitched battles contesting the maternity of this or that child, a skirmish over food that extended way beyond the presumed supper hour, and an exceedingly rocky surface beneath my bed roll. Whatever social glue had once bound together these women and children seemed to have abruptly come unstuck. Lighthearted spontaneity had turned to discord.

Beyond this, when the expedition leaders — the five Argolians, huddled in the morning to decide whether to head west or south from Warren, the two women who advocated a westward route, lost the debate and we began following former Route 11 South toward Youngstown. Freaked-out, with little experience in the wider world, I had no role in that decision. When I queried my spirit guide about the route, I got a muffled response as if his advice failed to penetrate the fog into which he'd disappeared three days ago. Hannah tried to explain but she might as well have been speaking Arabic. To me, this unfamiliar and terrifying geography and the routing seemed inconsequential.

Most of the town center of Warren had been demolished fifty years ago to make room for downtown parking. Cars I knew about; vast paved areas to accommodate them had never crossed my mind. From one of the few standing buildings — a stone three-storied former bank, emerged a bedraggled family of three scarecrow adults and several scraggly kids. As we drove past them, they gaped at us as though we were aliens. Shouting angry taunts, they begged for food. Ahead, I saw Jason lean out of the wagon that he and Nick were driving. He threw them several cobs of corn and said, "Sorry folks. This is all we can spare." They cursed and threw the cobs back.

Heading east to reach the road going south, we passed through desolate empty neighborhoods that Hannah referred to as suburbs. A monolithic five-story black-stained concrete hospital, surrounded by parking lots, was a grim reminder of the second pandemic twenty-some years ago, the one that overwhelmed medical facilities like this. A still legible sign, the words 'COVID-19 EMERGENCY' with an arrow, stood at one end of the building. I had never pictured vast tracts of mostly dilapidated homes, commercial businesses, and services such as this empty hospital. I saw a pack of feral dogs and tried to read the rusting signs: Wendy's, Walmart, Trader-something, names Hannah vaguely remembered from her girlhood. Apart from the dogs, there was no other life, as far as I could see.

At dusk, we pulled into a former city park in a place called Liberty, a ghost town among many. Silas and I sat on our bedrolls alongside the Conestoga wagon. The other three wagons were parked to form a sort of enclosure meant to secure the space where we lounged. We were trying to curate a few moments of peace and quiet amidst the tumult of women scrambling to calm and bed down children and a raucous pod of men at an impromptu fire pit. They were passing around a flask of something stiff enough to loosen their brains and tongues. "What do you make of your fellow males?" I asked Silas.

"That lot? Ach, I want nothing to do with 'em, especially those two monks."

Hannah tiptoed around the back of the wagon to join us. "Are you two as exhausted as I am?"

"Fully," I said.

Silas nodded in agreement. "It's a grind bumping along chuck-holed, broken roads. I walked most of the way."

"Get used to it," Hannah said. "Today is just the first of several long days. The plan is to zig-zag around Youngstown to mislead the trackers."

"Why are we so pressed?" I asked.

"I'm not totally certain because Nick and the others haven't been candid. I think they don't want people to be panicked about the chase that's probably underway."

"Hmm. I'm not the only one having nightmares about our pursuers catching up to us. In those dreams, what comes next isn't pleasant."

"It's that, yes, although we do have some hours lead on them."

"Also, I've been told there's a higher likelihood of bandits and desperate pickers around Youngstown, which is why we're avoiding it."

"Pickers?" asked Silas.

"Yes, people whose occupation is to steal and accumulate items from abandoned households, shops, and wayfarers. We've all been guilty of this practice at one time or another, I guess. But those who do this out of greed and avarice are not like us. We encountered three terrifying men of that sort last year. Fortunately, Nick, Jason, and Ezra dispatched them with a long gun and two pistols. The ring leader, a bully in a furry hat with antlers, wanted to beat and maim us before stealing our wagons and horses. He was left for dead with a bullet to his chest."

"Are our guys still armed?" Silas asked.

"Yes. And just before we left Andeferas they traded for another rifle owned by a Victor somebody. He seemed a bit daft and had no ammunition."

"Uh huh, Victor," I said. "Victor Graber. An older man, distraught over the death of his wife and daughter a few winters back."

"Armed combat is not what I signed up for," Silas said. "I'm glad the gun culture did not survive Omega. I wish we could obliterate all existing weapons."

"Me too," Hannah replied.

2

Mahmood Matthew O'Shea pushed his Arabian roan, Napoleon, to a gallop as the crumbling skyscrapers of Pittsburgh faded from sight. His mission accomplished, he now needed to put miles between himself and the urban riffraff who'd soon discover their leader dead. When he was a lad, he learned to sign his name M.M. O'Shea. People who had never seen him would thus assume Irish rather than hybrid blue-eyed, ochre-skinned Arab. That was decades back when racism saturated the land. It hardly registered anymore, so few were men like him. Men whose wits, discipline, and musculature enabled quickness and strength, and whose ruthlessness and instincts could irrevocably resolve disputes. Men who would never flinch in confrontations with desperate people, people who felt them inferior and underestimated their determination and artistry with weapons. At forty-eight, O'Shea was confident he still possessed these traits. After all, he was alive and the doubters were dead.

His sixty-mile journey would take more than a day. At nightfall, he found himself in a ramshackle neighborhood with few signs of life at the edge of the former city of Washington, Pennsylvania. Just beyond the intersection of old I-79, which he had been following, and I-70, which he would take in the morning, he rode down a ramp into the valley of a small creek where a stand of willows and pin cherries offered shelter. He led his roan to the softly flowing clear water. The horse slurped gallons. O'Shea bent over the creek to splash his own face and fill his sauce pan. As the sun set and the evening darkened and cooled, he fed and groomed the horse, gathered kindling and built a fire, cooked a modest meal, washed up, and climbed into his bedroll, the pistol at his side.

Hours later, stripes of vermillion and crimson marked the eastern horizon. He rose and hiked up the bank to the road. As dawn tinted the countryside, he squatted to study the rolling hills sloping toward the

Ohio River. It was mid-September. Nights were cool enough to remind him that in the weeks ahead he must either seek shelter or go farther south. He pulled binoculars from his pack and glassed the ridges and valleys. Nothing but forest and brush and the occasional high wall of an unreclaimed strip mine, all stitched together by thorny fencerows separating long fallowed farmlands. No movement, no smoke, no trace of humans. Still, he sensed this would not be a safe place to stay. He had no faith that others on the road would be well-intentioned. He returned to the campsite, boiled water for tea, ate his stale hardtack, and shared pocked apples with Napoleon. He packed his belongings into the saddle bags, tucked the Glock into his belt, attached the long gun to the saddle bag, and headed west on the public road.

Travelling at a slow gait on a sunny morning with patchy fog and nobody else on the broken asphalt, he allowed himself to imagine a more settled life. For thirty years he'd been a transient solitary operative, beginning with police academy training and assignment at nineteen to the Ohio Rapid Response Force, a sort of SWAT team to investigate terrorists, tamp down riots and protests, and protect the state's international border. When planetary systems went into freefall, he worked in counterintelligence for Europol until it too, in the wake of the second pandemic and nuclear war, triggered by Russia's aggression towards NATO, shuttered its operations.

Travelling back to the U.S. on one of the few international flights still operating, he was met at Dulles by the titular director of the CIA who hired him to work for the barely functioning federal government. When the People's Militia stormed the Capitol and assassinated the president and dozens in congress, surviving political leaders, federal agents, and a few civil servants retreated to the mountains in northeastern West Virginia. Out of a World War II-era bunker, O'Shea went afield to gather intelligence in remnant surviving communities and, when required, took down perpetrators of mayhem in Pittsburgh and other lawless places.

Years of working in the shadows meant three things: transience, anonymity, and social isolation. While he attributed his antisocial introversion to his work, he'd also realized since boyhood that this was probably who he really was. Growing up, he became known as a menacing loner, and for years he allowed it to define him. In the old days, he might have imagined retiring to a normal life when he'd no longer live in the shadows, no longer be that loner. He would learn how to socialize, how to love a woman for longer than one night, how to cope with the tedious ordinary rhythms of life, how to deal with the inevitable loss of control. The work he'd done for more than thirty years was the work of younger men. If he wanted to survive, he would have to change. But in these times, when across a land populated by sickly stragglers barely achieving subsistence, what exactly was normal? Where were people, anybody really, who might want to be sociable, might want to partner up? With no answers, he simply kept doing what he'd done — and done competently, one contract after another. So many killings he'd lost count. And now another.

Pulling off the road to stretch, empty his bladder, and water Napoleon, he took out his binoculars and scanned the road he'd just traveled. For the last hour, he'd had the sense he was being followed. Sure enough, far behind and barely discernable, was a two-horse coach accompanied by two riders on small horses or mules. Taking no chances, he took the first road off the highway going west toward the river. Calling it a road was a stretch; it was a really nothing more than a weedy rutted track with occasional lumps of bitumen. He coaxed Napoleon to pick up the pace. At darkness, he reached the river and pulled into a weedy graveyard. There were no signs of other travelers here in what used to be the northern panhandle of West Virginia. He dismounted, led the horse to a spot sheltered by a great white oak on a bluff overlooking the Ohio River. As the sun slipped below the horizon leaving behind a butternut sky, accompanied by a cricket symphony he found serenity among the graves of folk who'd died a century or more ago.

The next morning after a circuitous journey he crossed the river at the defunct rustbelt town of Weirton, then looped west and south toward his destination. At dusk he found the ranch house overlooking the river. It was exactly as his informant had described it, perched high on a bank with a view of Wheeling Island and the opposite bank, a landscape of decrepit twentieth century factories and refineries and vacant blue-collar neighborhoods framed in the distance by forested hills. The house on the bluff seemed a welcome refuge for a day or two, depending on the hospitality of its owner.

He hitched his horse to a post alongside a detached three-car garage at the end of the steep driveway. He ambled across the lawn to the front stoop.

"Hello? Ms. Kamal. Anybody home?"

From behind him, a willowy sand-colored woman dressed in crimson stepped out of the garage. She pointed a pistol at his chest. "Who's calling my name? Put both your hands above your head." Her voice projected jittery gumption. He raised his hands, scolding himself for being unprepared.

"Why are you here?"

"In Pittsburgh I met your colleague, Moises Marley. He said you may require a skilled professional to deal with a kidnapping."

"Who are you?"

"Mahmood O'Shea, ma'am. I have worked in intelligence and counterintelligence for thirty years. I plan and deliver resolutions to uncertain situations when evil doers amass power or require silencing. My resume includes work before the collapse for state and federal agencies and, before the second pandemic, the war, and the insurrection, for Europol out of The Hague and the CIA here."

"Your former employers mean nothing to me. Who do you work for now?"

"Myself."

"Why should I believe your story? It sounds contrived and impossible to prove." She stepped closer and steadied her weapon.

"If you give me a moment, I can document my history, at least that before 2021. I also have a letter to you from Moises."

Two hours later, they sat at her dining room table. Light from a chandelier spread a warm glow over a meal of roast lamb, mashed potatoes, and mixed vegetables prepared by a cook who popped in briefly to serve and clear away the dishes.

Looking up at the chandelier, O'Shea said, "You obviously have electricity."

"Yes, a friend helped restore and reconnect the solar array on the roof. There are batteries in the basement. It powers my fridge and other things as well. As far as I know, I'm the only house with electricity around here."

From there, their conversation stuck to mundanities: their ages — both in their forties, how each got to this place, their mental health in post-apocalyptic times, their families. Safiya told of the final days of her ex, the father of her daughters. After he succumbed, she and the girls tried to travel from South Carolina where he died, to their home in Ottawa. How their trip aborted in Wheeling. How she and Moises met. O'Shea spoke of family, his Irish aircraft technician dad and Jordanian mother with a PhD in philosophy and religious studies from University College Dublin. How he and his parents, together with a widowed grandmother and Cullen, his brother, emigrated from Dublin to New York in 1998. And within months, how they settled in a Dayton, Ohio suburb where his mother began her life in the U.S. as a professor of Islamic Studies and his dad landed a job at Wright-Patterson Air Force Base.

When the cook called out good-evening, they shifted to the deck overlooking the river. The night was balmy and moonless. Ripples in the wide river glittered beneath billions of stars splashed across the Milky Way. He said, "Everything these days is not dire. Skies like this never used to happen."

"Nor silence like this," agreed Safiya. "Brandy?"

"Sweet Jesus! I've not had a brandy in many moons. Where does one find brandy these days?"

"We distill it ourselves. The grapes are grown by growers nearby, growers in our, um, syndicate."

"You seem to be at the center of a local resurgence of sorts." O'Shea fished.

"One could say that. I have helped stimulate trade up and down the river, mainly in agricultural products. Traffic along the river has surged in the past few years. Some of it extends far beyond this place. About a month ago, a paddlewheel arrived at my dock from a place called Marietta, way down river."

"So, if you don't mind me asking, how is this connected to the kidnapping?"

"It's not. That's something else entirely."

"What, exactly?"

"Recently, in the middle of the night, a well-organized gang invaded an affiliated settlement two days north. They got off with horses and livestock and wagons. And they kidnapped a number of residents, including women and children. Although pursued, they seem to have escaped."

"And you want somebody to find them and return the stolen goods and captured people?"

"Yes, that's the task."

"If we get on this right away, I'm a good tracker. I can likely discover their escape route."

"That sounds like the beginnings of a plan."

The conversation moved to the particulars of where, when, and how much. Safiya answered most of his queries but dodged the question of why. "It's not something you need to know," she said.

"Is there a particular person, a ringleader or someone, you'd like me to capture or terminate?"

"I know very little about the perpetrators and who may lead them. You can do whatever you must to accomplish the mission."

O'Shea studied her more closely, scanning her classically proportioned Egyptian face in the semi-darkness. Beneath her arresting beauty, what he saw was a feral core and confidence in her power to control events. A formidable Cleopatra. "Okay, I can live with these ground rules," he said.

"Good choice." They shook hands, he holding the grip a moment longer. Her head tilting, her lips spreading toward a bemusing smile.

"Can you provide anyone to assist me?"

"Let me work on that tomorrow. For now, let's call it a night."

He nodded. "All right. By the way, have you seen any bison around here?"

"Bison? No. Why do you ask?"

"Just wondering. I crossed the river at Steubenville. Nothing to speak of there but somewhere down the road, I'm sure I saw a bison at the crest of a steep cliff. Strangest thing was that it was not like the shaggy brown beasts I'd seen in the west. This one was almost purely white."

He awoke to the sound of a two-way radio exchange, something he'd not heard in more than two decades. Back before mobile phones emerged, part of the tactical gear of anyone in his profession was a powerful two-way radio. Even after cell phones became ubiquitous, in places with no or weak signals, handsets using radio signals were still part of the kit.

He washed up, dressed, and met her in the kitchen. The cook had prepared biscuits, sausage, gravy and eggs. She poured coffee. "Hope you're not a practicing Muslim."

"Hardly. I appreciate your hospitality, Safiya. I've not slept in such comfort and so soundly in months. And I've certainly not had biscuits since the crash. They are splendid. Where did you get the wheat flour?"

"It is grown locally. I have so much, in fact, that I traded ten bags the other day for goods brought upriver by the steamer. Coffee, cooking oil, new bedding, other stuff."

"Impressive. Did I hear the crackle of a two-way radio just a few minutes ago?"

"You did." Before he could ask the next question, she said, "I've arranged for you to meet two people from the settlement that was raided. They will tell you what they know and lend a hand in recovering the stolen property."

Within the hour, he was on his way north. By mid-day he found the rendezvous site, a weedy urban park with remnants of a reconstructed 1780s fort built in what would become the center of Steubenville, Ohio. As was his practice, he arrived early for reconnaissance. He walked about the former park and the crumbling city blocks on three sides. Off toward the river, he saw a pack of wolves loping toward him. When they saw him, they veered north. Otherwise, there were no signs of life within sight of the park which was perched on an embankment with 360-degree sight lines. He explored a small stand of shade trees on the northern edge, musing once more on the pervasiveness and long-term outcomes of the second pandemic. Although its lethality peaked twenty years earlier, long-term debilitating effects of the disease caused death for years thereafter. Now, in the 2040s, there appeared to be no survivors in a city that once had been home to twenty thousand.

He led the horse into the trees and tethered him. At the edge of the stand, he climbed a buckeye to await his prospective partners. With so little time to judge the woman for whom he was working, he could not afford to meet complete strangers, likely armed strangers, without some surveillance. He scanned the main road. Around the bend where a Franciscan university once thrived, he saw two riders approaching at speed. They turned right just north of the park, and then left onto an access road and a small parking lot fifty paces from his perch. A prematurely balding man, probably in his thirties, wearing a brown smock and corduroy trousers, jumped down and lent his hand to a slinky young woman dressed in jeans, a sort of camo top, and what looked like an old-fashioned baseball cap. Her beige cornrows swished across her neck. They scanned the site cautiously and walked toward the quadrangle surrounded by decaying low-slung buildings of the former fort.

O'Shea shimmied down the tree, cocked his pistol, and ghosted to the back of a fortress building. He saw the man and woman venture inside a bastion on the southeast corner. While they were there, he strolled to the center of the quad and squatted near what appeared to be an archaeologic excavation site. When the woman reappeared, he called out, "Are you Salma?"

"I am. Are you O'Shea?"

"That's right." He stood up. "Shall we walk to those trees for some shade?"

Staying slightly behind them, he told them he was here to help them retrieve all that was stolen or kidnapped. She said, "Good. This is Brother Kornhower. We are here to assist you." O'Shea stepped forward to shake their hands, repeating his name each time.

Under the big buckeye, he explained that in the next day or two he thought it wise to backtrack to the place they had lost the thieves, then pick up their traces along the route they actually followed. "From there, we should be able to catch up to them."

Brother Kornhower, the technical genius who revived long distance communication and solar arrays on Safiya's house and at their community, demonstrated a bag of tools, including zip-ties and walkie-talkies. With that, they mounted and were soon putting miles between Steubenville and their destination.

At dusk on the second day, they set up camp on the shore of Kinsman Lake, a reservoir 100 miles north of Steubenville. In the morning, Salma and Kornhower led O'Shea to the westward trending road they had followed for a whole day. Salma said, "We found no traces of the thieves and ran out of food, so we returned home."

"So which way do you think they went?" O'Shea asked.

"I suspect that the party had taken one of three lesser-traveled roads that head south."

"Okay, let's try one of those for a few miles. If there are no clues, we'll go back and try the other ones."

They mounted up, heading south on old Route 7, a road with clusters of former rural properties fronting either side of the road. The houses had been gutted by pickers long ago and now harbored termites, rats, swifts, and organic rot. Quite apart from the chartreuse mold over everything, it's no wonder none of these houses were occupied — they offered no shelter from the elements and, aside from the pandemic, which undoubtedly killed or drove away many of the occupants, without upkeep these structures would never have made it intact halfway into this century.

Crumbling cultural landscapes like this were so much a part of life that the search party trotted on with barely a glance at the rubble and the myriad human tragedies it bespoke. *If you look back, you'll never survive in this troubled world, especially if you're an assassin,* thought O'Shea. He'd long ago concluded that his immunity to the suffering and death in these places must somehow be adaptive.

Leaving the lake behind, they moved at a pace slow enough to look for animal manure, wheel ruts, and other traces of a large party. Finding no clues in almost twenty miles, they set up camp just east of the former Youngstown-Warren Regional Airport, a somewhat risky treeless location. O'Shea said they'd have to head north again in the morning.

At sunrise, they chose former Ohio Route 193, a narrow overgrown track that paralleled the road they'd taken south. Passing through the former hamlets of Fowler and Johnston, both uninhabited, they found no spoor. At Johnston, the road crossed Route 6, the other main road heading south and the last secondary route Salma could imagine they would have taken. If they failed here, it would mean trying to pick up clues along the much more heavily traveled Route 11 that led into a complex network of roads in the former Warren-Youngstown area. That would be more difficult not only because of the road network but also because of highwaymen and bandits.

Along former Route 6 there certainly were traces of wagons and animals but the road turned out to be more heavily traveled than Salma predicted. The clues were not unequivocally those of their prey. As Route 6 crossed under a freeway, they were forced into the outskirts of Warren to cast about for places the perpetrators might have camped. Salma's previous travel had not prepared her for this and Brother Kornhower appeared to be overwhelmed by this former urban landscape. When they began to speculate and argue with one another, O'Shea had had enough. "You two are obviously lost in more ways than one. Gimme the map."

Salma handed over a brittle hand-drawn map based on a 2012 Ohio Road Map she'd somehow lost. O'Shea studied it, got his bearings and said, "No more bullshit. Let me decide where we go from here. What exactly is their destination?"

"We assume it's a place called Argolis in the south somewhere."

O'Shea had a vague memory of Argolis. In November 2013, as a twenty-two-year-old officer in the Ohio Rapid Response Force, he'd dropped out of a helicopter someplace in southern Ohio in the middle of the night to put down a student rebellion, and scuttle back to Columbus before sunrise. He scanned her map. Argolis was far south, just upstream from the Ohio River.

Pointing, he said, "We've got to get over to that river and follow it south."

3

Nick told us to continue to be wary. Choosing a series of secondary routes around the eastern and southern outskirts of Youngstown, we zigged a few miles east to cross into the former state of Pennsylvania. Nick explained that Youngstown was lawless space, driven by the deprivation of survivors and the trafficking of contraband to and from Pittsburgh. Our detours on small roads were meant to throw our followers off. We spent a night in a back yard in a hilly rural area near the former town of New Castle.

"They'll never find us here," Nick told us as we shared a meagre supper. Provisions were being parceled out in smaller proportions, and because of the pressure to keep traveling nobody had had a chance for wildcrafting, hunting, or fishing. The children were hungry and unruly.

"With these diversions, won't it be winter before we get to Argolis?" I asked Nick.

"I cannot really say, Hestia. If we were sure that our pursuers had given up, then we could get back on more direct routes. Let's take it a day at a time."

Over the next several days, the roads in western Pennsylvania proved to be a test of our mettle. Secondary paved highways three decades ago, now their asphalt was shot. The ruts of carriages and wagons had eroded the roads into elongated corridors of gullies and potholes. Collapsed bridges required hours-long workarounds, some of which we cleared by hacking brush and sawing up downed trees. Yesterday, it rained torrentially, throwing deep puddles and mud into the equation. It was slow going. At least we met few other travelers, no highway robbers, and no signs of Salma or her hench-brothers.

The expedition was wearing me down, and not just physically. I longed for guidance. The constant spats over children among the True Vine women and the plain truth that they were doing nothing to contribute to the common good offended me. Sure, these women had been sex slaves and unpaid field workers — a terrible plight. But somehow, once on the road to freedom, they resorted to sloth and the vilest of impulses toward each other and the brothers. And they chose to ignore the rest of us, their liberators. The only exception was the childless Giselle, a pretty waif of a woman barely seventeen. She had become my friend and confidant. Giselle had the courage to speak the unspeakable. She said the sexual appetites of the brothers were coarse and debased. "To put it plainly, we were raped, time and time again."

Around the edges of the True Vine dramas, Brothers Forthwind and Tybald both proved to be hopeless drunks. They arose morning after morning sullen and hungover, and then managed to do nothing but take up space in the wagons. When night came round, they were back at the bottle.

At last, the sacred bison materialized at twilight across a misty meadow in western Pennsylvania. In the moonlight, I hastened through waist-high grass and stinging nettle, crown-beard, ageratum, and asters. He twisted his neck to greet me with head nods and soft rumbling bellows. I ran to touch him, to scratch his shaggy mane. "How can we possibly survive such chaos?" I asked him. I stepped back to look into his eyes. His response came as a riddle: *When chaos mocks your day, how shall a dowsing stick point the way?*

We crossed the Ohio River over an old bridge and wended our way to meet the Ohio again at Follensbee on the West Virginia bank. From there, we began to follow the river south on former Route 2. A day later, we passed through the crumbling remnants of Wheeling: government buildings ransacked; empty churches, their steeples ghosting the gray skyline; the Royal Coach Bus Terminal a monument to social and economic breakdown, the final bus, a rusted hulk, trapped beneath a collapsed portico.

We stopped for the night south of the former city center on the grounds of a vast medical center and hospital. A sign on the front door read:

CLOSED

We regret to inform you that the pandemic has forced closure of our operations.
We will reopen as soon as we are able.
Stay safe.

Ohio Valley Medical Center, January 14, 2021

After dinner, Nick and Hannah came to me. I was stretched out on my bedroll dozing amidst the usual din of the evening. "It's time to take stock," Nick said. "Can you hear us out?"

"Of course." I felt honored to be included.

"I've had so many front-burner matters to deal with every day that I've not done enough forward planning," Nick began. "The size and composition of this expedition has seriously slowed us. There are frictions I did not anticipate. Unless things change, I'm not sure we can make it all the way with these people, especially if their former enslavers catch up to us."

"The True Vine women seem intent on stirring up conflict every inch of the way," Hannah said. "My forbearance has been put to the test."

"That's my experience too, except for Giselle," I added. "Plus, I had a terrifying personal incident a few nights ago."

"Can you tell us about it?" asked Nick.

"Only if you're comfortable doing so," Hannah added.

"Okay." I hesitated. "Um, about four days ago after dark, on his way to the loo, a tipsy Brother Forthwind sprung out of the bushes at me. He grabbed me roughly and groped my breasts and backside. 'Are you ready to fornicate, pretty maiden?' he slurred. I told him to get his hands off me. I managed to squirm away and shove him with all my might. He tipped backwards and rolled downhill, howling fiendishly. I ran away. The next morning, he greeted me as though nothing had happened."

"That's criminal, Hestia." Hannah wrapped her arm around my shoulders. I laid my head on her chest.

"Sorry, it's all a bit melodramatic."

"No apologies," Nick said. "What Forthwind did is off limits and he must be held accountable."

I pulled away from Hannah and leaned toward Nick. Speaking softly, I uttered this non sequitur: "Do either of you, by any chance, know what a dowsing stick is?"

4

Dawn broke beneath a heavy deck of stratus clouds and valley fog shrouding the far horizon. Safiya instructed her chef to cook a hearty breakfast while she prepared packs of foodstuffs and other provisions. Brother Kornhower had risen early. He was on the roof doing something with the solar panels.

Salma found her mother in the kitchen. "Are these packs for the trip?"

"Yes, my mabouba. There's enough for ten days or more."

"Mama, can we trust O'Shea? I'm worried about the children. Think of all the income and influence we stand to lose."

"Moises recommended him. I think he can be trusted. There may be bloodshed, hopefully not on our side. He is a skilled marksman and will not use his weapon carelessly. His job is to protect you so that everyone, including the kids, will safely end up back where they belong."

The others arrived for breakfast on the deck overlooking the river. Safiya and Salma chatted with O'Shea in English. Having been raised in Gaspé in Quebec, Kornhower's first language was French. Though he certainly could understand and speak English, he often remained silent when English was the mode. Instead of engaging he would nod and smile from time to time.

O'Shea said he'd been studying the map. "It's about 140 miles from here to Pomerance, the closest river town to Argolis. Assuming no delays, we could make it there in under four days."

"Pomerance is one of the towns Moises visited," Safiya said. "In fact, the couple who adopted the first two of our children live there. Moises' co-worker, a former medical student called Aram, is also somewhere down there. He has become a medic assisting the town doctor."

"Is this guy someone you trust?" O'Shea asked.

"Yes, he was a reliable and cheerful employee. Moises believes he fell in love. That's why he did not come back here."

"Okay. If we cannot intercept them enroute, we'll come up with a plan to seize your people and goods at their destination. It will be more difficult, of course. Aram could perhaps be a helpful insider."

Kornhower excused himself. He wandered to the deck railing with O'Shea's binoculars and scanned the river for birds. "*Merde alors! Qui est-ce que je vois?*" he exclaimed in a tone too clamorous for the circumstances.

Salma ran to him. He gave her the glasses. "Mama, across the river, there's a party in a two-horse wagon that looks familiar."

Safiya and O'Shea came to the railing. "How many women and children did you say were kidnapped?" O'Shea asked.

"We counted twenty-two missing women and a dozen babies and children," Salma replied.

"And they stole wagons and livestock as well?"

"Yes. Two farm wagons, four horses, and a number of goats and sheep."

"Well, though this is surely not the whole lot, it would be worth crossing the river and heading south on that road. Does it link with the main southbound road?"

"It does," Safiya replied.

"Alright, when we catch up to them, we'll find out."

5

At sunrise, Nick found Brother Forthwind in a patch of evergreens at the entrance to the hospital. He groaned and loudly expelled his queasiness over the juniper and boxwood. "Aaach," he moaned, wiping his mouth with the back of his hand. Nick wanted to back away. Instead, he said, "Forthwind. We need to talk."

The brother arose from his crouch, shielding his eyes against the sun and clutching the back of his neck with the other hand. "I'm in no mood, my friend. Can't you see? I'm not in top form at the moment. Can we talk later?"

"This cannot wait, Brother."

Ten minutes later, Nick strolled to the front of nearly all the adults gathered in a semi-circle near the wagons. At the far end of the parking lot, the children were tended by two mothers. Brother Forthwind skulked to the edge and slumped to the ground next to Brother Tybald.

"I'm here to tell you that our plan going forward will require everyone to help reshuffle gear and personal belongings. We're splitting into two parties. Each will travel separately and then we'll reassemble at a designated point for a day or two of rest before travelling the final leg to Argolis."

With four of us directing the reshuffle, an hour later, the advance party was on its way in the Conestoga wagon, driven by Em and Ezra, neither of whom had met anyone from The True Vine before this expedition. They were armed with Victor Graber's rifle and they represented the left branch of the dowsing stick. They would travel former Route 2, the main West Virginia road southward along the river.

The second group — the right limb of the dowsing stick — led by Nick and Hannah, included Silas and me and all the women and kids. Brothers Forthwind and Tybold were given a choice. Either walk behind the wagons or go the other way to seek their fortune someplace else. They chose the latter and began retracing their steps through Wheeling. As the two monastic louses faded out of sight, I murmured a benediction. "Good riddance, perverted brothers."

We left the medical center before noon, travelling eastward a few miles to climb onto the former I-470 bridge. We then headed west and crossed the river into Ohio. At St. Clairsville, we turned south on a back-country road wending its way far from the river. We were advised that it would be a tough journey and the narrow and rutted road did not disappoint. Even worse, the size of the party was ungainly and often wandered off road to herd the sheep and goats. Silas, Antonio — a strapping veterinarian and blacksmith who joined us in Warren, and I formed a rear guard, each riding a fleet horse and trailing the wagons by about fifteen minutes. Antonio carried our only weapon, a pistol with limited range and ammunition.

After a day of weaving slowly through empty country shrouded with tracts of hardwood forest regrowth, we arrived to find camp being set up in the encroaching darkness. The three of us joined Nick and Jason who were roasting a goat leg over a roaring fire.

"No sign of anybody trailing us?" asked Nick.

"None whatever," Silas replied.

"All good, then."

"Aye."

***

We three had had an inconsequential afternoon, keeping together by restraining the horses. Though they'd barely met, Silas and Antonio quickly lapsed into a friendly brotherhood and slung little sister taunts the whole way. I became intrigued by our newest fellow traveler, a Latin from a place called Argentina, a guy so unlike Jason, he took my breath away — a guy at ease in his own skin and adept in ways our expedition required. When one of the wagon wheel hubs failed, he rigged a fix over a hot fire that hardly delayed us; he was a good cook and cheerfully pitched in around camp. Occupationally, he was a self-taught veterinarian and an accomplished horse whisperer. Like me, he loved everything about horses. Like me, he cooed in their ears while scratching their withers.

Antonio! The youthful olive-toned face, a sun-washed hue burnished like that of a roasted chestnut. Strangely ancient, yellow-specked brown eyes of a priestly sage. Forbidden, hot, adventurous eyes. Shining black hair needing a trim; a limber long-legged gait. I secretly admired his muscular thighs, flat stomach, tight buttocks, large strong hands, and his manner of speaking — his Spanish-inflected English imparted civility and grace. No insecure overgrown adolescent, this man. We rode side-by-side for an hour or so.

"Would you say there's going to be a bright ending to this journey?"

"I'd say, from what little I know of you, Hestia, you already have the answer to that question."

Two travelers, about the same age, in the filtered sunlight of a canopy of fast-growing maples and poplars, shared gestures of new found friendship in a world of woe. Both born to such gestures, we offered them effortlessly, and so formed an immediate comfort in each other's company.

"What do you know of me? We've just met," I asked.

"I need little more than to bask in the glow of your good heart, your free spirit, your optimism."

"Optimism? I admit to little of that recently. Shame on me. But you know, after I received assurances from a trusted friend, I've begun to feel lighter. Witnessing the arses of those two retreating drunkards back in Wheeling — that has also lifted a burden."

"See, just as I said."

"Uh huh. Although we're supposed to be on high alert now, I feel relaxed riding next to you. I'm beginning to feel a smidgeon of hope. The new life Silas and I had imagined might actually happen."

"It will, Hestia."

I turned toward him, grinning shamelessly while realizing this man could be another reason for my rising spirits. Enough of the brothers, enough of the True Vine women and their squabbly kids, enough of the sullen and edgy Jason.

The camp was pitched at the edge of a forest called Blackwood. The oaks, the maples and beeches, the black cherries and walnuts were ancient and outsized, casting auburn and gold across the camp. After dinner and cleanup, when the sounds of humans took a backseat to cicadas and crickets and the hoots of owls, we gathered around the fire. Nick told us the story of how he and hundreds of his classmates at the university in 2013 saved this forest from plunder by the oil and gas industry. "At the time, Blackwood Forest was the largest patch of old growth forest in Ohio. But it is minuscule compared to the extent of forest before white settlers cut down more than 90 percent of the trees. When we walk through it tomorrow morning, you will understand why we staked our lives trying to save it."

He was right. It was the most awe-inspiring forest we'd seen anywhere — a sacred place.

"How on earth did your protest manage to prevail against powerful companies, the state, and the university?" I asked.

"Well, we outsmarted them. And when they retreated to lick their wounds, and decide what to do next, the world crossed into Late-K and began to go over the cliff — first the pandemic, the economic depression, the social breakdown, the 2021 insurrection, the war. All that. We didn't know it at the time but global collapse achieved protection for this forest in ways we never could have."

"What a gift to future generations, like ours."

"Yeah, despite all the heartbreak, everywhere we look we see that nature is healing scars inflicted by our grandparents and those that came before."

6

Safiya waved them good bye. "Safe journey, each of you. When you're on high ground, Kornhower, you will keep me posted?"

"Oui. Au revoir, Madame."

They trotted off the west bank of the Ohio River and spent the better part of an hour looping back to the former I-70 bridge that would lead them into Wheeling. From there, Salma, who harbored terrifying childhood memories of the place, confidently led them through former city streets, their echoing clip-clops the only sound. Nothing but abandoned warehouses and dilapidated commercial buildings in this part of town. When they passed the former Ohio Valley Medical Center, O'Shea raised his arm. They pulled up.

"There's a pile of debris out there in that parking lot."

"The whole lot's got debris scattered across it," said Salma. "Horseshit, cornhusks, plastic, something in the shrubbery by the hospital."

"Yeah, but it bears a look."

She shook her head. "It's nothing probably."

"You think they'd clean up their mess?"

"How in hell should I know?" Salma replied.

Leaving Kornhower with the horses, O'Shea and Salma proceeded on foot across the lot. The place was unnerving, revealing nothing but silence. And broken glass. The sky, streaked with cirrus wisps, was bright and blue, autumn sunrays refracting back to space. A fresh wind. Screeching, a fox skittered away from the rubbish. O'Shea bent over the pile and scooped two handfuls, brought them to his nose.

"Horses, sheep, ashes, charred kid's sock, melted plastic spoon."

"Has to be them."

The wind picked up, swirling a dust devil across the lot. O'Shea's eyes followed it. "Who's that?" He lifted his binoculars, glassed a line of trees at the edge of the complex. Two figures melted into the shadows. He could make out the contours of a small building.

"Okay, stay with me," he told her. He drew and racked his Glock. They ran to the back of the hospital building. He crouched behind a loading dock. She hunched to his left.

"I'm not seeing movement now."

"Me either. How should we proceed?"

"See that garden shed behind those low trees? They're in there."

"I see it, yes. How can you tell?"

"Never mind. Give me a couple of minutes to sneak around to the back of it. There's a door there. You creep up to the front. Flush them out the back."

"Wait, I have no weapon."

"Just shout something threatening and take cover."

She nodded. O'Shea skirted the edge of the stand of trees and disappeared into the shadows. He crept toward the shed. In the deep shade, he paused to let his eyes adjust. He moved closer. Salma ought to have been shouting by now.

At that moment, the building came alive with snorts, thumps, a rasping door. He heard Salma scream. He heard gasps and grunts as the little building toppled forward. A muffled cry, the footfalls and heavy breathing of men running. He came round to the front. His attention was immediately drawn to the head and shoulders of Salma, flat on the ground, pinned beneath the lintel, frame, and door. A head wound oozed blood across her forehead. She was unconscious. He found her carotid artery.

With care and as much might as he could muster, he lifted the timbers just enough for Brother Kornhower to draw Salma from beneath the ruins. Kornhower fetched water, an antiseptic tincture, and a flask from their saddlebags. Salma slowly regained consciousness. O'Shea cleaned the head wound, propping her up against his body.

She gazed up, squinting. "They get away?"

"Don't worry about that now. When you're able, have a slug of this."

Within an hour, Salma was alert and able to take unsteady steps with O'Shea and Kornhower on either side. By some unnamed grace, she had plenty of bruises but no broken bones. Her left wrist was sprained. She could remember almost nothing of the calamity, only that there were two of them.

In late afternoon, as day relinquished its light to dusk, they crisscrossed neighborhoods but found no sign of the fugitives. Giving up their search, they climbed onto former Route 2, cantered through South Wheeling, and at darkness, settled alongside the river at Benwood. Kornhower brought up Safiya on the radio and strolled away to the riverbank. When he returned, Salma, still suffering, was asleep in a pop-up tent. O'Shea gathered wood. From across his small fire, he gazed up at Kornhower. "You fill Safiya in on our day's misfortunes?"

"*Oui*. Seems that two of my compadres escaped and staggered onto her porch this afternoon."

"Them that were kidnapped?"

"Yes. And surely the very same who busted out of that shed and almost killed Salma."

In the morning, they proceeded southward on Route 2. Brothers Forthwind and Tybald, despite their alcohol-infused fog and irrationality, claimed that the kidnappers had split into two parties and that they planned to meet somewhere to the south. One wagon had definitely been dispatched to this road. By mid-morning, two men going north confirmed the story.

7

As the hours of daylight diminished, we crawled southward. Nights chilling to the bone; cold rain; rutted roads ankle-deep in sticky goo. One misty morning, I found the white bison at the edge of camp. Nonchalant, he came to me, urged us on with a hint of peril. Something about the rendezvous. I told Hannah about this. She'd pass it on to Nick.

At Woodsfield, we paused for two days. A former county seat with an impressively restored courthouse, Woodsfield's population seemed to comprise dozens of families living in restored homes in neighborhoods within walking distance of the town square. Surely, this was fantasy. I noted residents bustling between retail businesses, a doctor's office, a newspaper, and a stable and blacksmith. If I hadn't known better, we might have journeyed back a couple of centuries.

At the general store with polished white pine plank flooring and well-stocked shelves, we warmed ourselves around a potbellied stove, refurbished our supplies, and perhaps imagined a future of possibility. True Vine women and children filled the place with waves of positive energy we hadn't seen in weeks. Penny candy for the kids. Where did it come from? For me, just one slice of tangy gingerbread was the best treat since I closed the door of my kitchen so many weeks ago.

I wondered about this flashback place. I chatted up the proprietor, a rotund middle-aged guy about my height who seemed open to conversing with a slight girl with cropped hair and an attitude. "Folks seem to be doing better than just surviving. I'm impressed. How have you managed this?"

"Being isolated was a blessing during that second pandemic, way back," he said. "Our grandparents hunkered down and never left the county. Likewise, I guess very few infected folks passed through. The people of that generation doubled down on self-reliance; learned to home-grow most everything. I'm old enough to remember those days — I's one of nine kids. We pretty much got raised normally, dirt poor as ever. Mum and Dad lived into their eighties. Seven of us are still kicking."

"How about kids these days? Have women been bearing children?"

"Oh yeah. Most women your age have kids. We're only about two hundred people overall, so young folks would tell you that finding a good match ain't easy. A pretty girl like you might be horrified at the guys available here. Schooling's not mandatory so many of 'em are as fuckin' dumb as they are ugly — scuse my language. Too much inbreeding, I reckon."

I loved this guy's candor and wanted to ask more but Nick sidled up to interrupt us. "Tell me, sir, from here south, what's the next town with people?"

"Well, if you're following the Muskingum River down old twenty-six, there really ain't one 'til you get to Marietta. All them little towns are dead as a block o' granite. You're lookin' at nothing but deep woods between here and Marietta. Watch out for bears and cougars."

We went outside to sit on a bench in the October sun. Nick asked me about my hesitation around the planned rendezvous.

"It seems to project something ominous."

"How sure are you of that?" Nick was careful not to raise questions about what he thought was my affiliation with the occult.

"Enough that we need to come up with an alternative."

8

O'Shea led Kornhower away from the riverside camp. "She's putting on a brave face but it's obvious she's really hurting. We ought to give her a day's break. Then we may have to slacken our pace for a day or two."

Kornhower nodded. "Despite her needle arms and boney ass, she's strong-willed. Has the instincts of a vampire. I wouldn't underestimate her."

Forty-eight hours later, they pitched camp in a pasture behind a decrepit gas station south of the ransacked town of New Martinsville. It had been impossible to determine traces of the wagon they sought.

"O'Shea, we're on a fucking wild goose chase," Salma asserted. "Looks to me like we've allowed them to elude us. They may not even be traveling this way anymore."

"Hard to say." O'Shea ignored her tone.

"I think we should forget about them and just head straight for Argolis."

"I tend to agree," said Kornhower. "This seems like looking for a needle in a haystack."

"So, what are you, a couple of mutineers?"

"We want the best outcome, sir. We want to recover everything and everybody we lost." Kornhower tried to reason. "We don't want to waste time."

"Ambushing a small party is one thing. Attacking a village and trying to recover dispersed adults and children and animals is quite another. If it's the latter you're advocating, I don't like the odds. I'll cut my losses and leave you to it."

"Wait, wait." Salma said. "Don't be a jackass. We're simply pointing out that we may have been outflanked. If that's the case, we've got to reach Argolis before they do. Kornhower and I cannot do this alone."

"That last part is absolutely true. And so, I'd suggest you two quit your whining and we stick with our intelligence about the meeting in Marietta. If that fails, assuming we're not all dead, we'll go to your plan."

9

At dawn, Silas rode off on my chestnut mare. If all went well, he would find the wagon before the trackers did. The rest of us slogged southward on old Route 26 through the deep forest. I do love the feel and fragrance of a forest and this stretch was more redolent than most — mushrooms, lichens, mosses, rushing creeks — with more color than any autumn woods I'd ever been in. In my imagination I could see native people five centuries ago treading soundlessly in their rawhide moccasins along well-travelled paths. Sorrowfully those very people, who were obliterated by white settlers in the 1700s, got the last laugh. The ancestors of those white settlers living here have joined those long-gone Indians.

There were worrying omens too: the forest's claustrophobic dimness barred long views, there were few clearings, and the dankness of rotting vegetation set off my allergies. I saw signs of wild predators: a dead raven; the carcass of a coyote or dog reduced to a bleached skeleton; the skull of a buck, eight-point antlers intact; black bear spoor. I tried not to obsess, tried not to worry about our domesticated critters. My spirit guide advocated positive thinking. I forced myself to think of things for which I'm grateful: the spikes of sunlight pointing our way south, the late summer sunflowers and asters along the verge of the rutted road, the comradery of Hannah and Giselle, Nick's reassuring confidence, Antonio's night visits.

On the third day, we emerged from the forest after crossing an intact covered bridge. From there we wove our way through abandoned farmland and scattered rural homesteads, only a few of which seemed to be occupied. An hour later, we found the new rendezvous, a huge patch of green sward that used to be the Marietta Country Club. We set up camp at the edge of a weedy fairway in a copse of willows that offered clear sightlines and cover. Here we would wait for Silas and the other wagon.

10

On their fourth day out, on a hilltop at a bend in the road, O'Shea pulled up and peered ahead. Salma and Kornhower dismounted.

"We've caught up," O'Shea announced. He handed the glasses to Salma.

"That does appear to be our quarry. What now?"

"We keep our distance. With patience, we'll be rewarded. We'll be led precisely to their meeting place."

11

At the appointed place in a stand of mature oaks at the edge of the parking lot of a failed ophthalmology practice, Silas dismounted. Having pressed hard on his nine-hour journey through the forest, he and Hestia's mare, Farleigh, needed rest. He fed, watered and tethered her, then collapsed onto his bedroll on the forest floor. Out of sight and away from the occasional sounds of people traveling the road, he fell asleep. As the late afternoon bled out to dusk, he failed to hear the wagon. Em and Ezra hopped down, stiff-legged. They strolled around the building.

"Ah, it's good to be moving about," Em said.

"Excuse me a moment," Ezra stepped into the trees to relieve himself.

"That you pissing, Ezra?"

The rendezvous with Silas was brief. After warm hugs, Silas explained that they needed to get away from here as soon as possible.

12

Without cover, the three pursuers were forced to hang back most of the afternoon. Occasional long sight lines reassured them. Their prey was just a few minutes ahead. At St. Marys, they came upon the bridge across the river into Ohio. Riding point, O'Shea turned to the others. "I see the wagon crossing the bridge. It's getting dark. Let's cross over and stop for the night. Their meeting place is only a couple of hours ahead."

Leaving camp the next morning, they headed west along the river on former Ohio Route 7. With no other options, they rode directly into the business district of Marietta where dozens of residents bustled about the square. After several unsuccessful inquiries, one proved fruitful.

"Yep. That there eye doctor building is no more'n fifteen minutes from here. Yesterday afternoon I saw a Conestoga wagon parked at the back where there's a little oak stand. I saw three strangers: a black woman and two white guys. They'd two horses, they did."

"That barkeep seemed honest enough," O'Shea told the others. "Let's go."

They rode to the place. Though there was recent horse manure on the pavement, the site was empty. There was no evidence of a larger contingent. It was not the rendezvous they expected.

"Okay we'll follow their horseshit to Eldorado," O'Shea said. Though his allusion was lost on the others, they mounted and galloped up the road. Within the hour, they lost the trail just after passing the partly-collapsed golf clubhouse. O'Shea pulled up and dismounted.

"I suspect the lot are back at the golf course." They reversed course and rode to the clubhouse.

"Should we tether the horses here and recon the place?" Salma asked.

"Yeah. Are you strong enough to hike through thickets and tall grass?"

"I think so. Shoulders and back're sore, wrist stinging. Legs feel fine."

"Kornhower, look after the horses. Let me have one of those hand sets and my rifle. Here's my Glock in case you need it."

At the teeing ground for the first hole, O'Shea scanned the undulating landscape with weedy encircled former greens, scattered sand traps, and algae-infested ponds. He handed the binoculars to Salma.

"Nothing obvious. Perhaps they're down in that copse of willows, way out there near the big pond. That would likely have been the ninth hole with the back nine coming upslope this way."

She looked intently at the willows. "Although you may as well be speaking Chinese, I'd agree with your speculation. What I know about golf could be summed up as 'little balls bashed by men and their lethal clubs'."

"That's all you need to know. Nobody's wasting their time on golf now."

Staying low, they skirted the edge of the first fairway, O'Shea loping downslope two and three paces ahead of Salma. He swiveled round. "You doing okay?"

"Yeah, don't worry about me." He picked up the pace.

They stopped at a high teeing site for what must have been the seventh or eighth hole. From here, O'Shea spotted something at water's edge on the far side of the big pond. He handed her the binoculars.

"Evidence, there by the pond," he said.

"Alhamdulillah! One of our children."

"Arabic. You speak it?"

"After 'praise God', not a word."

They cut left and made a wide circle through brush and brambles to the wooded crest of a rocky ridge outside the course. He scaled a wind-torn maple. She caught her breath at its base.

"At last! The whole fuckin' camp."

He made radio contact with Kornhower, explained where they were and what they needed. An hour later, Kornhower crept up the ridge to the maple. He saw Salma dozing against the trunk. She startled awake, rubbed her temples. "Is it morning?"

"*Non. Où est O'Shea?*"

"*En haut,*" she said, pointing toward the sky.

Over the next five hours, O'Shea laid out the plan and they went over every minute detail, again and again. O'Shea made clear the objectives: to retrieve all the women and children; to capture at least one young man to invigorate the sperm bank; and to escape as quickly as possible.

They drank water, munched hardtack and dried fruit, discussed the risks, took turns napping. Kornhower paced in small circles, fingering his weapon, trying to calm his fear. Salma inspected and loaded her semi-automatic pistol. O'Shea shinnied down the maple for the sixth time.

In the willow shadows, dusk was approaching.

O'Shea told them it was time to go. No further explanation was needed; just two subtle bumps, each to O'Shea's outstretched fist. When they'd gone, he scaled back up the tree, calibrated his weapon. Awakened, his senses rushed to a familiar and exhilarating state of high alert. Intricate planning and hyperawareness had always kept him from the grave. This time, perhaps not. He realized the odds weren't exactly stacked in his favor.

13

The late afternoon sun warmed my arms and hands at the pond's edge where I scrubbed two of my three outfits and all my underwear. To my left, I spotted an earthen dam. Funny, I had not seen it before. Of course, there had to be a dam; the pond, like the golf course, was manmade. It was a curvilinear feature at least a hundred paces long and it created two distinctive habitats: the verdant aquatic life of the pond and its shores above it, and the parched rocky gorge below.

A sucking sound in the reeds interrupted my reverie. Something familiar. I tiptoed along the shore a few steps to see the hind end and tail of the white bison. He turned to me and pirouetted with astounding haste, soaking my smock as he shook off his wetness. I stood my ground. He jittered anxiously from head to tail, grunted and gargled with an urgency I'd never seen. "I get it, my beloved," I said to him. "But what is *it*?" I had an idea and it was terrifying.

I ran toward camp, cried out to my brother, the first person I encountered. "Silas! We're in some kind of serious peril."

"Peril? What should we do?'

"Quick, run! Tell Nick, Em, Hannah, Jason, anybody."

Pleased with the razor-sharp edges, Nick put aside his whetstone and bowie knives. He stretched toward the darkening sky, feeling relaxed and grateful that the expedition was back together and that they'd be in Argolis in just a few days. "Em," he called to his wife, "Come check out the sunset."

Just then, Silas charged across the grass. "Nick! Hestia insists we're in grave danger."

Nick spat out a flurry of commands. Silas ran to find the others.

A gunshot echoed across time. Nick slumped to the ground. Em emerged from the hut. A tiny hole in her husband's forehead oozed a rivulet of blood. She screamed, filling the air with French lamentations. She ran madly this way and that.

Jason, out of nowhere, grabbed her, held her with all his might. "What Mama? What's happening?"

A second shot. Another man down. Who?

Panicked shouts and screeches. Horses squealing. Flocks of birds squalling.

Jason could not calm his mother. He dragged her behind a cluster of spice bushes and honeysuckles. "Stay here, Mama; do not move." Dazed, she could only nod.

"I'll be right back."

He ran toward the wagons, dodging the body of Ezra in a pool of blood.

Rudi, Silas, and Hannah were huddled beneath the big Conestoga. Jason dived toward them.

"My dad's dead. Ezra too. Mom is out of her mind."

"Where are the guns?" Hannah said.

"Above us. In the wagon. I'll work my way there."

They saw his feet and lower legs as he hoisted himself into the wagon. Another shot pinged above them; Jason's legs crumpled. He dropped to the ground face down.

Witnessing homicide across the camp, the women and children thronged together. Kids bawled and screamed. Mothers scolded and consoled. There was pandemonium, but no bullets rained down on them.

Silas ran toward me down the path. I was cowering in the hollow of the trunk of a giant beech.

"Nick, Jason, Ezra. All dead."

"Oh god! Quick, go gather the others. Meet me down there." I pointed to the rocky gulch.

At the base of the ridge, from two directions, Salma and Kornhower crept into the dimness, packing their weapons, closing in on the women and children, the horses and wagons.

Rudi, in the Conestoga with Silas, grabbed Victor's rifle. He saw the two advancing across the compound. He recognized Salma. She brandished a fearsome weapon. Long the source of his fantasies and wet dreams, was she here now to kill him?

She called out, "Rudi, do not shoot me! You and I: we have a future together. Come to me. Now."

Rudi slipped out of the wagon, leaving the rifle behind. He closed the gap to Salma.

Grabbing the rifle, Silas screamed out to his friend, "Rudi, what in hell are you doing? She will kill you. Come back!"

Salma lowered her pistol.

In disbelief, Silas watched his best friend defecting. Salma, whispered something to him. He embraced her awkwardly, and they began to run toward the women and children.

"Stop or I'll shoot," Silas shouted. They didn't. He fired. Salma reeled around, slumped to the ground, a splotch of blood expanding across her blouse. Rudi gathered her into his arms and ran for cover.

Silas could not stomach or risk a second shot.

Kornhower scurried after the couple. He grabbed the handset. "Salma's been shot; get down here, *viens vite!*"

***

Darkness rimmed the sky but for a blood orange line at the western horizon. We huddled in the deepest part of the gulley. In Hannah's arms, Em wept without cease. Antonio wrapped his arms around me. I buried my broken heart in his embrace. Silas consoled Giselle.

Across the camp, we heard sounds that needed no explanation. The night air breathed low and clammy, like a throbbing frog. Then... stillness. They had departed.

At dawn, we buried our dead and briefly memorialized each — Nick and his son Jason, and Ezra. No one spoke of Rudi. Near the old clubhouse, I saw my spirit guide. He stood serenely grazing at the edge of a brush patch, the edge of terrifying heartbreak. He searched my eyes as though he had something to reveal. I heard the whimper of a child. I ran to him and swept a two-year-old girl into my arms. I returned to hand the crying child to Giselle. "Oh sweetheart!" she said, hugging her close.

We packed our few possessions and some food, as well as our trauma: trauma we could not offload, then or now. Making our way out, single file behind Antonio, we trooped toward Marietta — Giselle and the child, Hannah, Em, Silas and I. The white bison drifted toward the far horizon.

EIGHT

Prof and I

Argolis, 2042-2050

I MET STEFAN FREMANIS soon after I got to Argolis. From that day on, I called him Prof. In turn, he called me Hob.

"Hob?" I asked.

"You said you're Hestia, right?"

"Yes."

"Goddess of the Hearth in ancient Greece."

"So I've been told."

We were sitting in his log cabin at the dining table across from a massive fireplace at which he was now pointing. "See that little shelf in the fireplace — just off the hearth? That's a hob: a place to keep warm what's been cooked. That's you."

"Ah ha."

In those days, I came to know Prof as well as any other person in my life, including my partner. Of the many things I learned from him, the value of being authentically one's self has stuck with me longest. To be ineffably me, not some fairyland version of who I aspire to be, or who folks assume me to be, or to conform to some combination of respectability and propriety that our beleaguered society might demand. In lectures and discussions about the ways the world works, he would often halt mid-sentence and insist that I stop being a damned glassy-eyed student scribbling notes.

"I'm no longer your teacher now," he'd tell me.

"Erp," I bleated.

And then he would draw from me things I never knew about myself — intellectual things, philosophy of life things, insights about relationships and self-awareness.

The first time I brought him a slice of my honey buckwheat bread, a taste he told me he'd never tasted and had no idea how to make, he courteously implored me to explain how I created this delight. In my annoying nerdy tone, I started to explain the steps, one by one.

Unsatisfied, he shook his majestic head with its unruly mat of grey hair. He'd been a hot guy once; sort of still was with his chiseled cheeks, cleft chin, startlingly blue eyes. "Not words, Hob," he commanded.

"Alright, next time, I'll show you how."

When I arrived two days later with my basket, he asked, "What's in there?"

"Stuff to make honey buckwheat bread. "His face brightened like the sunrise. "How very kind," he said, as if everything between us and the morning itself had been freshly created. No metaphor this, for the fact is, Prof's brain had been bruised after a fall down ice-covered steps. It's not that he was senile. His brain still worked well in many senses and few in the village knew of his disability. He could remember details of lectures from thirty years ago and could rattle off definitions of terms word-for-word from whatever text. On the other hand, he could remember almost nothing in the short-term like when his daughter or his friend Aram had visited or what he ate for breakfast, or that he was wearing the same grimy shirt and trousers and mismatched socks he'd been putting on all week. He drew blanks on the names of people he'd known for three decades. His lesson that day was about how networks of fungi in the soil help trees in forests communicate with one another. When it came to an end, as usual, he said, "That's all I care to say about these matters now. Please check the syllabus and do your homework."

"Okay, now help me make the bread."

"The bread?" I reminded him about the stuff in the basket.

"Ah yes, the bread!"

Like a child, he was transfixed by each step of the process, looking on with wonder. He reveled in mixing and pounding the dough. He dabbed at drippings on the honey jar and smiled sheepishly. He licked his fingers. As the bread browned, he peered expectantly into the oven as if the loaf would reveal fundamental truths or resolve long-held quandaries, like the specific roles that mycorrhizae play in the carbon cycle, for example. It was one of many items in a brief ramble that also included the Riemann Hypothesis and what happens if Late-K leads to Omega. The vaults in Prof's deep memory never failed to reveal something to astonish and distract me. I then felt obliged to go straight to the library to find out what he'd dredged up.

As we shared slices, hot from the oven and slabbed with butter, he said, "I've never been more enlightened."

* * *

It had been a couple of months since I and six other wretched travellers staggered into the village of Argolis. Our journey had been brutal and I still hadn't dealt fully with the way it ended, nor the loss of friends I'd taken for granted. I was adjusting to this new place, living with my brother Silas in a recently abandoned cottage down the road from Hannah, who continued to be a life-affirming friend and, like me, suffered from the traumas of our journey. She had, at least, come home to a waiting hearth and a partner and daughter. Silas and I had no such things.

On the notice board at Holmes Mill, the community center, I saw a hand-written sheet that said:

Help Wanted

Caregiver and student for a professor, half-days, three or four times per week.

Please contact Kate in the library archivist's office two floors down

Bernard

When I knocked on the door, a youngish woman's voice bid entry. She stood behind her desk and offered her hand. "Hello, I'm Kate." I took her warm hand in mine — a hand with lovely long fingers, three of which bore rings.

"Hi, I'm Hestia and I'm responding to your notice about a caregiver."

She was a tall, long-limbed, appealingly proportioned woman dressed in a trim seafoam-green top over black pants that stretched tightly to her slim ankles above open-toed sandals. How could she manage to dress so stylishly? Brushing a tawny wisp of hair from her eyes, she tied it into her ponytail. I guessed her to be older than I but not yet thirty — no crow's feet or neck wrinkles and robust, smooth skin. As she came round her desk, she seemed to scrutinize me as well: my five foot-three girlish self in the one dress I managed to snag — a shapeless blue thing Hannah lent me — and scuffed black castoff pumps two sizes too big.

We sat facing one another. She cleared her throat. "If this were to work out, you'd be taking care of my father under the guise of being his new student. I have tried a couple of other young people for the job. Neither of them worked out and this is making me anxious. I plan to move soon and I'd like a person I can trust."

"I see."

"Tell me about yourself."

Without pause, I went through the short version of my biography I'd been spooling out recently — my childhood on the great Eerie Lake, the horror of the raid that killed my mother, abducted my father, and ransacked our village. Becoming an adult in the unnerving town of Andeferas, and the decision to migrate here.

"I've heard about your journey," she said. "I am heartsick at the loss of my dear friend Em's husband and son. I've known Nick and Jason all my life."

"The day they were murdered was terrifying," I told her. "I'd never experienced gun violence. Had never even heard gunshots. Fortunately for me, my brother Silas and Antonio both survived."

"I have met Silas. Who's Antonio?"

"He is the father of the child I'm expecting. We might be a couple but we're proceeding with caution, if you get my meaning."

"I surely do. How wonderful that you're pregnant. We have so few children."

I did not want to talk to her about that. I still haven't expunged all the superstitions I grew up with. Plus, the last thing I wanted to do was to think about the dreadful failure of our mission to revive this village with new mothers and children. I dared not hex the fetus growing more prominent by the day.

"And your father? What kind of care does he require?"

She told me about his icy spill last winter, how he threw out a hip, broke his ankle, and then became more testy and forgetful. The doctor concluded that the purple lump near his left temple revealed a blow severe enough to have caused brain damage.

"Dad can take care of his personal needs, though his choices of what to wear leave something to be desired," she said. "Mostly, he's fine on his own. He's happy doing his research and writing. He needs companionship and a bit of housekeeping. I've been stocking his pantry and preparing him one solid meal a day. After I move, those tasks would become part of the job."

There was something disturbing about the breezy way she spoke of her dad's situation. Her cheer seemed overblown, perhaps contrived. Her hands were nervously turning over in her lap, seeking out one another. She avoided eye contact, though occasionally I saw her casting glances in my direction. She seemed desperate to get out of here. I received vibes saying *he's all yours, girl.*

"You're asking that the caregiver also be his student?"

"Yes. Before the collapse, Dad was a professor at Gilligan University. That's why we're here. Since then, he's been a valued teacher and mentor for the kids who've grown up during these times. That is so much a part of his persona that inevitably whoever spends time with him ends up a participant in one of his seminars. Some people find that tedious. Would it put you off?"

"Oh no, not at all. I am an intrepid student," I said almost too emphatically. I spoke of my experience as librarian in Andeferas and my insatiable appetite for reading and notetaking.

"Perfect! And would you consider becoming the librarian and archivist here after I leave? The job pays almost nothing but there's tons of work to do. We haven't even unboxed all the books we brought over from the university."

"Oh yes, definitely. I'd be really good at that kind of work."

"When can you start?"

***

Two months later, in the midst of a lesson on resilience, Prof broke his stride and uncharacteristically asked me a personal question. Staring at my midriff, he said, "Hob, I've seen that you're, um, expanding there.

I've been wondering about that." The book he'd been quoting dropped to his lap.

It was late afternoon on a warm spring day. Through the west-facing windows, the sun streamed into Prof's study, striking his bookshelves broadside. It was a room with books on every wall and piles of yellowed documents, offprints on the carpet and every other surface. There were other items that sparked my imagination: a world globe on a metal stand, some framed photos, an artist's rendition of a black man with a white baby in one arm, a black baby in the other. The room was cluttered, but when I tidied up, I dared not shift things for I sensed hidden order in the chaos. Though he could hardly remember the name of this little village, Prof was always able to head straight to a book or journal when the need arose. One day when I managed to extract him from his study to do a bit of deep cleaning, I was not surprised to find all manner of detritus beneath and behind the furniture and in the dark corners: dust bunnies, hairballs, pencils and pens, crumpled papers, the odd sock, and an old notebook I had not yet brought to his attention. By contrast, Prof's desk was uncluttered. It was a grand writing surface for exercises he'd devise for me to launch us into a case study or hypothesis.

Stroking my expanding tummy, I said, "What you've observed, Prof, is true. All evidence points to a baby becoming part of my life soon."

"A baby!" Prof leaned toward me, the book slipping to the floor beneath his desk.

"True."

"How soon might I be able to meet this new citizen of our hapless planet?"

"In four months or so." I stopped there and held my breath. I feared he would find the event troubling or even threatening to our arrangement.

He dipped his chin and ran his hand anxiously through his hair, as if trying to penetrate a fog that had darkened the scene. A long minute passed. As the setting sun fingered its way up the bookshelves and I turned my notebook over and over in the mellow light, finally, he looked up at me. A broad grin gained ground across his face. "This calls for champagne," he bellowed.

He made haste toward the pantry where I was quite sure there was no champagne. Right in character, Prof proved me wrong. Somewhere back there he came up with a bottle of sparkling rosé. I followed him with glasses and before I began to cook supper, we had a proper toast.

Lifting his glass, he said, "Here's to the baby of Hob. What are we to call this child?"

"For the time being, we're calling it Cha."

"Cha, as in cha-cha-cha?"

"Yes, Child of Hob and Antonio."

"Would Antonio per chance be the father?"

"He would."

"Have I met him?"

"No, but I will bring him to meet you soon."

Prof looked troubled. After a pause, he spoke softly. "Antonio is a fortunate fellow. If I had to recommend anyone for him to marry, Hob would be my first choice."

I reached across the space between us and for the first time I laid my hand lightly on the bruised side of his face. He did not recoil, as I feared he might. "How very sweet of you to say that, Prof."

"It was easy," he immediately replied. "Hob is a glowing ember, caring for me more warmly and kindly than my own daughter. Um, Kate.... And now Hob is bringing me a grandchild."

What? How confusing, potentially troublesome, and yet how tender and memorable this embrace of my pregnancy. Despite the man's dodgy memory, he somehow knew what I really needed. Often alone in this dilapidated little village far from the place I was raised, I have occasionally felt blue. Antonio tries to show compassion but he does not really understand how to help. Prof's unabashed happiness is different. It's an elixir and exactly what I would have expected from the father I can hardly remember. I could not stem my tears.

"Oh dear, have I made you unhappy?"

I dabbed my cheeks. "No, Prof, you will be the best grandfather ever."

As I became more and more rotund and began to walk like a bow-legged pensioner — whatever that may be, thank you Mr. Dickens — the intellectual and emotional rewards of my days with Prof blossomed in ways my mentor, Freya, back in Andeferas, would have called serendipity. Prof's short-term memory was erratic. There was more vagueness about what he does in my absence and all things not intellectual. He cannot remember Antonio's name but often asks how Cha is doing. Then there's his charming silliness when covering memory lapses. "Oh goodness," I said one day when he appeared with his underpants on top of his trousers.

He belly laughed at the sight of himself. Then, he said, "I've just got to eat more fish." Was this a non-sequitur? I never really knew because he couldn't remember saying anything that foolish and the next day his undershorts were apparently back underneath.

On the other hand, his passion and acuity for my lessons seemed only to intensify. A strange cocktail, this. But my love for him, in both his confused childlike and thoughtful professorial modes, only grew.

He could be grumpy. This is true. One morning, after I'd washed the dishes, hung his freshly washed sheets out to dry, and tidied up the great room with the big hearth, I knocked on the partially closed door of his study.

"Hmm, what?" he mumbled.

I pushed open the door and looked in on Prof hunched over his desk, his reading specs halfway down his nose. As always, the study smelled of books and documents, the air stagnant and light dim at this time of day. Prof had a broken yellow lead pencil in hand, his straight-up cursive crawling across a lined notebook.

"I'm sorry to disturb you. I wonder if we'll have a lesson today."

His back still facing me, he harrumphed again. "Oh, who is this interrupting my studies this morning?" He turned to me and cast a thousand-yard stare beyond my right shoulder. I saw blankness and it scared me. As I backed away, light crept back into his eyes. "Ah, Hob. So, you are back."

Although he'd greeted me with the same words an hour earlier, I'd long ago learned not to mention lapses like this which only served to confuse or upset him. He lives in the present moment and that's good, I keep telling myself.

"Good morning, Prof. Just wondering about a lesson this morning."

"Yes, my dear. Please sit there and take out your notebook. Um, now where the devil is my folder?" He began to scurry about exploring various piles of papers and documents.

"Could it be right there on your desk?" I asked, pointing.

"Oh maybe. Hmm, yes, here it is. You're spot on."

As always, when he opened the dog-eared folder marked 'HOB' he exclaimed, "*Voila*! This is exactly what I've been looking for."

After that familiar routine, which was both comforting and troubling, he proceeded precisely from where we'd left off two days earlier. He had recently been bent on discussing how and why the world went over the cliff more than two decades ago and where we might be headed nowadays.

Last week I told Prof that my mother had explained collapse by telling me that a fatal illness everywhere in the world was the cause.

Prof said, "Well, that's not entirely the case." Then he added, in a softer voice, "With the greatest appreciation and respect for your dear departed mother, Hob."

No wonder I loved this man.

From there we discussed the mind-boggling intersection of influences, including pandemics that put the world in a precarious state at the beginning of the century. In a relatively short time, Prof said, we saw societies and nations and international institutions toppling one by one. Some of this history was a bit beyond my reach and Prof's disability left gaps I haven't been able to bridge in the library. What, for example, were *Google* and *Twitter*?

Here's what I wrote in my notebook: *In the two opening decades of this century, because of rapid climate change, the world's ecological systems that enabled human societies to thrive for a hundred thousand years began to unravel: forests, grasslands, coral reefs, surface and ground water systems, ocean currents, the ice covering the North Pole, and so forth. This unravelling hastened the onset of famine, human starvation, infant and childhood deaths, severe storms and floods, drought, wildfires, and sea level rise. In less than a decade, two global pandemics killed 50 million people and then nations lobbed nuclear weapons at each other. In other words, almost everywhere Late-K devolved toward Omega.*

Now, two generations beyond collapse, Prof explained that we need to think about whether we'll remain stuck at our present level of barebones survival, or whether we can slowly climb toward a way of living that would be respectful of all life.

"After Omega, what could happen next?" Prof asked.

"Well, the next phase in our model," I said, "is Alpha. Alpha is the stage when life is challenged to start all over again, maybe from scratch. The new order may be partly like the old or be something new and full of promise. On the downside, Alpha can be bleak. If the land and water are so tarnished, some regions could be trapped in a state from which they may never recover."

"Good," Prof agreed. "When we moved here we realized we were among the very few survivors in this region. Do you think we landed in such a trap?"

"Well, that was way before my time. I'm only twenty-seven."

"Oh my gosh," Prof said. "How did you manage to stay so young?"

To that, any response I might have come up with would have been futile. Prof was not well oriented in either time or space. I continued, "To me, Prof, it is obvious that our little valley was not severely tarnished. Though the river may have been polluted and in the past was subjected to flash flooding and basin erosion, it seems like a half century of being left to its own devices has been good. It's clean enough to swim in and has not flooded in my time here. A healthy river has allowed tall forests to grow right to its banks with all their resident animals, insects, birds and butterflies. If this is really Alpha, many new species and ecological combinations may evolve. That spells the promise of a better future, especially if we humans can make more babies."

"Yep," Prof uttered softly. I wanted him to respond to my last point. He didn't. So, I asked, "What can we expect next?"

Prof sat there still and muted, as if his own mind had crossed back toward Omega. After more moments of silence, he recovered. "Ah Hob! Your inquiring mind is a joy to behold! Just pay attention in the coming lessons and I think you'll have some answers. But don't take what I say as gospel truth. I'm just an old professor."

For Prof, unanswered questions were the very grist of our lessons. Great questions never have simple answers, he would say. "I want to know your reasoning. Speak in sentences and paragraphs, my dear."

***

In the fifth month of my time with Prof and the ninth month of my pregnancy, Kate returned to Argolis. Apart from one brief letter, we'd not seen nor heard a peep from her. In my mind, this bordered on callousness. She certainly did recognize her father's disability and might have suspected that it could be worsening. But you'd never know that. Before she left, when I asked how I should get in touch with her in case of an emergency, she replied, "Oh, I refuse to buy into catastrophic thinking. Dad's in good health, strong as an ox, and he's only sixty-two. He's just a bit daft at times."

When I unlocked the back door, I found her in the kitchen alcove, stirring milk into a mug of tea.

"Kate! What a surprise. How are you?"

"Just fine," she said smiling. Her tone was polite, not warm.

We went on to exchange pleasantries and small talk — the gorgeous spring weather; how the dogwoods were blossoming at the edge of forests; how things were going at the library and archives. Our chatter was certainly sociable but strangely, so far, she had not commented on my very obvious pregnancy or asked any questions about her father. When she waxed lyrically about her mare, my heart pumped full with remorse. For the first time in weeks, I thought about my beloved Farleigh, the horse abducted on our fateful trip. When I told Kate the story, she seemed distracted, offering no comment or condolence.

Prof appeared as usual around nine, wearing the same clothes he'd worn every day since the last wash. His hair desperately needed a trim — a skill I had perfected by practicing on Silas. As he gazed back and forth at the two of us, he seemed to be frightened, as if aliens had landed in his kitchen.

In fact, from the moment he stepped into the kitchen, I'd sensed something harrowing, something drumming like a heartbeat; it emanated from Kate. Prof stood there motionless.

"Dad! It's me, Kate."

Prof's blank face darkened. He seemed agitated. He acknowledged neither of us.

Kate's tongue darted back and forth across her lips.

"I had no idea," she managed to murmur, her voice wavering.

I tried to reassure her. "This will pass shortly and the father you know will pop back into place." We were silent for several more anxious moments, all three of us frozen in space. I gently guided Prof to the table. "Time for breakfast," I ventured as cheerfully as I could.

Obediently, he sat down and wrapped a napkin round his neck. "What have you got for me, Hob? And who do we have here?"

The awkward moments had passed. Prof found his words. His face opened to the new day. He realized we had a guest. With a bit of coaxing, I helped him identify his daughter and invite her to the table.

Kate complied but any illusions she held of her dad, strong as an ox and only a little daft at times, had been dashed. I have to say that she didn't handle the situation with grace. She accused me of withholding information and frostily went silent when she was unable to participate in a conversation Prof initiated about the bright morning, his breakfast, and the day's lesson. Now I feared that she viewed me as an interloper. Were my future and that of her dad in jeopardy?

The next day Kate returned with Dr. Aram. Aram was in practice with Dr. Todd and the midwife who was looking after my pregnancy. I'd met him soon after I arrived, and from the Argolis rumor mill, I had picked up something of his history with Kate. This morning the two seemed edgy in each other's company.

As for me, I've been awestruck by both Aram and his senior partner, Todd, especially after I'd learned that neither had finished medical school. It was our good fortune that both these men were gregarious and serious students of medicine. They constantly had to improvise to deliver health care to us — without proper equipment, supplies, or manufactured medicines and drugs.

I told them Prof was in his usual place. Wordlessly, they headed straight to the study. I timidly followed. "Stefan, how's it going?" Aram asked.

Prof swiveled around. A smile spread naturally across his face. "Aram, hello. What's brings you here this bright Tuesday morning?"

How intriguing that, without hesitating, Prof recognized and named his visitor, and was fully oriented in time. And equally mystifying was that he failed to acknowledge Kate, standing next to Aram.

"Well, Stefan, I just want to do a quick checkup this morning. Are you okay with that?"

"Yeah, sure. As long as you're not intending to stick me with a long syringe or something."

"No worries there."

"Dad, I'm here, just to be with you for the checkup."

"Ah, alright, no problem. Where's Hob?"

"I'm here, Prof." I fluttered a wave from the doorway.

"Great, the whole gang's here to witness what exactly?"

Aram unraveled his stethoscope and proceeded to listen to Prof's lungs, heart and stomach. He took his pulse and checked his mouth and throat with a tongue depressor. He then pulled a small card out of his shirt pocket.

"Here are three words, Stefan. After I say them, please repeat them back to me."

"Is this some kind of game?"

"You can think of it that way. Ready?"

"Sure."

"Apple, sunrise, chair."

"You want me to repeat them?"

"Yes."

"You must think I'm losing it or I'm some kind of dingbat."

"Not at all, Stefan. You are my dear friend. So, what were those three words?"

"Apple, sunrise, and chair."

"Right."

"Okay, next I want you to draw me a clock."

"Oh, come on, Aram. Why are you wasting my time? This is something for Hob's baby when it grows up a bit."

"Just do this for me, okay?"

"A clock. Okay, I'll just draw a flipping circle. That good?"

"Yep. Now put the numbers on it."

Prof did so without hesitation. "What about the hands?" he asked.

"Good question. A clock without hands wouldn't be helpful, would it? So, draw me the hands that show the time to be 11:20."

Prof did so with precision.

"Great. Now, can you remember the three words I asked you to repeat?"

"You mean, draw, and flipping, and circle?" Prof could be a rascal.

Aram suppressed a smile. "No, the words I first asked you to repeat."

"Ha. You think you've distracted me with that clock business. You are wrong, my friend. Apple, sunrise, chair," Prof called out.

"Very good. I'll not bother you further, Stefan. You can get back to your work."

"Thanks, Doc. Come by for a beer sometime."

"You bet."

We three retreated to the kitchen. In hushed tones, Aram said, "Well, he passed the cognitive checkup with flying colors."

Kate said, "Thank goodness. He had me worried last night."

"Hestia," Aram continued, failing to acknowledge Kate's comment, "since you're with him more than anybody else, have you noticed any of these things about him — trouble making decisions, losing interest in daily life, general lethargy, repeating stuff over and over, forgetting what day or month it is, indecision when trying to solve problems or, say, trouble turning on the water, opening a window, or locking a door?"

I folded my arms atop my baby-to-be, stared briefly at the ceiling, then took a deep breath. On the outbreath, I said, "It depends on the day, Aram. Yes, he does experience some of these things at one time or another. But I'm never sure whether I'll find him amazingly lucid as he was just now or distracted and behaving like an exaggerated version of the absent-minded professor he might once have been. I never know what to expect."

"Absent-minded professor. You nailed it," Kate said. "Imagine being raised by him."

"Can you give me some examples?" Aram asked me, again ignoring Kate.

I told them about the undershorts episode and his blanking out occasionally on the name of my partner. How he could be crabby and was often disheveled. I also said, "Without fail, he is incredibly thoughtful and lively during our lessons. And he's been tender about my forthcoming child. He just indicated he could imagine my baby drawing a clock. Now, wasn't that amazing!"

Aram stroked his chin. "Yeah, it *is*! It's just fascinating how the human brain works and doesn't work after traumatic injury. If I were practicing medicine forty-five years ago, I would have ordered some scans to learn more about Stefan's condition and how to treat it. But now all I can tell you to do, Hestia, is to keep doing what you've been doing, and let me know if there are abrupt changes in Stefan's daily health and basic functions like getting out of a chair, walking and keeping his balance, using the toilet, dressing himself. Stuff like that."

"Okay."

What on earth are scans?

The next day, Kate stopped by. "I'm reassured that Dad's in good hands," she said. "Aram will help if you need him." After a five-minute conversation with her father in his study, she passed through the kitchen and said goodbye. That was that. It was the last time that she, her father, and I were together in his cabin.

Three nights later, my water broke. I'll not say much about the birth except that the midwife arrived in time to help me through way too many hours before a six-plus pound reddish-brownish human plopped into an uncertain world. We named the boy Che — namesake of one of Antonio's heroes who was also, long ago, from Argentina. Throughout my labor, Silas and Antonio paced the floors as the obligatory worriers. Afterwards, Aram came by to pronounce Che a 'healthy little bloke' as Che began suckling on the biggest breasts I'll ever have.

***

Antonio agreed to look after Che and feed him milk I laboriously extracted on the first morning I returned to Prof. My maternity leave had been eight weeks, during which Hannah, Astrid, and Em, all former students of Prof, gladly took on his care. They told me not to worry, that each had fallen in love with Prof before I was born.

I was sitting in his little kitchen drinking hot tea when he shambled across the great room in his pajamas. He locked into my eyes and shook his head, a crooked smirk enlivening his mouth and smoky blue eyes. He was a sight for my own sore eyes.

"Jumping Jesus! My dearest friend and student is back. Is this for real?"

I expected that he might have forgotten my name, so I said, "Yes, Prof. Check out the new, improved, slimmer Hob and let her give you a big hug."

Without delay, he spread his arms like the wings of an eagle and embraced me with such tenderness, I almost wept. "Hob, I've really missed you," he whispered.

"I've missed you too, Prof." With my sleeve, I wiped my eyes. "But, guess what? I've done something unbelievable in the time since I last saw you."

"Something…?" Prof murmured.

"Yeah, something. I gave birth to a baby boy. A boy named Che."

"A baby! That *is* unbelievable. How did you manage that?"

I cleared my throat. Prof didn't need a birds-and-bees recap. What to say? "Um, yeah, you know it can happen when a girl like me gets together with a guy like Antonio."

"Yep, it can. Well, damn! Can I see this little fellow sometime?"

"Of course, but first let's have breakfast and plan our seminars, okay?"

Prof smiled again and almost skipped to his chair at the table.

Between that first day back and the day I finally brought Che with me, Prof thrived in what turned out to be the best of times. With his say-so, I performed a targeted upgrade of his appearance, beginning with a haircut and proper shave, nose and ear hair trims, nail clips, and concluding with fresh sets of almost never worn clothing discovered at the back of his wardrobe. When we looked at him in the mirror, he gave me a thumb up and off we went for our first lesson.

In the next few weeks Prof seemed reborn and blissful in his role as my professor. We soared through lessons on the precariousness of human society — then and now; the reality, even before the crash, of declines in human reproduction; climate change; and several extraordinary days strolling along the Shawnee River while Prof plucked and identified dozens of wildflowers and shrubs and trees, told me about the historic river and the vast Ohio Valley region. When we'd climb the steps to his cabin, Prof would take off his boots and collapse on the couch. Before falling asleep, he'd say, "Holy hell, my body's seriously unfit. I've got to eat more fish."

Several weeks later, I brought Che to meet Prof. I opened the kitchen door and there he was, dressed and ready for the day. When he saw my babe in arms, he smiled broadly and rushed across the kitchen, wrapping us both in the most memorable hug of my life — the pure emotion, the three of us bound together as one. Bewildering as it seemed at the time, this moment of crystalline lucidity — so unusual and so welcome, is a moment I shall forever cherish. As I write this — Prof long since dead, I still bask in his unconditional love for my son.

Even as his cognition slipped, he unfailingly greeted my son by name. He would ask, "So, little Che, what shall we learn today?"

As Che became a toddler, he could not wait for his days with the man he called Abuelo. By the time he was four, Prof had read him dozens of books from a shelf once meant for Kate. She told me that he had rarely read to her, and that's why she learned to read at age three-and-a-half. With each book, there were lively conversations around Che's sense of wonder, his questions, his giggles, his boundless imagination. When Prof was still mobile, we three strolled around the village where Prof would chat with almost everyone he met. When he could no longer walk, we pushed him through town in a wheelchair Aram loaned us. By then, Prof typically drew blanks on the names of villagers who greeted him, but to the very end he almost never forgot Hob and Che.

Looking back, I remember a sparkling fall day when Che, and I guided Prof's wheelchair toward Holmes Mill for a picnic. The air was crisp; a mere breeze rattled the oranges and flaming reds of the forest across the river. We all wore sweaters. At the Mill, we aimed toward the radiant, spreading sugar maple in the courtyard. As I spread a cloth and began to set out lunch, Prof invited Che to sit in his lap. Che cast an inquiring glance my way. "Do you think this would be okay, Mom?"

"Just be careful, Chiquito," I replied. "Abuelo's legs are weak."

Che climbed aboard and the Prof wrapped his frail and trembling arms around him. "Look over there," he said, pointing at the grand statue of the Greek God Pan just a few paces away. "One day long ago, we hauled Pan over here from the university. And ever since, Pan has been looking after us and the river and the forests, even the wildcats and coyotes and bears — all the animals, fish, birds, insects, and little critters in the soil. He loves them all. Now, every time you come down to the Mill, take a moment to visit Pan. He will be grateful, and he will know that you are thankful for the ways he protects us."

Che was too young to comprehend the deeper significance of those few moments. When they'd passed, he hopped off Prof's lap and swept his arms toward the tablecloth laid out with his favorite foods. "Abuelo!" he exclaimed. "Time to eat."

It was a wonderful afternoon, a flavorsome, though certainly not extravagant or elegant luncheon. In light of what was soon to come and the sunny timelessness of that afternoon, it was the most memorable picnic of our lives. As the October sun sunk toward the horizon and the day chilled, we wrapped prof in a wool blanket and with all our strength, we pushed him up the hill and into the lane where his cabin looked down on Argolis. We helped him up the steps and guided him to the couch in the great room, now shot with pumpkin-colored spikes streaming in from the west.

"My boy," Prof called out to Che. "You won't forget Pan now, will you?"

"No, Abuelo, I won't."

I looked on from the kitchen where I'd begun to fix dinner. For all the wonderful moments of that afternoon, that turning point sent shivers down my spine. Had Che's very name now disappeared from his memory?

***

On November 4, 2050, exactly thirty-seven years after the cataclysmic storm that marked the beginning of the end for Argolis and the world beyond, Professor Stefan Fremanis died peacefully in his bed. He was 68. I found him the next morning. Bereft as never before, I sought out Hannah. She took the reins from there. Kate returned for the memorial that drew more than a hundred survivors from across the region.

Abuelo's legacy lived on. Prof would have been elated to hear that eleven years later, Che, at age 18, began his career teaching at the Buckley Farm — an environmental education center at the edge of our little riverside village. Surrounded by the verdant fields and forests of the Ohio Valley, all of us continue to be sheltered by the Great God Pan.

NINE

Running Bear and the Jitney

Argolis, 2050s

1

CROUCHED BENEATH the open window, your ears strain to hear fragments of a heated conversation. Agitated exchanges calm down to whispers after Ma says, "Hush, Wes. You'll wake him." How could she believe you sleep through these nightly bouts of venom slung back and forth across the porch? How could your perpetually agitated Iroquois mother fail to realize you inherited a measure of her disdain, or should you call it defiance? For months, you've known that little is going right and much is going wrong. The village, the few kids my age, the new fellow Pavel, everything's haywire. Rivalries appear you never knew existed, with lines drawn that make no sense; lines you don't get. And people look at you — kid of the mad scientist, as if you're part of his plot to overthrow the order of things.

You long for the old days, embraces in the kitchen, the way the family surrounded you with love and rendered you secure and assured, the ordinary kid of mixed parentage that nobody used to notice. Now who are you? Running Bear — a half-breed with a ludicrous name, in Pavel's words. You're no longer a kindergartener nor a single-digit kid. But if you try to empathize with Ma and be as assertive and outspoken as she is, you could make things worse. *Grow up. Stop your sniveling and get on with the life of a fourteen-year-old in this hollowed-out village.* You and your dog walk alone along the river all the way to the confluence. You try to clear your troubled mind.

From your house at the top of Armitage Ridge, you can see the whole village in one sweeping glance: the big curve of the Shawnee River; the dam and falls at the mill; potholed roads along the river's north and south banks; the narrow bridge over Mildred Creek to the road that splits the village in two; the little grid of narrow lanes with their partly restored houses with leaky roofs and sagging front porches; the towering Holmes Mill, its red metal roof, white clapboards, and broad grassy yard. Former commercial buildings at the northern outskirts, mostly abandoned, the exception being Pa's workshop, a former auto repair and tire shop. You stare across the mile or so from here to there and imagine the shabby village has taken to glaring back at you. You can see people coming and going; you imagine them casting looks and nods and cynical smirks at the sight of you. You take in their cunning.

You work at fitting in during lessons in the schoolroom. You are in a group that ranges in age from six to sixteen. Seven to ten kids on any given day — none your friends. You do the schoolwork to please Ma and Pa. Esteban, almost twenty, is the only boy who ever became a good friend. But he left classes three years ago to work on his parents' farm. You fancy a girl, Samantha, who is a year older and pays you no attention. You fantasize stroking her silky black hair, your other hand on her cheek. Whatever. She's out of reach. Her parents may have ganged up with others against you because they believe, in spite of how much they love Ma, that Pa is bent on toppling poor Ma as well as their presumptions about the future. Toppling Ma?

Pa often works late into the night. After dark, you lie there either hearing them argue, hearing more than you'd like, or waiting for the man to come home from the workshop. On one of those nights, you hear Mom's muffled sobs down the hallway. Kayé, our big Newfie, gets up to clop across the kitchen for water. After she slurps, you hear her returning to her pad near the stove. Kayé means two in the Oneida language of the grandparents you never met. You were two when Kayé wandered into the family. Dogs in your grandparents' tribe are guardians of other worlds, like the world you seem to be living in now. This is why you and Kayé are best friends.

You hear footsteps up the long path and the creak of the back door. Pa's work boots squeak across the kitchen. Lying awake waiting for the arguments to begin is agonizing, like bathing in a tub of cold water. You strain to hear their whispers. You wait attentively for the shouting, the tension, fearing that in your anticipation, you yourself are somehow bringing it on. You want to jump out the window.

What you hear leads to no good place. Pa is tired and edgy. He takes exception to Ma's claim that Pavel has come to divert Pa from his good intentions, to steal from him and ruin our village. "Don't bring Pavel into this," he says.

"The man is a selfish boor," Ma counters. It goes on like this and you learn that Pavel is an immigrant from someplace called Buffalo. Ma says he's little more than a vagrant who wandered here after jumping ship downstream from Marietta. "It is rumored," she claims, "that he made off with a stash of silver stolen on the paddle wheeler." Her voice rising, she says that in Marietta, he worked out of what she called a brothel. "He was a vile pimp, Weston, a pimp!" Your vocabulary falls short and you can only imagine.

Pa yells back. "That's a bunch of rubbish. Whatever Pavel did before is of no interest to me. He's a hard worker and a good engineer."

2

When you were a lap-sitter with a bizarre imagination and nothing but happiness in your heart, you whiled away the days alongside the creek. The possibilities seemed endless. Your little world made sense. On Ma's lap, rocking on the porch swing, you learned about things. Looking sad-eyed and girlish, she told you about what happened when she was a young woman, before she mated with Pa. "The earth," she said, "was out of balance. Forests had been chopped down and burned, plants and animals and birds were killed until many were gone for good. The rains, winds, clouds, seasons and the oceans were sick and began to haunt humans in response to their wasteful and dirty lives. There were terrifying wildfires and storms and droughts. The wellbeing of Mother Earth, Father Sky, and the rest of creation got worse and worse. As our ancestors predicted, things began to topple. Bad diseases spread around the world infecting and killing many people and causing everything to come apart. And as students," Ma said, "we protested, but it was too late. Your dad and I survived the disease. We wandered into this little village and began to live our lives in balance with the Great Circle. We wanted nothing to do with the awful things that brought down our Mother Earth and killed all your grandparents."

As a scientist and inventor, Pa told Ma that he wanted to develop what he called systems that honor the earth. "He knew — we all knew — that the horrible times we'd barely survived happened because we humans committed the biggest sin of all. We fractured the circle of life. We knew we needed to make amends. We needed to put things right."

"One summer, before you were born, everyone in the village gathered for a Powwow in the big field next to Beasley Concourse — that big dome that has partially collapsed. We had many discussions about the future. We celebrated our river, and the fields and forests, and winged and four-legged with drums and dancing and singing and prayers. We decided we needed to learn how to close the sacred hoop."

"By that time, millions of machines from the old times had been asleep for years — earth movers, field tillers, transporters, devices that could fly. Laying there, everywhere, they were being taken back into the earth by the plants and termites and ants and worms. And for a very long time nobody had heard their ceaseless whirring or had to breathe their awful fumes. Without their noise and smoke, we learned to be calm; we learned to move more slowly as do Mother Earth's beings. With less poison from those machines and all the factories that produced them, the waters and the air became cleaner and fresher. Our eyes no longer sting when we swim in the river and the plunge pool up the creek. In the dark of night, we can count many stars and constellations."

And she continued, "Before we till and plant our gardens nowadays, we know we must offer sacrifices and prayers not only for a good harvest but also for the health of the soil and all the caterpillars and worms and insects and tiny others who thrive there. We promise never to put anything poisonous in our gardens, so that what we eat will be pure and good. At the Powwow, we pledged never, *ever,* to fire up machines, never to burn oil or gasoline, never to dig in the earth for coal, never to rush helter-skelter through life. And before we take any action, we always sit quietly to converse with our relatives — the trees of the forest, the cougar and bobcat, the eagle, all of nature. Since they share their home with us, we need their advice so we can honor their needs. We must not be selfish by thinking only of our own needs."

Ma pauses to give you her beautiful smile and run her fingers through your curly hair. For a moment, she holds your cheeks in her palms and kisses your forehead.

"I believe you understand these things."

"Yeah."

You decide you've had enough. You climb down. Ma says we can continue the story another day. You tell her you want to think more about the ancestors and relatives. How you are related to them.

A few days later, you are back with Ma, this time stretched out on a blanket under the shade of the big maple at Holmes Mill. There is a basket of potatoes and another of apples and a big bag of cornmeal Ma picked up at the weekly food distribution. Ma polishes two apples and, as is our custom, we each take our first bite at once. "Are you ready for more of the story?" You say, yeah.

"Okay. One day, with the help of village oxen, your dad dragged a heavy machine out of the river. Over the next weeks at the workshop, he took apart the rusted machine, cleaned all the pieces, including a big winged spinning thing he called a turbine, rubbing and cleaning everything with grapeseed oil. Then he put all the pieces back together. When people asked about the machine, he told them they'd be surprised once he put it back into the river. Using wire that he'd been saving for something like this, he connected the machine to a box in Holmes Mill."

Remembering, she said, "It was fall. Days were getting shorter. Late in the afternoon on a dreary cold day in November, he invited people to witness his accomplishment. Many villagers huddled together in the community room. Pa gave a little speech, then, like magic, when he flipped a switch on the wall, a string of little bulbs lit up the room like a birthday cake. From then on, the mill became the only place in the village with electricity for lighting. We could plan things like concerts and plays and dances after dark. Do you remember going to plays starring kids you know?"

"I do."

"Well, electric lights at the Mill were so successful that people began to discuss stringing wires from house to house to have light at night everywhere. Your dad got angry. He refused to help. He said the machine in the river was not strong enough for that, and besides, wires would invite evil spirits into our homes and mess up the lives the ancestors granted us — when we go to bed, when we wake up, when we eat: those kinds of things. If that happened, we might begin to slip back toward the times of ruin when families no longer sat at the table to eat with one another. Ma and Pa thought alike in those days. And so did many, if not most, of the people of the village. You remember that Ma and Pa went to university with several of your friends' parents?"

"Yeah, I remember that. Those friends have even come to our house, right?"

"That's right. Like your dad, they were opposed to the idea of lighting up the whole village. We all believed in living our lives within limits; it is how we've managed to resolve problems year after year and still provide food and clean water, nice warm dry homes, a school, a clinic and doctors to care for you kids, and much more."

You look up at Ma who's gone oddly quiet with a faraway look in her eyes. Your face is pressed against her shoulder; you take in her lavender fragrance; you can hear her slow, deep breaths, her heartbeat. "Are you alright, Ma?"

"Yes, little Bear. It is just that the story from here follows a twisted and scary path. I will wait for you to grow up a little more before I finish telling it."

You were young and naïve enough to forget her foreshadowing, if that's what it was. But after Pavel came to the village and after Pa and Ma began to argue, you knew it was time. Being fourteen, you'd think you'd be capable of staying calm when you heard Ma's version of how we got to this moment. You'd be wrong.

3

As he made his way home from his workshop, Weston Churchill watched the moon rise over the ridges east of the village. It was a frosty April evening. He pulled up the collar on the sweater his wife, Abby, had knitted along with the matching mittens and tuque. As a former nerd with diverse mechanical skills, scientific interests, an obsessive encyclopedic memory, and a childhood diagnosis of Asperger's Syndrome, he knew this month's moon would be a pink super moon, a name his wife and other Native Americans spoke when the full moon coincided with the nearest point in its orbit around the earth. *Darn it, at breakfast, he'd forgotten to mention the pink moon.* Now he was dismayed that he wasn't home with his ten-year-old son.

Crossing the shaded old bridge over the river, he walked along the running planks careful not to fall into gaps and land with a twisted ankle on the cross beams below. As he was about to step off the bridge into the moonlight, he skidded to a stop after brushing against a scruffy, bearded man in a long wool coat. Pavel Symanski was urinating against the parapet and singing a shanty about a drunken sailor.

"Wha's zup?" Pavel slurred.

"It isn't exactly couth or sanitary to be pissing into our river."

"Aye mate, thash true. Uncouth. But a homelesh man has little choice and thish is as good a place ash any." After a vigorous shake, he put his pecker back into his tattered trousers and took a couple of wobbly steps toward Weston before slumping against the side rail.

Weston gazed down at him, searching for clues of how a young man, obviously inebriated and filthy, could have ended up in a heap on this particular bridge. Pavel lifted his bloodshot eyes, casting a look at Weston that was more pitiful than malevolent.

"You need to sober up, man. Where will you spend the night?" Weston asked.

"Why would you care? You look like you're all well and good — set in life"

With no response, Weston abruptly turned his back and headed uphill toward home. Though he tried to put the encounter aside, his mind stuck on what the guy was doing here, how he made it to this point, how he had endured the adversities that had dashed hopes and presumptions for the future. And whether the man's judgment of him could be accurate. Certainly, he did have it better than most people. He had a strong loving wife and healthy child, a secure home, enough food, and an occupation that suited him. Should he be feeling guilty about his good fortune? Should he have been more hospitable?

Setting off to the workshop the next morning, he wondered where the scruffy man on the bridge had gone, but willed himself no speculation about the hopeless vagrant. Approaching the door of the shop, he noticed the hasp and padlock had been torn away. He pushed it cautiously. It creaked and yielded inward. The subdued light of early morning cast ashen shadows across the shop. Nothing seemed out of place. As he crossed toward his work bench, the familiar dusty metallic odor and utter quiet calmed his nerves. Early sun rays brightened the corners and far reaches of the shop.

Just as he pulled up a stool and sat down, a disembodied gravelly voice drifted across the room. Someone, a male, was concealed beyond a stack of plywood.

Weston picked up a long crowbar from the back of his workbench and walked cautiously across the shop. He peered around the stack into the darkness of a small adjacent room with floor to ceiling shelving bearing thousands of sorted automotive, plumbing and electrical contrivances, fasteners, nuts, screws, bolts, and supplies. In the dimness, Pavel Symanski sat, elbows on his knees, on an overturned five-gallon bucket. He hiccupped. Weston found himself flinching at the stench of the fellow. *I don't need this,* he thought.

"What you need," the man said, reading his mind, "is sommon to talk to — a bit o' friendly conversation." His voice was wheezy, his throat clogged. He spat up a ribbon of phlegm.

"A friendly chat? How's that possible? You're a drunk. You broke into my shop and violated my private property. And now you spit on my floor."

"In these times, mate, you know as well as I do that there ain't no legal ownership of property. That's why you people tend to ignore my type."

"And what type is that?"

"People with nothing but the rags on their backs. People with histories, and maybe skills that are invisible to the likes of you."

Weston relaxed his arm and hand, allowing the crook of the crowbar to hang loose in his palm. Though he leaned casually against the door frame, his body was poised to spring.

"The likes of me?"

"Yeah, chief. You people. You've illegally assumed, that is, stolen all the assets and means of production. And you've seized the reins of power in piss-hole places across the country. Far as I can see. Where's the fairness in this?"

"Fairness? That's a bunch of claptrap! Everybody's had to absorb massive blows to our former ways and now we're just trying to survive and maybe rebuild. Life isn't some zero-sum game. We've worked our fingers to the bone here. And we're not opposed to share what we can with new folk who are willing to pull their own weight and contribute to the community."

"You want to know why I landed here and chose you?"

"Not especially. I've got about all I can handle, but if it will hasten your departure, speak your piece and make it brief."

"First, would you mind putting that bar aside? What were you planning to do with it anyway?"

"Defend myself. I'll set it down, as long as you promise to stay calm."

"Look man, even when I was a bit drunk last night, did I seem the aggressive type?"

"A bit drunk? I'd say you were wasted."

"Yeah, it goes back to being a broken loser."

From there Pavel spun his tale of three years of wandering through widely scattered settlements between Buffalo and Marietta — a place he came to detest. He'd survived a raid in a town in western Pennsylvania by a mob of mad monks who absconded with most of the village maidens, had been beaten and robbed in Pittsburgh by a huge

Jamaican, was a stowaway on the paddlewheel steamer between Wheeling and Marietta. For the past two years he'd cobbled together part-time jobs in Marietta.

"Jobs? What kind of jobs?"

"Nothing highly skilled. Not worth bragging about."

Before all that, he claimed that he studied four years toward a degree in engineering from Syracuse University. The year he was to graduate, the coronavirus nearly killed him. The university shuttered and his degree was never conferred. He still suffered from muscle and joint pain, severe headaches, and brain fog. "Alcohol helps deaden the pain," he said.

"The drinking could be making it worse."

"No, not the drinking. I've got remnants of the virus, I'm sure."

"What kind of engineering?" Weston asked.

"Mechanical."

"And your particular interests?"

"Moving goods and people over land. Transportation. I know a lot about vehicles and systems of mass transit. I did an internship at an electric vehicle plant. All that is useless now."

"Maybe not."

"That's what I thought."

4

Abby contrived an excuse to disappear every third Tuesday morning after Weston went to work, and Running Bear moped out the door toward school. She had no intent to inform either of them that she'd been attending meetings of the Good Works for the Future (GWF) group at Antonio's barn. Proprietor of Hob Livery, Vet, and Blacksmith Services, Antonio was Hestia's partner. Trying to walk a fine line, Abby risked a double failure. On the one hand, drumming sense into her husband's thick skull often felt futile — notwithstanding his short fuse. Though she did still love the stubborn bastard. On the other hand, staying true to the Iroquois values rooted deep in her bones and aspiring a decent future for her confused, angry son seemed a far reach in this world of exhausted survivalists.

She descended the path off the ridge, crossed the river, and weaved her way to the backroom office at Antonio's livery. When she arrived, there were seven others gathered in a circle, drinking tea and chatting about their families and village news. The steamy aromas of stabled horses next door wafted about the office. Hannah handed her a piping mug of comfrey tea. The mug bore the faded logo of Gilligan University.

Hestia rose to speak. "Alright, GWF friends, it's time to catch up on news of Weston's workshop among other things. Are you ready, Abby?"

"Sure, thanks Hestia. To start, Weston's workmate, Pavel, has spent the past few weeks travelling to sites where cars, trucks, and buses had been ditched. I don't know exactly where he found it, but he and a farmer from Pomerance discovered a well-preserved vehicle in a garage next to a partially-collapsed farmhouse."

"What kind of vehicle?" asked Hannah.

"A mini-bus, like the ones that used to circulate around Argolis in our Gilligan days. They hoisted it onto a farm wagon and, after sunset, Pavel brought it here to the workshop."

"Have you seen it?" asked Astrid.

"Yes, as part of our détente, Weston and I came to an agreement that, with a little notice, I can visit the shop. I went there to see what he's been calling his 'jitney'."

"Jitney. Now there's a word you don't hear much." Astrid said. "What did it look like?"

"Well, I was not impressed. The bus had been torn apart, the engine removed. That morning they were sanding the outer shell — the metal — to remove rust and old paint. Weston told me that the project was long term. Years maybe. Pavel disagreed but otherwise he hardly acknowledged me."

Sean, Dr. Todd's partner, frowned. "The longer timeline would be better. We'd have time to think clearly about our response. My own emotions are whirring; I'm anxious and fearful. I'll need time to work toward a more peaceful place."

José agreed. "Peace. That's a damn good goal, man. The key question for me is what kind of power are they planning to use?"

"I've dodged that question for the moment," Abby replied. "The engine they removed, of course, ran on either gasoline or diesel. As far as I know, Weston has no intention of reverting to those fossil fuels, even if he could find and refine them. He'd prefer electricity but he says he's never found an electric vehicle worth restoring nor a battery with any life. And he doesn't know how to make a battery."

José jested, "Why doesn't he just google 'batteries' for instructions?"

"Shut up," said Astrid, José's partner.

Hestia wondered aloud, "What's google mean?"

Astrid rolled her eyes. "Forget that word; José's gone bonkers."

"Okay," agreed Hestia. "What was that about Pavel?"

Abby continued, "Pavel? He thinks I'm trying to get him sacked. I consider him a wild card. I'm not sure he's honest."

"Are you afraid of him?" queried Hestia.

"Not so far."

"What does he do in the shop?"

"Besides helping with organizing and clean up, Weston says he's looking into natural gas. A few rural people with old gas wells use it in their homes. But not for vehicles as far as we know."

"Natural gas!" exclaimed José. "Oh my god. I'm seriously opposed to natural gas. As some of us may remember from Dr. Zielinski's class, because of methane, natural gas is at least as bad for the climate as gasoline."

Hestia replied, "Again, when we know more, this will be something to investigate. Anything else, Abby?"

"Yes, I am troubled by how this controversy is affecting Running Bear. He's quite angry at his dad and, what?, almost paranoid about the way people in the village seem to have shunned him. He thinks they hate him because of what they believe Weston is doing in his shop — that Weston is on a path to disrupt our lives and that he's bent on returning us to the world of 2013. Despite my loyalty to Weston, I'm in sympathy with my son. I'm being torn in two."

"I have someone who might help Running Bear. Let me get back to you," Hannah said.

5

You can't believe how many weeks you've been dogged by the sense of not fitting in, of falling out with the only village and people you've ever known. Taking the long view from the front room window, you gaze down at the only tiny settlement for miles and miles. Down there, people are probably feigning friendship but quietly harboring anger and jealousy toward my Pa and, by extension, his family. Me. They're lying. They're undoubtedly fomenting a reprisal or something. That's how it looks from here. And that's why all that you're sure about and all that you are suspicious about bear down upon you like the weight of a corpse.

After a hug, Ma whispers, "You're looking awfully sad, little Bear."

"How many weeks of school left?"

"Three," she says. "Three weeks."

You turn away silently. Three weeks seems an epic challenge. Three weeks of spurns and seclusion. Three weeks before you're finally released to the woods and swims beneath the falls. Walks with Kayé. Time with Ma in the garden and kitchen. Stealthy avoidance of Pavel. Maybe catching Pa in a good mood.

Ma puts a tentative question to me. "Can we finish the story sometime? It might help you feel better."

"Yeah, but don't expect me to keep my mouth shut."

After dinner a couple of days later, we sit facing each other at the kitchen table. Pa is working late.

"Alright," Ma begins. "We left our story when the people of the village and your Ma and Pa were living mostly in harmony with each other and trying to do so with our Mother Earth. When questions came up about whether to apply ideas and tools and technology of the world we left behind, we would gather to discuss the pros and cons, and we would almost always agree that we should reject a tool or technique or substance that Mother Earth had no way of digesting and turning into further life. If we had old stuff from the past, like things made of plastic, we could use them until they no longer functioned. Then we'd take them to the recycling lot. Unfortunately, plastics do not degrade easily."

"Everything was wonderful then?" Your wily cynicism surfaces.

"Yes, mostly. But here's an example of something we could not agree upon. You remember Mr. Isaac Wample, right?"

"Uh huh. The old fat farmer with gobs of land somewhere near… What's that place called?"

"New Marshfield."

"Yeah, New Marshfield. What about him?"

"At the time you came into our lives, Mr. Wample had long been trading food with us for things like honey, mushrooms, and herbs that our village could supply. In turn, he provided cornmeal, wheat flour, oats, sugar, soybeans, and potatoes. Stuff we could not grow enough of here. Then one day at Village Council when you were about six, Astrid and José asked whether the workers who produced the food we eat from Wample's farm were treated justly."

"No one could answer their question. The only way was to visit the Wample operation. So, a group from here traveled there. Mr. Wample conducted a tour of the farm which is vast, as you said — at least five-hundred acres. The group returned with evidence that at least some of the food we'd been eating from Wample's farm was produced by farmhands who seemed to be made up of indentured if not enslaved people. They saw several overseers on horseback with leather crops riding among the farmhands. And their living quarters were rudimentary."

"Rudimentary?"

"Places you and I and Pa would not want to live in. Houses — shacks really — that were not insulated, open to the wind and rain and snow. Dirt floors. Shared outdoor toilets that were dirty and unsanitary. No proper piped water for drinking, cooking, or bathing. They saw filthy children in rags. Those kids were too weak to play."

"This new information led to disagreements. On one side were people who had become accustomed to having Wample's goods. Partly because Juan and Pauline Herzog were friends of Mr. Wample, they argued strongly for keeping things the same. One or two other people took their side. They said we'd never had success growing wheat in our small fields and sugar beets were well beyond our capability. 'It's his farm to run in the way he wants. What's the harm in letting him supply us?' they argued. On the other side, people like us wanted nothing to do with produce that came from a farmer who mistreats his workers and their families. Burt Zielinsky, one of our most avid defenders, argued that, sooner or later, Wample's bad treatment of his workers might involve us because they will run away and try to take shelter here. He said it would be immoral to continue to do business with the man."

Ma pauses to search your eyes, her dark irises boring into yours.

You squirm and ask, "So what happened?"

"First, there was a village tragedy. One moonless night, sometime after midnight, a fire broke out at Burt Zielinsky's big two-story home. Burt, one of my former professors — a very lovely man — and several of his pets perished before anyone even realized the blaze was lighting up the village skies. I think you know where the charred ruins of his house are."

"Over on Claybourne, right?"

"Yes."

For years, you had heard about that fire. Tempers had flared at the meeting when the village decided to shut down trade with Wample. The Herzogs wouldn't change their minds and apparently stormed out. You ask a deliberately baited question. "So, did the Herzogs or somebody on their side torch Mr. Zielinski's house?"

Ma will have none of it. She reprimands your implied bias. "One cannot jump to conclusions just because the Herzogs and Mr. Wample were friends. The ancestors tell us it is unkind to think bad thoughts about people in our tribe. Your Pa believed the fire started in a faulty stove pipe Burt had been complaining about. In these old houses, fire is a risk we all face."

Your cheeks feel hot. You pound the table. "Bullshit! Didn't anyone try to find out what the Herzogs and their sympathizers were doing that night?"

"Do not use crude language in my presence, Running Bear. Do not!" Ma stared you down. "I'd appreciate it now if you would let me finish my story."

Staring at your shoes, you mumble, "Sorry, Ma."

"To answer your question, no, there was no formal inquiry about the possibility of arson. But after the fire, we reached consensus that some of the better gardeners ought to try growing wheat and oats again, and we agreed to increase our corn and potato harvests. Several of us offered to add hives to produce enough honey to substitute for sugar. All that has worked out. But I so miss Professor Zielinsky."

You hold your tongue and raise no further comments on that part of the story. "But what about the poor kids of the farmworkers?"

"Although we were all sympathetic, short of some forceful act, which nobody advocated, we couldn't figure out what to do about them. We are a small village struggling every day to make better lives for our own children. We have no courts or judges. We don't even have a constable. A year or so later, we learned that some of the workers rose up and held hostage two of Wample's overseers. They tried to escape. The farmworkers chased them and beat them. Wample was furious. With neighboring farmers, including Juan Herzog, Wample organized a posse to overwhelm the rebellious farmworkers. And here, my son, the story becomes ghastly. Maybe I should stop until you're older."

You'd been expecting something like this. "Don't hold back, Ma. I'll be alright."

"You sure?"

"Yeah."

"Well, four of the ringleaders of the insurrection were imprisoned and severely beaten. Then, in the presence of the surviving farmworkers, those four limp bodies were dragged across the workers' compound and burned at the stake. Can you imagine? Burned!"

"And Wample, what has happened to him?"

"His brutal response has forever stained him and his farm. We've had nothing to do with him since."

You said nothing and avoided eye contact with Ma. You thought, but did not say, *How could any human be that ruthless and not pay a price? He ought to have been scalped.*

Ma reached across the table and placed her hands on each of yours. Her doe-eyes were misty. "Do you see how conflicts can spiral into darkness? If Pavel and Pa ever roll out a jitney that runs on gasoline or diesel or even natural gas, who knows what might happen? This is why people are upset; it's got nothing to do with you. You are a good boy, Running Bear."

The next day after school, you pour out your self-doubts and anguish to your new friend Samantha, Hannah and Manuel's daughter. The girl you thought had no interest in you. You tell her about Wample and those poor workers burned at the stake; how Ma chastised you for talking about arson; how you fear that Pavel might draw Pa and the village into another clash; the tedious schoolwork before summer.

You sit side-by-side on the river bank looking into the darkening forest, a wall of deep green right down to the opposite bank. The air is cool and smells like honeysuckle flowers.

"You should trust these things to the ancestors, Ruddy Bear," Samantha advises. Sometimes she calls you Ruddy Bear. It's alright. "Whatever your Pa and his mate are up to is beyond your control," she says.

"How can I do that? Dire thoughts about the future are turning me into Katshituashku — the stiff-legged bear, a weird character in Indian lore."

Samantha turns toward me with a coy smile. "'Stiff-legged' does not apply to you, Ruddy Bear. But 'stiff-something-else' does seem to happen rather frequently."

"I wish I'd never heard the word jitney."

"I get it. But there's more to it than that. Maybe what you really want is more time with your Pa, like you used to have."

"I'll grant you something there."

"Maybe you should just tell him."

You sigh and look at her slender arms resting on her knees, her back a willow whip, her black hair swishing around her ears in the downdraft off the river. Pan, you cannot get past her loveliness, her smarts. She's not quite sixteen and speaks like your wise old auntie. Your imagination rambles. Thoughts you'd never think about your auntie, if you had one.

"Yeah, thanks, Sam. I'll try talking to Pa."

6

A mild autumn breeze flowing through our hair, Samantha, me, and our six-year-old, Ahanua, ride along the woodsy trails of Bailey's Run on what used to be Wayne National Forest. Ahanua, meaning 'she laughs', reins in her pinto. She turns to me giggling, "You fart, Daddy?"

"Never happens. However, I do smell something sulphury. Let's tie up the steeds and have a look."

Following our noses, we hike up to a high ridge beneath the tall canopy. At the top, we see a clearing downslope a few hundred paces north with the rusted remains of the fossil fuel era — a fracking drill site. Although this is not an unusual sight in these parts, something is different here. Pulling out the scope Pa found in the rubble of the old Hawkins house, I snap it open and scan the site.

"There's a couple of mules down there. Behind that recently built cabin. Also, that tower, which is called the rig, has black puddles around it. The rusted tank hasn't been touched for years."

"Dad, are those puddles making the poopy smell?"

"I suspect so. Here let's have Mom check it out."

"For sure," she says. "Jeez Ruddy Bear, this well appears to be producing oil. But how?"

"Must be why they have mules," I reply.

Ahanua, now scrambling over sandstone boulders, turns back to ask: "Dad, what's oil?"

That night after supper and bedtime reading, Sam and I drink tea at the kitchen table of our cozy cottage, a wedding gift from Samantha's parents, Hannah and Manuel. They'd secretly restored the house from top to bottom before the wedding. It's small but plenty adequate for our little family and just a short walk to visit Ahanua's besotted grandparents.

I tell Sam that my sense of dread is creeping back. "I'm computing the odds in these times, in our region. Pa denies he'll ever consider oil or gas as fuels. Pavel has never committed to that. And less than an hour from the village is a functioning rig. Thinking about this makes me furious."

Looking my way, she's probably thinking I'll go bat-shit crazy all over again. After a long pause, she reminds me. "It's been more than seven years, Bear. Last time your Ma looked, the jitney was still up on blocks, no engine, no tires."

"Not sure that's up-to-date information."

"Well, there's the Good Works for the Future group. Your Ma attends their meetings. They're keeping a close watch. You need to trust them. For your sake, trust them."

"For my sake?"

"Actually, for all our sakes. Sometimes, Bear, I feel as though you're under siege. I know it's all those haunting memories of your parents' fights, your obstinate Pa and his remoteness even to his granddaughter. After you and he put your animosity on pause, you've both discovered that neither of you can quit remembering those harsh times. Your whole life, I feel, has been clouded, twisted really, by those two or three years."

Taking a long breath, I rub the back of my stiff neck. It's true, adolescent angst can seamlessly seep into every cell of my body, immobilizing me. Great Pan, I am 22, my adolescence is long past! The achy neck and stingy skull bones are alarm bells. Dropping my hand, I look at my wife. "Sorry, Sam. I seem to be reverting to my dumb shit days. It's wrong."

Sam nods and looks away.

7

When Weston bounded down the stairs, Abby greeted him in a way proven to soften the day and extend his lenience. It's worked for years.

"Come on, Wes, let's have a hug."

"How're you?" he said, then dropped his arms and pulled away from her hips.

"*Wakata'kalí:te: kih!*" She replies, which means *feeling great!*

The morning ritual completed, Abby turns to practicalities.

"I saw mouse or rat droppings in the pantry. Could you have a look? Also, these scraps need to find their way to the compost, the new kitten seems to have peed in the corner, and the hook on the back screen door has gone missing."

"Real men's work. Alright, I'll take care of all that when I get back this afternoon."

"So, what's happening at the shop today?" Abby wheedles half-truths every so often. Occasioned by Samantha and Running Bear's discovery at Bailey's Run, she needs data to share with GWF.

"Uh, nothing too exciting. Pavel's got the engine back together. Not sure where that's going. Too bad he drinks so much, he's brilliant. I could never have reassembled it so quickly and efficiently."

"That's the original engine?"

"Yep."

"Has he installed it back into the jitney?"

"Nah. It's still on saw horses. Needs to be tested."

"How is that possible? Doesn't he need gasoline or diesel?"

"We'll be trying out my new biofuel. If that doesn't work, Pavel found some petroleum."

"Wait a minute. I thought you were adamantly opposed to powering anything with oil or gasoline. Where did he find it?"

"My opposition to fossil fuels hasn't changed one iota, Abby. What Pavel is doing is experimental. There's no way we're going to scale up a fossil fuel-driven engine."

"Where did he get the fuel?"

"I don't know," Weston lied. "As I mentioned, the first option is to test the engine with biofuel. Better still, I recently got a new lead on a 2015 Tesla-S in a building on the campus of that old college near Nelsonville."

"What's a Tesla?"

"An electric car. At the time of Late-K, there were over twenty-thousand Teslas on the road. They had limitations: small batteries that could only run the car for 100 miles and they occasionally exploded. They also cost a mint."

"All this is really beyond me, Weston. I just hope Pavel is not going to spring a dirty surprise on us."

"That won't happen, Abby. I promise."

As usual, Weston power-walked to the shop, a mile or so of exercise he looked forward to each morning. Compared to Pavel, he was far more fit and trim. Not bad for a man in his mid-fifties. The clarity and crispness of the autumn morning and its resplendent foliage boosted his spirits. At the bridge, he took a moment to stare down at Mildred Creek. Not much water there; a trickle stringing together small pools in the midst of the channel. Droughts in recent years extended farther into fall and then were often followed by rain bombs — big downbursts that erode everything in sight. At least the Shawnee River, into which Mildred flowed, still had enough water to power electricity. They would need it.

He opened the shop and started his day by looking over notes about the design of the jitney's interior. A few minutes later, Pavel drifted through the door. He slumped into a chair and groaned, gingerly massaging his forehead and eyes.

"Rough night?"

"Yeah, boss. Hussy from Pomerance brought up some apple jack. We drained a bottle and went on to the next. I can't remember how she seduced me."

"Anybody I know?"

"Doubt it. Avery somebody. Hot but slightly nuts."

"Are we going to be able to test the engine soon?"

"Maybe by the end of the day."

"Good, this could be significant, especially if my biofuel fires up."

Later, bent to the task, Pavel said, "get me some of that wire over there."

"This spool here?"

"Yep. The green one."

For the next several hours, they wrestled with the wiring, installed fuel lines, tinkered with the fuel injection system, and pondered how to rig the ignition to the inverted hydro power which Weston had quietly extended to his shop — a fact few villagers, including his wife, knew.

As darkness began to engulf the village, Weston dipped the fuel line directly into a container of biofuel. Pavel attached the green wire to the starting motor. Upon contact, the starter turned over and over and over. After several more iterations, they shut it down.

"Either there's no spark or the fuel is not combusting. Or it could be that the fuel-air mix is off," Pavel said.

"Let's test to find out which," Weston suggested.

After an hour of checking each spark plug and the integrity of the fuel lines and the air intake ductwork, they concluded Weston needed to go back to the bench to reformulate his biofuel.

"That will take a few days," Weston estimated.

Pavel raised his eyebrows. "Days? Alright. In the meantime, let me try my cocktail."

"Your cocktail?"

"Yeah, the stuff I brought back and refined from Bailey's Run. It's in the fifty-gallon drum by the door. Plus something else. I've mixed in some aviation fuel I found behind the old airport terminal. Ratio of three gasoline to one aviation fuel. For additional combustibility, I plan to add a portion from that can of starting fluid I found in the back room. That stuff is alcohol based."

"What? Jumping Jehovah, no, Pavel! I won't have you breaking the promise I've made to everybody in this village. For anything."

"Okay, okay, boss. But let's think of this as a necessary step to see if my rebuild of the engine has been successful. If it runs on the fuel I've made, we can then be assured that once your biofuel is reliably combustible, we'll be able to argue that our jitney will be a sustainable mode of public transportation."

"Hmm. I guess if we frame it that way, we might be able to avoid a revolution. We'll just do a limited series of bench tests with your fuel, then install the engine in the jitney and go from there using biofuel. I get your logic. Do you think your mix will burn?"

"Yes. Yesterday, I put a candle to a saucer of the fracked gas mixed with aviation fuel. It flared nicely; then it was hard to douse. Adding the starter fluid should only make it better."

"Alright. Let's give it a shot."

***

In the living room, Ahanua and I stretch out on the shabby carpet, playing checkers. Sam is in the kitchen preparing supper for five. Ma and Pa promised to join us. As though she doubts the plan, Ahanua repeatedly asks when her grandparents Aksót and Laksót would be here. Something in the distance grabs our attention. First, we hear a subtle crack, as though the limb of an oak is being severed in a storm. But there is no storm. Seconds later, the house rattles and vibrates on the heels of an unworldly whoosh and deafening thump — sounds no one here has ever heard. More concussive than the nearest thunderclap, the explosion is followed by kettle drums, cymbals, gongs and one final detonation that seem to reverberate forever.

The metal roof, the steel beams, the fabricated cladding of the workshop blow into millions of molten bits, some of which reach the river sizzling. Pavel's remains are never recovered. The jitney is just a mass of twisted fragments.

***

When I decide it's time to work on reconciling my differences with Pa by explaining to him the depth of my and Ma's suffering and by inviting him to share his grief, when I finally get to that gut-wrenching place, it's too late. Pa lies unconscious on an operating table at the clinic oozing puss and pooling blood and emitting the stench of death from burns that cover his body. His face is grotesquely disfigured; I can hardly look. I'd wanted everyone, including Ma and Samantha, her parents, and especially Ahanua to be in harmony — be at peace in the great circle — returned to themselves, safe and contented, the way it used to be. Now it is impossible.

Running through the brush to the river's edge, the halo around the full moon lights my way in gray softness, triggers my deepest despair. When I return, Pa is dead. Ma, horror-struck at his bedside, beckons me. I wish the image in my memory was of his confident yet dreamy self, the geeky smile hiding unbounded belief in the promise of tomorrow, the father who once loved me as I am. Not the memory of my mutilated Pa.

Bernard

I feel as though I'd witnessed the final chapter of a world that tried vainly to rise again. I cannot imagine Pa contriving a way to be part of that world — ever. It had to be Pavel.

TEN

Another Version: Hestia's Destiny

Argolis, 2060s

No matter who you think you are; there is always
another version waiting to show up.
— Bindu Madhav Tata[6]

1

JUST LAST WEEK I'D DISMISSED HIM out of hand and paid scant attention to his public lecture, although his cause was worthy. His eyes paused on mine it seemed, about halfway through or perhaps not. In either case, I feigned interest and continued jotting impressions, questions, and new information in my notebook. At the reception in the Holmes Mill rotunda, I was a silent citizen in a cluster in conversation with the speaker, Cameron Caldwell. I showed up because I felt a civic

---

[6] https://ownquotes.com/profile/bindumadhavtata/

responsibility. My conscience is clear. I've made it past forty. And still, I'm living.

The next morning, as I wrote a summary of his talk and his responses to questions from the audience, I paused to wonder about him. He was a tall man with a shock of gray hair going to white, and what my friend Hannah described as the manner of a southern gentleman. Such a manner meant nothing to me but apparently it was an apt description. Raised in Virginia, he attended the formerly famous university there, graduating with a law degree a few years before the world went topsy. He married, started a family, and took a job in the West Virginia Attorney General's office. After losing his wife to the coronavirus, and after everything shut down, he and his children moved across the Ohio River.

"He is wont to brag about his lineage and education," Silas, my brother, told me. "The guy has a sense of entitlement that has zero relevance these days. It's a local joke. I mean people like us have had no opportunities for education and highfalutin careers. We've all sunk to the lowest common denominator. We are sort of a classless society. We've had no friggin' choice."

"Probably a good thing," I ventured.

Across the table, my partner Antonio said, "Yeah, that man's a crusty hombre. One time a couple of years ago, he left his lame horse with me. It took a while, but I helped that old gelding get better. When he went out the door, he could even gallop. The man bargained me down, paid his silver, and hardly said thanks."

As a Latin born in the barrios of Buenos Aries, Antonio perpetually saw the world through the eyes of someone who rose up in extreme poverty, as if that's so unusual now. He was surely not in that man's league, nor would he want to be. His mind constantly swirled with class-based recrimination. It was my lot to absorb more than my share of his tirades.

As I now put the finishing touches on my minutes, my gut continues to roil over Antonio. To our partnership of more than a dozen years, he brought a bizarre cocktail of anger and empathy, compulsion and remorse, fatherhood and philandering. It was a cocktail that proved too toxic for my taste, too misogynist even for these barren times. I used to be aroused by the swagger — the singular Latin ostentation. I loved that *tío.*

I turned to making breakfast for Che, packing his lunch, getting him off to school, and hitting the trail for my early morning run along the Shawnee River. Twenty minutes in one direction, twenty back. After that, I'd be good to face whatever the day might bring.

***

On a summer evening a few weeks later, I'd noticed that the Virginia lawyer and I were at opposite ends of the raucous summer solstice crowd at Astrid and José's farm out on Harmony Road. A makeshift band with a half-dozen musicians trying their best to blare out tunes from generations past — *Let There Be Love* at the moment — added to the merriment of the one event each year when everybody could put aside their cares to relax and forget their inhibitions. There were easily fifty people crowded around and boogying across the dance floor which extended away from the 1898 barn that had been Astrid and José's home for almost four decades.

At forty-three, I was in my increasingly familiar new role of 'that poor sweet woman whose partner ran off.' Tonight, I willed myself to put that aside. I was in a jovial mood and happy to be free of the philanderer, the father of my son. He left town a year ago. And so far, he's reneged on his promise to be present for his son. I don't want to talk about him anymore.

Seeing me tapping my toes, two dear friends dragged me onto the dance floor: Giselle, my age-mate and fellow survivor of the True Vine bloodbath, and José himself, the once flamboyant theatre and dance major who had the grace not to dance circles around us. These were rare moments of abandonment in my otherwise humdrum life. Then, Che, my sixteen-year-old, took the obligatory turns around the floor with his mum for a waltz or two. "You're a pretty good dancer, Mamá. I never knew."

"How would you have known? Before you were born, your father taught me Latin movement. He was a smooth dancer."

"Ah," Che said. These days he refrained from saying much about his dad.

When Che delivered me to the buffet table, I found myself at Cameron Caldwell's side.

"Hello," he said, his eyes, the color of an Indigo Bunting, searching mine. "Aren't you the village clerk?" He extended his hand and I responded hesitantly with my own, immediately engulfed in his great fleshy palm.

"I'm Cameron Caldwell."

"Hi Cameron or should I call you Mr. Caldwell?"

"Ah no. Just Cam or Cameron." He smiled down at me in a disarming way.

"Okay, Cam. I'm Hestia, and yes, I *am* the council clerk. I took notes at your lecture last month. The challenges of stemming the ongoing traffic of young children along the river are certainly daunting." I withheld my history of landing in the midst of what, looking back, was lethal thuggery aimed at recapturing 'assets' — the heart of such traffic. That day we lost not only our beloveds to gun violence, but also the promise of a regenerated society with new moms and kids.

"As I mentioned in my talk, yes, I'm trying to find a way to stem the child trafficking," he said. "It's clear from people along the river that the cartel, or whatever it is, has already delivered children to childless couples for quite a while. Most of those kids, now in their teens and twenties, have become, pardon the expression, potentially successful breeders boosting one's sense of the future. On the other hand, those kids certainly landed on various farms at a rather steep cost — incredible amounts of silver per child. And the toll on their birth mothers in the baby mills could not have been anything but heartbreaking."

"To say the least. The whole scheme is morally reprehensible."

"Indeed."

"Giselle, groomed to become one of those moms, is my best friend. She managed to escape and single-handedly brought up an orphan girl likely born in one of those mills. She might be a useful informant."

"I've met Giselle. Yes, she's been helpful. Her daughter is considering joining our expedition upriver. I've also spoken with Aram Masood, a doctor at your clinic. He suspects that his former employer near Wheeling is likely still behind the trade. She is the target of my investigation at the moment."

"I would trust Aram's opinion."

"But let's not talk anymore about that now," Cameron said. "Would you care to join me? Grab a plate and we can take our food over to one of the tables under the oaks."

"Alright." I felt awkward, but better to have a dinner companion than to be at the periphery alone.

"This is good," he said as he folded his legs beneath the table. He seemed to be studying me. "I don't know many people here. I feared eating alone. I'm grateful you accepted."

"I've heard you are an outgoing, confident, well-educated man. I wonder why you would want to chat up a diminutive waif like me. I've had very little formal education. Things had come unhinged when I was a kid. My brother and I were orphans."

Cameron Caldwell gazed a long contemplative stare across the lawn toward the dance floor. The band had almost everybody else out there, hips swaying and arms stretched to the sky waving like wheat in the summer wind. "Well, yes, I was both fortunate and curiously ill-prepared for the bad times, born as I was with lots of privilege way back in the eighties. At times I might have been too full of myself. But I'm a different person now."

"Different?"

"Yes, the years since the collapse have been humbling."

"Everybody who's made it through those years has had to adapt or perish." I hesitated, then said, "My late friend, Professor Stefan Fremanis, believed that whatever one thinks of one's self at any given time, there will always be another version ready to manifest itself.[7] It has surely been true for me."

"My wife died in the second pandemic. I was cut adrift and devastated. With help from my daughter and two sons, I've slowly adapted, I think. I've became a softer but not a very effective single parent. Since my daughter moved into her own place, I've probably wallowed too much as a lonely old man. And now I miraculously find myself talking with a sprightly attractive woman named after a Greek Goddess."

"Yeah, the Goddess of Hearth and Home. I hope that doesn't mean you're interested in someone to cook your meals and wash your socks."

"Huh, no. Just companionship."

My mind drifted. What would Che think of this? As always, it was Che I most worried about. The shattered world he's inherited, his father's abandonment. I wondered if Cameron had parallel concerns about his daughter.

***

Some weeks passed. My jogs along the river had become routine, not like other summers when I would be fully present every day in the efflorescence of nature — the eye-popping green of everything, the spring and summer wildflowers, the buzzing and chirping and rippling daily symphonies, the glittering sun dancing on the river. All this nature and so much more unobserved in the soil beneath the forest used to make me blissful. I can identify a bird by its nest and by its song, name a tree by its bark and leaves and fruit. I know what kinds of wood are best for construction, for fence posts, and for harboring morel mushrooms. I know that copperheads are near if I smell something like cucumber. I love the spring peepers, the noisy cicadas on summer nights, and the joy of walking through a meadow of oxeye daisies.

---

[7] This wisdom has been paraphrased by the author. The original, written by Indian author, Bindu Madhav Tata, is this story's epigraph.

Now I seem somehow immune. I never thought I would lose my fascination with the resurgence of the natural world, which would mean I'd have to forego one of my best arguments for hope. But here I am trudging in at least partial oblivion. My brief time with Cameron offered the only recent evidence that I might be able to get back into life. I thought of his dead wife and of my own brush with death more than twenty years ago. How we'd both suffered.

Going to work on a Monday morning, on the Holmes Mill stairway, I came face-to-face with the very man. He was ascending as I was heading down to my office.

"Oh, hello Cameron. What brings you up to Argolis?"

"Hestia! Hi. I was just at your office door. Two things. Thanks to your friend, Giselle, there are some young people here who are interested in joining my mission up the river. I'm here to interview each of them. And second, I wanted to ask you about something."

"Okay."

"Um, would you like to have dinner with me tomorrow evening?"

I paused, a beat too long.

"If you're not comfortable doing so, I'd understand," he said.

"No, I would love to. It's just that nobody has ever asked me that particular question. Until recently, there's never been a restaurant any place I've lived. I've always been the one to prepare dinner for guests, especially men."

"Well, I'm honored to be first. I've been told that a new place has just opened overlooking the river. I thought we might eat there."

When I mentioned the invitation to Che that night, I told him I had been unsure about whether to say yes. "He is, after all, old enough to be my father and both Uncle Silas and your dad had fairly negative things to say about him. On the other hand, his wife died, his daughter's moved out, and he's lonely. I'm sad for him. But are you alright with me doing this?"

"Well, Mom, I've never met the man. I have to trust that he'll be kind and honorable toward you. Yeah, go ahead and have dinner with him. Why not? You'll have fun."

We met outside the restaurant, once the home and office of an architect. It was July with more than two hours of daylight to go. Samantha, Hannah's daughter and one of the proprietors, met us at the door. "Oh, you must be Mr. Caldwell along with one of my dearest relatives," she said, closing the space between us with a warm hug. "Hestia, welcome to our little restaurant."

"How are you two related?" Cameron asked.

Samantha quickly replied, "She's my Nickleby Mother."

Cameron crinkled his brow. I told him I'd explain later. Samantha escorted us to a table on the open deck high above the Shawnee River, tumbling over the historic dam with Holmes Mill on the other bank. From here, I could see the wrap-around windows of the library and my office. Neither of us spoke as we took in the view. In the silence it occurred to me that we knew little about each other and I worried we'd find nothing to talk about, generations apart as we were.

He ordered a bottle of wine. He said it came from a vineyard near his home. "Mama Riah is our only choice but that doesn't mean it's bad wine. In fact, it's quite nice. Two of my daughter's best friends are the vintners."

Sitting diagonally from him, I realized how big Cameron seemed at this little table, something on the order of Jason, the boy with whom I said goodbye to my virginity. The teenage version of me dreamed of having a brawny brood with Jason — poor gone Jason. It would have been an interesting blend: the genes of a bird-boned, pinkish girl of nineteen and those of a giant brown-sugar boy, two years younger. So much for that dream. A troubling thought cropped up. Not about Jason. I wondered what it would be like in the arms of this older large man, a scenario I hadn't been part of for more than a year, as though I'd signed a vow of abstinence when Antonio flew the coop. Would a seventy-something man be at all interested in partaking of this fantasy?

"Goodness, you came through life as an orphan," Cameron said. "That must have been hard."

"Not as difficult as you may imagine. The raid on our village obliterated my parents and chased us away from the Eerie lakeshore; there were several kids like me. The village pitched in to raise us. A wise woman named Freya was as dear to me as any grandmother could ever have been. When I left her to come here, it was one of the hardest days of my life."

"I would imagine."

Surely, he could not. Instead, I said, "And here in Argolis, the same thing has happened. Loving big sisters like Hannah and Em have shown me how to be as I head into middle age. I pay their care-and-nurture forward. That's why Hannah's child, Samantha, is my Nickleby daughter."

"I get the idea of paying forward but who or what is Nickleby?"

"We probably don't have time for a full explanation. Suffice it to say that I, as a Nickleby Mom, have pledged to shelter and love Samantha in the same manner godmothers did in the past. What's different now is that we've dispatched that scary bearded-male sky god. In this instance, Katja Nickleby has taken his place. She's not a goddess in any traditional sense. I'll find a copy of her book to lend you.[8] You'll see why we hold her in high esteem."

As dinner progressed, we spoke of more personal things like our childhoods and his marriage. I found it comforting. Though I'd had many such conversations with close female friends, none of the men I've known, including my brother, have been comfortable talking of personal and emotional issues. In other words, age-old male hang-ups seemed to have transferred across the generations. Or has it been baked into their evolution as *males*? Is Cameron an exception? Survival seems to have reinforced, for better or worse, many conventional gender-based roles and attitudes. Mine is a history of bucking those behaviors. And it always discombobulates the men I've been around.

I remembered one night in the Antonio version of my life, having put Che to bed, I dozed on the brink of deeper sleep in the sitting room when Antonio burst through the door after having one too many *cervesas* with his mates. It was late. He sat on the couch, propped me against him, and began, with his large brown hands, to stroke my breasts.

"Have you been yearning for me today?" he asked.

"Have you felt at all guilty about missing Che's bedtime, about not reading to him the way you used to?"

"Ah, I've just been thinking about these lovely pink buds and how I want to suck them. And go from there."

"Can you imagine suppressing your libido long enough to accomplish something for the good of our family?"

"Well, *mi amor,* I can easily imagine anything," he said.

"Try that another night."

"Alright, I'll come home and be the good *esposo.* You can go to the bath and put on a sexy robe for me." He blurted this in a repetitious, irksome way.

"I feel like you're mocking me, Antonio. Am I simply your *amante?*"

Later, after we'd had sex, I would not let up. "In your experience as an allegedly downtrodden *compesino* with a big heart, how long can a relationship last on misogyny, machismo, and a love letter written years ago?"

"Forever, as long as the man does not lose his *cohones.*"

---

[8] Katja Nickleby. *Over the Cliff.* Winona: Spring Fountain Press, 2005.

I shared a condensed version of this story with Cameron and deliberately withheld the name of my partner. His only response was, "When and where did you learn words like libido, misogyny, and machismo?" In itself, this was as perfect an indication of the man's chauvinism as I could have conjured. And a depressing one; Cameron is *not* an exception.

I said, "I'm grateful that my grandmother taught me to read, to love words and sentences, and to think for myself."

After what I took to be an apology, I decided to restrain myself. We both obviously needed someone to talk to, someone to listen, and from there we did that in equal amounts. Cameron never mentioned his Virginia education, nor his career as a prosecutor. He did speak more about his reverence for his late wife. We finished our dinners, talked more until Samantha brought out two brandies, and we sat there with our nightcaps, the gurgling Shawnee beneath us, a backdrop as soothing as any I could imagine in the wreckage of the days we'd been reflecting upon.

The next week we met for lunch at the café in Holmes Mill. The harsh daylight of mid-summer sent shards of glare through the south-facing windows. We moved to a table away from the annoying shimmer. The little café's atmosphere at midday was far shabbier than Samantha's new restaurant in the twilight. Cameron appeared to be exhausted and our conversation seemed forced with awkward dead spots. As we finished our salads, things took an unexpected turn.

I was in the midst of spilling details about how Antonio's abandonment had impacted our teenage son. "At this point, after all these months, I have to assume Antonio is far away. Maybe he caught a riverboat that took him all the way to the Gulf of Mexico. I don't know."

Cameron averted his eyes. He seemed to be staring at someone in the doorway. After that person departed, his unfocused gaze was still a thousand paces off. He cleared his throat. "Um, the times we met before, I did not think it appropriate to be asking questions about your life. I had no need to know why you were by yourself at the *soirée*, why you were available to chat with me. I feared that knowing might be the kiss of death for the next occasion. I didn't want that to happen."

"Well, I'm all about being open and honest, Cameron. Antonio bailed out. Simple and tragic as that. I've dealt with it for more than a year and I'm still trying to get through the fog."

"I admire your pure intentions and transparency, Hestia. But, but my stomach churns."

"What is it? Are you feeling ill?"

"No. It's that I possess disheartening knowledge I never imagined had any relevance for us." His face clouded over revealing dozens of craggy lines I had not noticed, a droop that extended from his cheekbones to his jawline and chin on down to his neck wattle.

"Relevant how?"

"Antonio." He blurted the name as though spitting out rotten meat.

"What? What? Have you met Antonio?"

"Regrettably, I have." He told his story in a short burst of sentences. I stared at him, grimly absorbing shockwaves that rattled my brain. He looked away, despairing, about to weep.

I paused a few seconds, then blurted, "Oh, my fucking word!" A curse that reverberated across the café and into the kitchen. Resorting to foul language was typically a red flag for me. I was more riled than I realized.

He buried his face, his long fingers rubbing his temples.

"That baby is your grandchild?"

"Yes, she is." Cameron nodded twice, hung his head, could not look me in the eye.

"You obliged that putrid womanizer?"

"What could I do, Hestia? It was a one-nighter, she told me. I could not, I just could not order my daughter to abort or to leave Pomerance in shame. The very daughter who's been desperate to have a child. The very moment when we need babies to replace ourselves and sustain the recovery."

"It's not your fault, Cameron. But shit, I'm sitting here agitated and confused. I don't know what else to say." I got up and walked slowly toward the door. Over my shoulder I cried out, "You cannot imagine how unhelpful this is in my effort to purge Antonio."

"No, no, you don't understand," he pleaded.

"You are spot on there, Cameron. I don't." I slowly walked toward the door, straining to calm myself. Though I really wanted to slam it, I silently closed the café door behind me.

***

A couple of weeks later, Giselle stopped by the library to pass on a note from Cameron. Before handing it to me, she asked, "Are you and Cameron becoming an item to toss around the village?"

"An item?"

"Yeah, we know you had a dinner date at Samantha's restaurant."

"Oh that. It was definitely not a date, dear. The man's a grandfather. He's needful and I happened be the first person he came across at the *soirée*. He asked me out. He's an old-school bloke whose life experience doesn't seem to have anything for me."

"What? Why won't you give him a chance? I believe he likes you and respects you."

"I don't want to talk about it."

"Well, you won't have to for at least a couple of months." She handed me the note.

Dear Hestia,

As Giselle will explain, we'll be setting off upriver in just a few days. I don't know how long this trip will be. I wanted to say that when I return, I would very much like to meet with you and see if we can fix the regrettable situation we've found ourselves in. In the meantime, know that I do care deeply about you and your son,

Cameron

Giselle looked at me expectantly. "So?"

"Nothing. By the time he gets back, we'll both have moved on."

Giselle had no response. She said she needed to meet her daughter to catch a ride on the postal wagon to Pomerance. I told her I'd been worrying about Cameron's expedition. "Our experience with those rogues years ago was hideous, as you well know. They killed Ezra and Jason and Nick. They kidnapped Rudi. Who's to say they won't resort to violence again? And why would Holly want to face that risk?"

"Do not worry, Hestia. It's an information-gathering mission."

"And you entrust your daughter to Cameron Caldwell?"

"Yes. Besides, Holly is twenty-two, Hestia. She's plenty able to make her own decisions."

2

Trying to raise my son while dealing with continuing blows of renunciation makes me a battered woman. When alone, I cannot help but relive the argument the night of Antonio's fiery departure. Over and over. And the aftermath: the throbbing headache, the fluttering heart of a trapped bird, the fright. Che will soon be gone. The bleakness of a life alone is almost more than I can bear. And now knowing that a love child is less than three hours away is driving me crazy: Che's half-sister, born of a seduced, desperate woman. A woman I've never met. She basks in the glow of her fatherless newborn, knowing nothing of me or my pain.

At the very edge of drowsy consciousness, I feel safe and secure. My slowing breath, my arm propping my head on the soft pillow, the luxury of my own bed. I'm awake enough to realize I'm sailing off the cliff toward deeper sleep as another reality kicks in — the gathering mists of a dream that's already begun.

I am clutching two hands: Hannah on one side, Giselle on the other. Em is behind, her arms embracing us three. We are crowded with two others in a tiny cavern behind a mat of tree roots in a deep gully. Gun blasts and screaming children send recurrent waves of terror over each of us. We women are gasping and weeping; the men stoic, heads bowed. This familiar nightmare is different. There's one more woman in it. It cannot be. We four are the only women meant to be in this dream. The new woman is transparent. Gazing at her chest, I can see the root mat behind her, no, inside her. She extends her hand; I take it. It is crimson; her blood oozes between my fingers. The ethereal woman is Salma of the True Vine Sanctuary. Salma, the stunning ecru-skinned girl with beaded cornrows and a surly attitude. Now I see blood spurting from a wound in her gut. She weakly wheezes: "Have mercy." As I try to reach her, the word *mercy* fades like an owl's distant call. Before my eyes, she fades to ripples of scarified, blood-soaked skin that envelop and seek to suffocate me.

I awake in a cold sweat, heart pumping, breath shallow. The mystical appearance of Salma evokes menacing flashbacks that include a witch cremation and a violent bloodbath that leave me woozy. I shiver, roll over, and try to fall back asleep. I cannot. Two decades have passed since the events that spurred that terrifying dream. That's half my life, almost. Antonio claimed to have witnessed the shot that hit Salma, fired, we now know, by Silas. Rudi, we inferred, had been drawn away, caught in Salma's web. His infatuation may have been the death of him. No one knows whether either he or Salma survived. The True Vine Sanctuary obviously has.

***

Silas is on the front porch when I trudge up the lane. He rides up from Pomerance once a month and always brings me surprises from Thad Symonds' shop on the river. I never know when to expect him.

"Got some coffee beans, Emmental cheese, and Mexican salsa for you. Boat from New Orleans passed through a couple of weeks ago."

"Oh Silas, thanks. Coffee, my gosh, what a treat! We'll brew some in the morning."

After dinner and a chess match with Che, Silas and I sit on the porch. The sun has long since dropped below the horizon tugging twilight behind it. The night is alight with fireflies.

"Lightning bugs," Silas corrects me.

"So, how're you doing overall?" he asks.

"I've been better."

"Still mourning that scumbag?"

"Not mourning. Mostly angry and blue. Also experiencing flashbacks from that bloody Saturday in Marietta so many years ago. Sooner or later, I will come round to equilibrium, though being alone is not how I imagined I'd be spending my forties."

"What about Mr. Caldwell?"

"Oh, Cameron. He's gone up river to find out more about child trafficking."

"Yeah, I heard. People in Pomerance are split on the subject. There are maybe ten kids and young adults in town who were provided by that commerce. But what about him?"

"Nothing much, really. When I responded to his invitations, it seemed like the universe was telling me his company might brighten my life. That was what Prof would have called 'fantastical thinking'."

"Well, maybe it's for the best. As I mentioned last year, I had some issues with the man. Poor match for you. You need to find a younger stud."

"Yeah. Know of any good candidates?"

"I'll keep my eyes open. Maybe Lester will have some ideas."

Lester is Silas' cynically hilarious, irrepressible partner — the opposite of my sulky brother of few words. Back in the last century, Lester would have been tabbed a drama queen. Today, people don't quite know what to make of him. Lester and Silas are quite a pair in these times when procreation is top of mind for young couples. Lester argues that his acerbic wit would irreparably tarnish a child — if there were a child to be had. Silas has never expressed an opinion.

He excused himself and stepped inside a moment. He came back with what looked like a tabloid newspaper. "Here's something for you, the first issue of *Ohio River Currents*."

"Hmm. What's this world coming to?" I leafed through its pages, almost all of which were covered with columns of text rather than graphics. Of course, I had seen newspapers — yellowed ones in the stuffy back reaches of libraries. I knew that by the time of collapse, many newspapers had gone out of business. People were getting their news online. What that meant has always been unclear to me. I had no idea someone could put together an old-time printed paper nowadays.

"Who's behind this?"

"Spencer Caldwell, one of Cameron's sons. As a kid, he yearned to be a journalist. The old printing press had been collecting dust in the former offices of the Daily Sentinel. He cleaned up the place and figured out how to get the press going. Not sure where he sources the ink and paper. He's got two or three part-time writers and one journeyman. Kate is part of the project."

"Kate, as in Prof's daughter?"

"Yep."

ANTI-CHILD TRAFFICKING GROUP IN WHEELING

July 15, 2060

Kate Fremanis

The exploratory mission to stem the Ohio River trade in young children left the Pomerance town dock more than three weeks ago. Leader Cameron Caldwell sent this dispatch via the Sternwheeler Muskingum earlier this week. . .

On July 9th our team of seven met with a small group of Wheeling citizens who are working with authorities to stem child trafficking on the Ohio River which they deem to be illegal and socially destructive. The problem around Wheeling is the same as where we live. There are no legally sanctioned officers or courts of law. The group is dependent upon a self-appointed sheriff who may himself be implicated in the scheme.

Tomorrow, July 9th, we will interview a locally influential woman called Safiya Kamal. Some people suspect that she's the brains behind the trade.

She is a successful entrepreneur who coordinates and owns many agricultural enterprises, and commands a fleet of vessels that move goods up and down river. People on the Ohio side, where she lives, have said they could not feed themselves without her produce and network. They trade and barter with her throughout the growing season. And they argue that she is a fair-minded communitarian who could not possibly be a child trafficker.

"Good grief, Silas. This cannot be a coincidence — two women named Kamal in a small part of what used to be Ohio. This really troubles me. Cameron has no idea about the darkness of the Kamal we encountered or of our history with her. And there's no way we can warn him."

"Calm down, Hest. Salma Kamal is probably dead. Thanks to me, she took a bullet in the belly. If she *is* dead, it's surprising that Rudi has never found his way back. I'm guessing Cameron's group will be stonewalled or gaslighted and return empty-handed."

"If they're lucky. By the way, I know the meaning of those two antiquated verbs. Where in Pan's name did you learn them?"

"Lester the Jester. Where did you think? He's stonewalling and gaslighting me every chance he gets."

As the days rolled by, I could not stop thinking about the Kamals. Silas returned to the arms of the incorrigibly cheerful Lester and their lives in Pomerance. Che and I were left to our own devices. He relished his time with a wagonload of kids attending the annual summer camp at the Buckley Farm. I despaired into the wee hours. It was wearing me down and I often found myself napping in the library after lunch.

"Hestia, are you in here?"

I startled to semi-awareness. I looked out the window and saw the sky was neither blue nor black. It was gray. What time of day is it? How long have I been asleep? Someone's calling my name.

"Ah, Giselle, is that you? Sorry, I've been so exhausted, I dozed off. Come, I'll make a pot of tea and let's catch up."

I confessed that my dismissal of Cameron was premature. I told her that Cameron had revealed that his own daughter had given birth to Antonio's love child. I told her I was embarrassed that I'd walked out on Cameron at the café.

Giselle giggled softly.

Bernard

"What's so funny?"

"Oh Hestia, I'm not laughing at you. Don't you see the paradox?"

"Paradox? All I see is Antonio's impudence and irresponsibility and lust. All I think about is how much suffering he unleashed on Che and me. Anger and fatigue are about to take me down."

"Well, while everybody's having trouble conceiving and there's a freaking mission to shut down some kind of baby mill, here's Antonio jumping on Avery Campbell one night. He runs off. Nine months later, she drops a healthy child. That, to me, is classic irony."

"What about my three miscarriages? A laughing matter too?"

"Not at all. Those miscarriages happened; they're real and very sad."

"And they deprived Che of a sibling and killed our sex life."

"Hestia, humanity is and probably always has been a crucible of suffering. I don't deny the pain you feel. I do say you could learn from it. I think if you enjoyed being in Cameron's company, you should open your mind to working this out."

"Working it out? What do you expect me to do? Go knocking on his daughter's door? Tell her that her little girl has a big brother?"

"That sounds like a plan."

Later that afternoon, I took a long walk along the Shawnee to try to sort out the jumble of emotions stirred by Giselle's visit. Torrential rains in the past few days caused the river to be up to its banks and running fast. I remembered years ago assuring Freya that I felt strong in the face of the future. Now, middle-aged and more jaded than joyous, I feel disoriented. I fear the future. The distortion that has robbed me of optimism and my typical good nature is Antonio, whose absence I cannot rationally address until I admit that the pit in my heart is beyond mending.

Antonio appears frequently in my dreams. They always begin with the epochal argument and my misjudgment that a rage he'd never before seen in me would be the motherload that sent him packing. In these dreams, Antonio is back from New Orleans. His neck is enveloped in colorful bead necklaces that he gathered during Mardi Gras. He makes no mention of Che. His mustache is flecked with gray; he limps across our sitting room toward me. He limps and limps but never gets closer. He claims he's glad to be back. He remembers nothing of a colossal quarrel.

None of this makes much sense either in the dream or in reality. What is Mardi Gras anyway?

"Antonio!" I exclaim. "Where have you been all these years?"

"Ah Hestia, you must be looney." He laughs. "I was gone just one night."

I break up as well, a teethy burst. I'm not angry at Antonio; I want to forgive him. I'm just glad he's alive and I'm happy we can laugh over our difference of opinion. Laughter had long been absent between us.

When I wake up, my intent to forgive him has vaporized. As always, I am pissed.

Yet the Antonio in the dreams, though older, sounds and smells and looks like the Antonio I remember. He's not the sinister Antonio I conjure when I am awake or the philandering one or the deadbeat one. Since the Antonio of my dreams is vibrant in ways I cannot remember him ever being, I'm prone to think about the dreams as both illusion and benediction. If I can embrace the latter, perhaps I can move on. Perhaps the next version of me will show up.

By the time I got back home, the sun had set. With Che gone for three weeks with the kids at camp, this has become a forbidding time of day. The darkness and empty house magnify my gloom, causing hours of sleeplessness. What a damn shame. I used to love long summer evenings, relaxing in the twilight with a chilled drink, windows wide open, the cool damp air drifting through rooms, the mystery of night sounds — caterwauling cougars and howling wolves, sounds our great grandparents would never have heard. Sounds Che loves. Sounds of a recovering world.

3

A month down the road, Giselle is back with something — either news or not news. Over the weeks, I've tried to discipline myself not to think about the expedition or Cameron. The mission was risky even for a younger man. I allowed that he'd not be back. If he did manage to return, what then? I would owe him an apology and I doubt he'd just forget the rude way I walked out on him. I'd been foolish. Cameron is not the man I would have chosen in other circumstances. Nor would Cameron have been attracted to me. But there we were on the deck on a magical summer evening relaxed in each other's company, achieving closeness. I had not had an evening so pleasant in years.

"Pomerance is abuzz about the expedition. Somebody heard that it's on the way home," Giselle said in measured tones.

"Is that somebody a reliable source?"

"Not sure. In fact, I have no idea who that might have been."

"Is that the only rumor?"

"Um, no. Lester told me he heard there was trouble of some sort. His source insisted there's no evidence of anyone from the expedition on the Memphis Queen, the next sternwheeler coming downriver."

"And what about Lester's source?"

"A family drifting downriver on their small flatbed. They left the dock at Wheeling at the same time as the Queen."

"Geez, are you worried about Molly?"

Giselle teared up. "Molly. Oh Molly. Hestia, you warned me." All I could do was embrace my friend and try to stay positive.

***

I look out the kitchen window on a chilly December Saturday morning. Fog and freezing rain have descended upon our village; a glittering coat of ice accumulates on trees and walks; icicles gain length on the porch roof. I stoke the wood burner and sip my morning tea. A crinkled anthology of poems, dated 2017, lies open on the table staring back at me. The words of Holly Hughes bring me round once again to where my heart, not my mind, should have been all along.

> *But the mind always*
> *wants more than it has—*
> *one more bright day of sun,*
> *one more clear night in bed*
> *with the moon; one more hour*
> *to get the words right; one*
> *more chance for the heart in hiding*
> *to emerge from its thicket*
> *in dried grasses—as if this quiet day*
> *with its tentative light weren't enough,*
> *as if joy weren't strewn all around.*[9]

4

Two more years had passed with no word about the fate of Cameron's expedition. A party of three young men, including both Cameron's sons, traveled to Wheeling last year. They found Safiya Kamal's house overlooking Wheeling. It was locked; nobody there. Through the windows, it appeared to have been occupied recently. Inquiries yielded

---

[9] Holly J. Hughes, from "Mind Wanting More," *Poetry of Presence: An Anthology of Mindfulness Poems*, eds. Phyllis Cole-Dai & Ruby R. Wilson (Grayson Books, 2017).

no one with memory of Cameron's party, and nobody willing to speak about the woman who lived on the bluff. Empty-handed, the group returned to report their findings to a hushed gathering at the Pomerance Court House. The acting constable declared the case closed.

Giselle, who moved back to Argolis, has joined the clan of the walking dead. She claims to be utterly unable to stay on task or focus on anything but the loss of her beloved Molly. Aram says she's clinically depressed. Giselle and I have tripped on multiple crying jags that seemed cathartic at the time but ultimately have been unhelpful for either of us. I've somehow managed to move on, staying close to my sisters, including Giselle, Sam — my Nickleby daughter, and my son; losing myself in my work; rejoining the community of nature in this little valley. I'd achieved a subtly pleasant, low frequency equilibrium.

That is, until I responded to a knock on the door that icy morning.

There in the watery light stood a tallish, slim white woman of uncertain age draped in a shit-brindle winter coat big enough to harbor a couple of stowaways. Drenched, her dark hair dripped rivulets across her face. She seemed a harbinger of utter defeat, bleak prospects, dystopian congregations. In her arms, a frail child rested her head against the coat's fur collar — a girl with a rust-colored complexion, gargantuan brown eyes and straight black hair. The hair, the shape of her face, her pursed lips, her roman nose seemed familiar.

"Are you Hestia?" the woman asked.

"I am."

"Dr. Aram sent me here."

"Oh my, are you and the child ill?"

"No, nothing serious. Sniffles. He said we could perhaps rest here before returning home."

"Of course. Come in out of the rain."

As she crossed the threshold, I noticed her oversized work boots. She asked whether she should remove them.

"Oh no, don't worry. Though, if they're wet, you can put them next to the wood burner."

She carried her boots to the stove, set down the child, instructing her to sit on the floor. She removed her coat, tried to straighten her hair, folded shaking hands. Her faded artichoke dress hung loosely on her frame, calling up images of skeletal prison camp survivors. Her stunning lime-green eyes gazed right past me.

I set the kettle on the stove and unwrapped a loaf of honey buckwheat bread.

"So very kind of you to make a total stranger and her child feel welcome."

Who knows why we offer hospitality when we do? In this case, the woman seemed needful beyond anything I could fathom. When she wiped away tears, more flowed. She cleared her throat and finally focused her blurry eyes on mine. A long pause followed. The room and all it contained held its breath. The child was utterly still.

"Hestia," she said. "I am Avery Caldwell and this is my daughter, Naomi."

***

The early weeks of December, as always, catapulted toward the holiday season. Our community celebrated Winter Solstice at the Mill, topping off a grand feast of fish and poultry, lamb and pies of all sorts with a walk at sundown along the Shawnee. Daylight, we knew, would now begin to lengthen just as we were assured that the New Year of 2063, also my birthday, would make its appearance Monday at one second after midnight.

When Cameron Caldwell briefly squired me round Argolis, I was forty-three. Now, forty-seven looms. In these three-plus years, I have been forced to reckon with the death of Cameron while navigating the choppy waters of Che's teens and the mulish pathway to friendship with Avery and her daughter, Naomi, Che's half-sister whom he is reluctantly coming to accept. Che completed his education in July and has taken a teaching job at The Buckley Farm — the environmental education center at the edge of town.

Prof would have been very proud of his protégé, Che, now a young man who is deeply in love with Ahanua, Running Bear and Samantha's daughter. On a sparkling fall day, a village-wide ceremony outside the Mill sanctified their relationship, sending them headlong into adulthood. I could be a grandmother someday. Don't hold your breath, they advised.

Yet more drama crept into my life. Aram Masood, our family doctor, launched an awkward courtship. People in the village chattered, hopefully and incredulously, that it was about time the doctor — not quite fifty — found a soulmate. And, in whispers among a shameful few, "Thank goodness he's not gay like the other doc."

"Hestia, I know you're not a virgin," Aram whispered across the table on our first date.

What? Why did he open the evening with such a conversation stopper? "Do you want details about my previous lovers, Doc?"

"Oh no, please don't think that of me. I know this will come as a shock but I wanted you to know that, despite some opportunities, I am, myself, at this ripe age, a virgin. Circumstances led me to hold to a standard that has nothing to do with these times. I long ago put aside the religious baggage that repressed me and led me to that choice. In the years since we collaborated on Prof's health and well-being, I've always held you in the highest regard."

"Goodness," was all I could come up with. My own decades of adulthood would have been painfully barren without a man around the house and in bed, even as Antonio almost drove me to madness. But being held in high regard by a learned and deeply interesting man I myself had venerated was quite another matter.

As one 'date' led to others and Aram began to stay the night, I found him a passionate, eager lover. So much so that in response, like a giddy teen, I often lost my bearings. Our closeness bore an erotic spark I'd never experienced and a growing comfort in our more mundane moments around the house. I found in Aram worldliness in his expansive intellect and the way he spoke of his upbringing in Canada and deeper roots in what he called, "the Middle East." Every evening he brought stories of folks he'd healed, kids he's followed through life, and the still rare expectant mom. In those times, I found myself aroused: the lines of his face, his sensual mouth and sleek brown body, his touch and where it led.

Aram, for his part, let me know how remarkably easy he found our long conversations, not only because he said I listened and I spoke truths, but also because he believed I prompted him to want to respond in kind. Beyond that, he said that for years he had found me so attractive he felt obliged to look away when what he really wanted was "to drink in my loveliness." *His words.* After the tragic final chapters of my previous relationships, I couldn't fully fathom my good fortune and I worried that this too might plummet in some heartbreaking way. I had no reasonable justification for such thinking and because I had long pondered Prof's axiom of 'another version', my apprehensions waned. A month went by without worry about a tragic denouement, and then six months, and a year. I concluded that in the arms of Aram, a new girl had indeed blossomed. She would never again be haunted by yet another miserable version. Content and fulfilled, she could be herself.

THE END

Acknowledgements

THANKS FIRST to Donna Lofgren, my long-suffering partner. I can hardly imagine how she managed over countless Covid-sheltered days to abide a detached mate lost in a world, decades from now, plagued, among other things, by two pandemics---how she stayed true to her loving, upbeat, compatible self. She did. These stories would never have jelled without her.

Heaps of gratitude are also due to Alexa Miller for her evocative art, abiding interest in the project, and uplifting optimism and smarts; to Danielle Aubrey, my editor, whose keen sense of storytelling and intuitive rigor added immeasurably to this book; to Peter Geldart of Petra Books, for embracing this love child of Late-K Lunacy; and to Michele, Geoff, Willlem, and Bernhard, whose friendship sustained me like no other. Despite the pandemic, we five managed to find ways to swig our share of craft brews and swap stories on the patios of one or another of the breweries of Argolis.

Beyond these, for their moral, intellectual, and editorial sustenance, I wish to thank folks in the Lofgren, Postma, Bernard, and Chaulk clans; Merrill Cragin, Joe Brehm, Nedra Chandler, Ann Barr, Amy Rock, Sam Crowl, Jr., Eden Kinkaid, Rachel Cook, Nancy Pierce, Linn Forhan, Pattie O'Brien, Carol Waltz, Reber Dunkel, and Ella Zimmerly. Though they had reason and despite the strangest of times, not one of these beloveds ever told me to get lost.

Finally, I fondly remember my old Niagara Peninsula buddy Brian Gibson for his friendship and intellectual comradery extending across three continents and four decades. He crossed to the other shore before I could share these stories with him.